Erratum

The sentence starting on page 11, line 17 should read:

In Latin America and the Caribbean it is 5.0 years, in Africa 3.5 years and in Asia and the Pacific 3.0 years (ibid).

What Makes Women Sick

What Makes Women Sick

Gender and the Political Economy of Health

Lesley Doyal

MACMILLAN

First published 1995 by
MACMILLAN PRESS LTD
Houndmills, Basingstoke, Hampshire RG21 2XS
and London
Companies and representatives
throughout the world

ISBN 0–333–54204–5 hardcover
ISBN 0–333–54205–3 paperback

A catalogue record for this book is available from the British Library.

10 9 8 7 6 5 4 3 2 1
04 03 02 01 00 99 98 97 96 95

Copy-edited and typeset by Povey–Edmondson
Okehampton and Rochdale, England

Printed in Malaysia

For Len

Contents

Acknowledgements

As usual, the creation of this book was a more collective enterprise than appears from the front cover. Much of the work was completed at the University of the West of England and I owe many thanks to colleagues there. The Women and Writing Group in the Faculty of Health and Community Studies was a continuing source of intellectual nourishment, good food and lots of laughs. Philip Wookey made it possible for me to have a much needed sabbatical. Arthur Keefe took on a lot of extra work so that the book could be completed and was always there when the going got tough. Malcolm McEachran tolerated my technophobia, helped me search out obscure references and allowed me to have more than my fair share of inter-library loans. Helen Jackson came to the project late but with great enthusiasm, helping me during those final and painful stages of the birthing process.

Outside the university, Carol Marks worked with great skill to transform my scribbles into a legible document while Kate Woodhouse checked both the text and the references with consummate dedication. Sophie Watson, Ann Hammarstrom, Nancy Worcester, Marianne Whatley, Sue Lees, Kate Young, Mary Haslum, Tamsin Wilton and Norma Daykin all made extremely valuable comments which helped to improve the final text. Steven Kennedy was an understanding and supportive publisher whose gastronomic generosity and skills also contributed significantly to the eventual outcome.

My son Dan Wilsher continues to be an unfailing source of support. His fish pies sometimes rescued me from the worst depths of despair while our debates about question marks raised the art of punctuation to new heights. Hannah Doyal matured with the book and her solidarity and friendship made a major contribution to its development. Finally, without Len Doyal's faith, love, feminism, determination, word processing skills and dogged commitment to intellectual rigour none of this would have come to fruition.

Thanks to all of them.

LESLEY DOYAL

1

In Sickness and in Health

Introduction

There is a widespread belief that doctors are the 'real' experts on women's health and that biomedicine holds the key to improving it. This book demonstrates the limitations of such an approach. Instead of exploring the interior of female bodies, it steps outside to investigate the ways in which women's lives can make them sick. Through examining economic, social and cultural influences on their well-being it identifies the major obstacles that prevent women from optimising their health.

There are obvious differences between male and female patterns of sickness and health. Not surprisingly, these stem in part from biological differences between the sexes. But as we shall see, the situation is more complex than might at first appear. All societies continue to be divided along the 'fault line' of gender and this too has a profound effect on the well-being of both men and women (Moore, 1988; Papanek, 1990).

Gender differences are especially significant for women, since they usually mean inequality and discrimination. Though female subordination can take many forms it is an extremely pervasive phenomenon, demonstrating 'both endless variety and monotonous similarity' (Rubin, 1975). This does not, of course, mean that all women are worse off in every way than all men. But it remains true that in most societies the male is valued more highly than the female. Men are usually dominant in the allocation of scarce resources and this structured inequality has a major impact on women's health.

Material discrimination against women has been extensively documented. Worldwide, they do more work than men, yet their labour is seen to be of less value. Typically they receive about 30–40 per cent less pay than men if employed and no pay at all for most domestic work. They hold only 10–20 per cent of managerial and administrative jobs and are very poorly represented in the ranks of power, policy and decision making (United Nations, 1991, p. 6). As a result, many face

1

major challenges in acquiring the material resources needed for a healthy life.

Cultural devaluation is also important, though more difficult to map. All social groups operate through a variety of discourses that naturalise gender differences and inequalities. Women have to create their identity – their sense of themselves – within the framework of these culturally constructed and sometimes conflicting definitions of womanhood (Martin, 1987; Ussher, 1989). They may be revered as mothers for instance, or as the guardians of morality, while also being regarded as 'sickly', neurotic, polluted or just fundamentally less valuable than men. The dominant message is that women are not just different, but physically, psychologically and socially inferior. In a world defined by and for men, women are 'the other' (de Beauvoir, 1972). Under these circumstances it is hardly surprising that many find it difficult to develop the feelings of competence and self-worth associated with positive mental health.

However these similarities do not mean that women constitute a unified and homogeneous group. Though they share a gender identity and a common biology, women are differentiated by factors such as age, sexual preference, race, class and, very importantly, geopolitical status – the wealth or poverty of the country in which they live.

> no-one 'becomes' a woman (in Simone de Beauvoir's sense) purely because she is female. Ideologies of womanhood have as much to do with race and class as they have to do with sex . . . it is the intersections of the various systemic networks of class, race, (hetero)sexuality and nation . . . that position us as women (Mohanty, 1991, pp. 12–13).

These differences between women are clearly signalled in both national and international health statistics (Momsen and Townsend, 1987; Seager and Olson, 1986; United Nations, 1991).

This book will describe variations in patterns of health and illness between women and men, as well as identifying the inequalities in health status and access to medical care that separate groups of women from each other. It will then explore the complex processes shaping these biological and social realities. If they are to be effective, strategies for improving women's health must be based on a clear understanding of how these differences are created and sustained. The remainder of this chapter provides a preliminary framework for developing such an analysis.

What This Book Is and Is Not About

This is not a book about the health of both sexes. It is quite unapologetically a book about women. Though men are present, they appear mainly as actors in women's lives rather than as subjects of the analysis itself. However this should not be taken to imply that men's health is unimportant or that it cannot be subjected to the same methods of analysis. Indeed it would be one measure of the book's success if the framework presented here were adapted for a similar study of the influence of gender divisions on male health problems.

Neither is this a book about women and medicine. A comprehensive treatment of this important topic would require a very different approach with extensive coverage of issues that have hardly been addressed here (Lupton, 1994; Martin, 1987). In particular it would include a more detailed analysis of how doctors and other health workers 'treat' women in the context of individual medical encounters (Miles, 1991, Ch. 6; Roberts, 1985; Fisher, 1986).

Instead the analysis will focus on two specific aspects of modern medicine. First, knowledge generated within a biomedical framework will be combined with that from other disciplines to develop a more holistic understanding if women's health and illness. Second, the impact of medical practices on women's health will be critically reviewed and compared with that of other factors influencing their wellbeing – for good or ill. Though doctors sometimes play an important role in their lives, we will see that modern medicine is rarely the major determinant of women's health status.

This analysis will not produce a detached and objective account of women's health problems – if such a thing were even possible. Instead it will be explicitly feminist in the broadest sense. This claim to feminism does not derive from the use of specific methods of data collection or particular styles of argument (Harding, 1986; Harding, 1987; Maynard and Purvis, 1994). Indeed the evidence marshalled throughout is eclectic, both in its disciplinary orientation and in the manner of its collection and presentation. It includes both quantitative and qualitative data, some of which have been produced by people who would not define themselves as in any sense feminist. However, the analysis itself is shaped by a fundamental concern to identify – and change – those aspects of women's lives that cause them serious harm.

Physical and mental health are basic human needs yet they remain unmet for millions of women. As we shall see, the reasons for this are rarely 'natural' in the sense that they are unavoidable; too often they are, quite literally, 'man-made', requiring feminist imagination(s) for their understanding and ultimately their transformation. But to declare one's feminism in the 1990s requires further elaboration. In particular it necessitates a clear statement on the thorny question of 'difference', which has been at the heart of recent feminist debates.

In this analysis of women's health we will reject both crude universalism and crude difference theories. Instead we will attempt to identify the commonalities in women's situations while at the same time remaining sensitive to the complex social, economic and cultural variety of their lives. In other words, we will focus on their 'common difference' (Joseph and Lewis, 1981). Only in this way can we construct a theory that makes both moral and political sense.

Rejecting Crude Universalism

During the last decade, women from many different constituencies – working-class women, lesbians, black women, women with disabilities and women from third world countries – have challenged the white, western, middle-class domination of feminist theory and practice (Humm, 1992, Ch. 5; Lovell, 1990; Segal, 1987; McDowell and Pringle, 1992). In particular they have been critical of those feminists who prioritise gender over other social divisions, representing all women as members of the same oppressed group, unified by their experience of male domination and their uniquely female emotionality. This political critique has been reinforced by a shift towards post-modernism in much feminist thinking. Women working in this tradition have emphasised the dangers of inaccurate and inappropriate generalisations, stressing instead, the importance of 'hearing many voices' (Barrett and Phillips, 1992; Braidotti *et al.*, 1994; Mohanty *et al.*, 1991; Nicholson, 1991).

In response to these arguments, many feminist writers are now placing much greater emphasis on the differences between women. Rejecting the ideas of 'universal sisterhood' that characterised much feminist thinking in the 1980s, they have begun to develop a more sophisticated understanding of the relationships between race, class and gender. The analysis contained in this book should be seen as a contribution to that process, with the social construction of health and sickness offering important examples of how such links are forged in concrete historical circumstances.

As we shall see, there are very marked inequalities in the health status of women from different classes and racial backgrounds and these will be explored in detail as the book progresses. However the greatest disparities are those that divide the majority of women in the developed countries from the majority of those living in what is often called the 'third world'. Though the diversity of social forms in 'third world' countries is immense, they are similar enough to generate comparable patterns of disease and death for the mass of their female populations. It is important therefore that we specify these common features, as well as defining the term 'third world' more precisely.

About two thirds of the world's women live in countries where per capita income is low and life expectancy relatively short, where the fertility rate continues to be high and a comparatively small percentage of the paid labour force is female, where class and gender inequalities in income and wealth continue to be very great and the state provides few health and welfare services. Though they are both culturally and materially heterogeneous most of these countries do share common experiences of colonialism and imperialism, which have resulted in varying degrees of subordination within the world economic system. Geographically they are located in the southern part of the globe in the Latin American, Caribbean, African, Asian and Pacific regions.

All the terms currently used to summarise the complex reality of these economic and social divisions are problematic. They tend inevitably towards over simplification – there are huge differences for instance, between the newly industrialising nations of Asia and Latin America and the majority of African countries. Such terms also have the potential to reinforce economic, cultural and ideological hierarchies (Mohanty, 1991). Yet it is difficult to avoid their use altogether. 'Third world' is probably the most frequently used and widely understood of currently available options (Mohanty, 1991, p. 75, note 1; Sen and Grown, 1988, p. 9, note 3). It also continues to be employed as an affirmative identification by many political activists around the world, and will therefore be used here (with care) to locate women's lives within a broader geopolitical context.

However we need to acknowledge that this categorisation of global reality into first and third worlds excludes those countries that used to be called 'second world' but are now 'post-communist' or 'desocialising'. A number of recent texts have made the lives of women in Central and Eastern Europe much more visible outside their own countries (Buckley, 1989; Corrin, 1992; Funk and Mueller, 1993). Though health has not been their major focus, most of these accounts imply that the rapid social changes now taking place in this part of the world have been detrimental to women's well-being.

Both the political realities of the recent past and the economic and social pressures of the present have contributed to a situation where the life expectancy of women in the countries of Central and Eastern Europe is five years less, and that of women in the Newly Independent States (the former Soviet Union) six years less, than that of women in the European Union (WHO, 1994, p. 4). In some of these countries life expectancy has declined further since 1991, and female deaths from cardiovascular disease are a particular cause for concern (ibid, p. 6). Attempts to make sense of these differences and to explore more qualitative aspects of women's health are now beginning, but detailed evidence remains sparse. Hence women in the second world are seriously underrepresented both in this text and in most other discussions of women's health.

Rejecting Crude Difference Theories

It is clear that women's lives vary enormously and recognition of this reality must remain at the heart of any analysis of their health and welfare. However this rejection of crude universalism does not mean that we should embrace crude difference instead – that we should deny any possibility of women having beliefs, values or interests in common.

A number of strands in contemporary women's studies contain within them the implication of radical difference, the belief that we cannot make meaningful judgements about the relative situations of women in different cultures. For some, this relativism reflects a political commitment to the acceptance of all 'other' cultural beliefs and practices. To do otherwise is said to denigrate those who live their lives in accordance with values that are different from our own. In the context of women's health, this can mean a refusal to engage with the hazards of procedures such as genital mutilation because they are defined as 'traditional' practices. It has also led in some instances to a reluctance to condemn male violence in cultures where it is widely condoned.

Similar tendencies are evident in the work of some post-modernist writers (Maynard and Purvis, 1994; Nicholson, 1991). Their rejection of any universal criteria for determing what is right or wrong, good or bad, real or unreal, implies that the situations of women in different cultures cannot be compared in any meaningful way. Thus even 'worse' or 'better' health cannot be measured, except perhaps by the crudest measure of all – survival. According to some writers even the category 'woman' is itself so culturally variable – so discourse – specific – that it is not a useful category for social analysis. Thus the very project of feminism is called into question as women are seen to have radically different interests.

This has led in some parts of the world to a political paralysis that is becoming increasingly intolerable (Maynard and Purvis, 1994; Ramazanoglou, 1993). Despite their undoubted heterogeneity, women do have important things in common. All share broadly similar bodily experiences, even though the meanings they attach to them may vary dramatically (Martin, 1987). Their bodies are not merely social constructs as some post-modernist writers seem to imply (Haraway, 1991). Nor are they infinitely malleable. Bodies do impose very real (though varying) constraints on women's lives as well as offering enormous potential, and this is evidenced by the fact that the fight for bodily self-determination has been a central feature of feminist politics across very different cultures (Jacobus *et al.*, 1990; Lupton, 1994, Ch. 2; Morgan and Scott, 1993; Pringle, 1992).

Women also share the reality of occupying (more or less) subordinate positions in most social and cultural contexts. Though this subordination is linked in complex ways with divisions of race, class and nationality, women do have common experiences as the objects of sexist practices. Some of these are psychological, as women struggle to construct their sense of themselves in the face of cultural messages about their intrinsic 'otherness' and inferiority. However they also have a material dimension as women deal with the consequences of poverty and economic inequality between the sexes. Again, women in very different cultures have identified similar processes of gender discrimination as powerful obstacles to their achievement of both mental and physical well-being.

As we shall see, it is a common recognition both of their need for control over their own bodies, and of the social origins of many of their health problems, that has led many women into political action. Physical and mental health are universal and basic human needs and all women have an equal right to their satisfaction.

Why Is Health Important?

At first sight the answer to this question might seem obvious. Even minor illness can be temporarily distressing, while serious illness can have a devastating impact on how individuals feel about themselves, others and the world. Indeed it may eventually kill them. For someone to be 'happy' and to be seriously ill is usually a contradiction in terms. Illness is feared not just for its physical consequences but also because of the distress – the pain, fear, anxiety and depression – it can engender. It is not surprising, therefore, that health is generally regarded as a 'good thing' – a state of being that everyone would wish to achieve and maintain. However the benefits conferred go beyond immediate feelings of subjective well-being.

In order for women or men to flourish they must interact with others. It is only through social participation that people learn what they are capable of and how these capabilities may best be used (Sen, 1985). Personal identity is forged through family relationships, friendships, waged work and a variety of other communal activities (Braybrooke, 1987). Any artificial and sustained constraint on an individual's ability to relate to people in these and other areas of social life will constitute serious and objective harm. This harm derives not just from any subjective feelings of pain and unhappiness they might have about their situation, but also from the fact that arbitrary limits have been placed on the realisation of their capabilities – on their potential as human beings.

Health and Human Needs

Whatever their culture, individuals have at least two basic needs that must be met if they are to minimise such harm (Doyal and Gough, 1991). Their first and most immediate need is to survive and be physically healthy. Death is clearly the ultimate harm, while physical disease may seriously impair both their ability to interact with others and their capacity to benefit from it. But physical health is not enough. Both men and women will also be prevented from realising their potential when their need for mental health is unsatisfied. This will occur when their ability to make informed choices and to act upon them is limited over sustained periods of time by their cognitive and/or emotional incapacity to negotiate physical and social realities.

Thus inequalities in health between social groups are not simply inequalities in desired states of subjective well-being. They also represent objective inequalities in the capacity of individuals to play an active part in social and community life – to realise their own potential and help others to do the same. For those who wish to improve the situation of women, physical and mental health are therefore strategic issues. They are important goals to be sought in their own right, but they also provide the key to women's effective participation in attempts to create a fairer and healthier society.

Comparing Health Across Cultures

Cultural variations in concepts of sickness and health are now well documented and their significance will be obvious in future chapters (Baer, 1987; Kleinman, 1988; Lock and Gordon, 1988; Lupton, 1994; Whelehan, 1988; Wright and Treacher, 1982). However they do not mean that we cannot compare the health status of women in different societies. This can still be achieved if we distinguish as clearly as possible between the objective manifestations of 'disease' and the subjective experience of 'illness' (Eisenberg, 1977). These two elements will certainly be inextricably intertwined in the minds and bodies of particular individuals. Yet we can still measure the social distribution of disease and death while also understanding and respecting the cultural relativity of illness.

Women in different cultures who contract tuberculosis or pelvic infection for instance may well experience these diseases in very different ways. However they will also have a great deal in common. Some will die, most will 'feel ill' (in some sense or other), all will show similar physiological signs (albeit in varying degrees) and all will respond in broadly similar ways to scientifically tested treatments such as antibiotics. It is these commonalities that we can measure, and use to compare the health status of different social groups (Doyal and Gough, 1991, pp. 56–9).

What western medicine defines as mental illness poses more difficult problems of interpretation and measurement since usually there are no objective 'signs' independent of the subjective symptoms. But again, similarities in its effects can be identified across cultures. Whatever the form of their distress, or the words and concepts used to describe it, women with poor mental health will all experience a significant reduction in their capacity for successful participation in their culture. Though each will have their own contribution to make, all will be disabled to a greater or lesser extent in the exercise of their cognitive and emotional capabilities. It is this disability that can be compared between societies (Doyal and Gough, 1991, pp. 62–3).

A Picture of Health?

All women whose physical or mental health is damaged will therefore be harmed in broadly similar ways, and morbidity and mortality rates can give us a preliminary indication of the global distribution of this harm. Of course such statistics can provide only a partial picture since they are not measuring the subjective or experiential aspects of illness. Moreover they offer a negative view of sickness and death rather than a positive picture of well-being. However they do represent important points of reference between societies and social groups as well as offering clues to structural factors underlying any perceived inequalities.

Inequalities in Mortality

In most of the developed countries women can now expect to survive for about 75 years (United Nations, 1991, p. 55). However this average conceals significant variations in life expectancy between women in different social groups. In Britain women married to men in semi-skilled or unskilled jobs are about 70 per cent more likely to die prematurely than those whose husbands are professionals (OPCS, 1986). Similar social divisions are apparent in the United States, where black women now have a life expectancy of 73.5 years compared with 79.2 for white women while their risk of dying in pregnancy or childbirth is three and a half times greater (US National Institutes of Health, 1992, pp. 8, 13). In most underdeveloped countries the social inequalities in health are even more dramatic.

There are also major differences in mortality rates between rich and poor nations. In Latin America and the Caribbean average life expectancy is lower than in developed countries but still relatively high at around 70. In Asia and the Pacific it is 64 and in Africa as low as 54 (UN, 1991, p. 55). The lowest rates recorded for individual countries are in Afghanistan, East Timor, Ethiopia and Sierra Leone, where women can expect to live for only about 43 years (ibid.) These inequalities are at their most extreme in deaths related to childbearing. In developed countries mortality of this kind is rare, with less than five deaths for every 100 000 live births. In South Asian countries, on the other hand, the rate is more than 650 deaths per 100 000 with the African average a close second at around 600 deaths (UN, 1991, p. 56).

Though these figures are extremely dramatic they do not show the true extent of the inequalities in reproductive hazards facing women in different parts of the world. The maternal mortality rate reflects the risk a woman runs in each pregnancy. However we also need to examine fertility rates to assess the lifetime risk to an individual woman of dying of pregnancy-related causes. Recent estimates suggest that for a woman in Africa this risk is 1 in 23 compared with only 1 in 10 000 in developed countries (Rooney, 1992). Pregnancy causes almost no deaths among women of reproductive age in developed countries but between a quarter and a third of deaths elsewhere (Fortney *et al.*, 1986). Reproductive deaths are therefore an important indicator both of the different health hazards facing men and women and also of the heterogeneity of women's own experiences.

Turning from mortality to morbidity statistics – from death to disease – we are immediately faced with what appears to be a paradox. Around the world, women usually live longer than men in the same socio-economic circumstances. In most of the developed countries the gap between male and female life expectancy is about 6.5 years (UN, 1991, p. 55). In Latin America and the Caribbean it is 50 years, in Africa 3.5 years and in Asia and the Pacific, 30 years (ibid.) Only in a few countries in Asia do women have a lower life expectancy than men. Yet despite their generally greater longevity, women in most communities report more illness and distress. This pattern of excess female morbidity is reasonably well documented in the developed countries and we examine that evidence first. The more limited information on women in third world countries will be considered later.

Sickness and Affluence

A number of studies in the United Kingdom have found that women's own assessment of their health is consistently worse than that of men (Blaxter, 1990; Whitehead, 1988). Similar findings have emerged from studies in the United States (Rodin and Ickovics, 1990; Verbrugge, 1986). US women are 25 per cent more likely than men to report that their activities are restricted by health problems and they are bedridden for 35 per cent more days than men because of acute conditions (US National Institutes of Health, 1992, p. 9). In community surveys throughout the developed world, women report about twice as much anxiety and depression as men (Paykel, 1991; Weissman and Klerman, 1977).

Women also use most medical services more often. This fact cannot be taken as a straightforward indicator of the relative well-being of the two sexes since admitting illness may well be more acceptable for women than for men. However it does highlight certain important features of women's health status. The most immediate reason for their greater use of medical care is longevity. Deteriorating health and increasing disability are a frequent, though not inevitable accompaniment of the ageing process and women make up a large proportion of the elderly in the population – especially the 'old old' (Doty, 1987). In the United States 72 per cent of those over 85 are female (US National Institutes of Health, 1992, p. 8). Older women appear to receive less assistance from relatives and friends than older men of the same age, despite the fact that they suffer higher rates of certain disabling diseases, including arthritis, Alzheimer's Disease, osteoporosis and diabetes (Heikkinen *et al.*, 1983; Verbrugge, 1985).

Because of the incorporation of birth control and birthing itself into the orbit of doctors, younger women too make more use of medical services. This is not usually associated with organic pathology but reflects the growing role of medicine in the management of the 'normal' process of pregnancy and childbirth (or its prevention). Women also appear to experience more problems with their reproductive systems than men, and again this is likely to bring them into more frequent contact with the formal health care system.

Finally, evidence from across the developed world suggests that more women than men consult doctors about psychological and emotional distress. In the United Kingdom, female consultation rates with general practitioners for depression and anxiety are three times and nearly two and a half times, respectively, those of males (Office of Health Economics, 1987; UK Royal College of Practitioners, 1986). Over the course of a year one British woman in every twenty aged between 25 and 74 seeks help for emotional problems from her GP, compared with one in fifty men. There is also evidence from a range of countries that women are at least twice as likely as men to be prescribed mild tranquillisers (Ashton, 1991; Balter *et al.*, 1984).

Broadly speaking then, the picture in the developed countries is one where women live longer than men but appear 'sicker' and suffer more disability. They are ill more often than men and use more medical services. Men do not suffer such frequent illness though their health problems are more often life-threatening. But sex and gender are not the only factors influencing women's health status, as we can see if we look again at the differences between women themselves.

Even within developed countries there are major variations in the health of women in different social groups. In the United States, strokes occur twice as often in black women as in white women, and they have the highest incidence of gonorrhoea and syphilis (US National Institutes of Health, 1992, p. 13). Though black women have a lower incidence of breast cancer than white women it is significant that they are more likely to die from it (ibid.) In the United Kingdom women in the lowest social class are much more likely to experience chronic illness than their more affluent counterparts. In a national survey 46 per cent of unskilled and semi-skilled women aged between 45 and 64 reported a long-standing illness compared with 34 per cent of professional and managerial women (Bridgewood and Savage, 1993). Women in the lowest social groups were also more likely than those in the professional and managerial groups to report that illness limited their daily activities (30 per cent in comparison with 20 per cent) (ibid.)

Sickness and Poverty

However it is in the poorest countries that the state of women's health is at its worst. Though some affluent women are as healthy as those in the developed countries, it is clear that millions of others live in a state of chronic debility, afflicted by the diseases of poverty and the hazards of childbearing (Jacobson, 1992; Smyke, 1991). Estimates suggest that for every one of the half million women who die of pregnancy-related causes each year, at least 16 suffer long-term damage to their health – an annual total of about eight million (Royston and Armstrong, 1989, p. 187). Reproductive tract infections are also extremely common (International Women's Health Coalition, 1991). In some African countries gonorrhoea is estimated to affect as many as 40 per cent of women (WHO, 1992). These diseases are not just distressing and disabling in themselves, but often result in chronic infection with serious effects on women's overall well-being.

Millions of women in third world countries also have to cope with the broader health consequences of poverty – communicable diseases and undernutrition. While they risk contracting the same endemic diseases as men, both biological and social factors may increase their exposure or worsen the effects. Malaria, hepatitis and leprosy, for instance, can be especially dangerous during pregnancy, while women's responsibility for domestic tasks increases their chance of contracting water-borne diseases.

The extent of undernutrition in girls and women is dramatically documented in the incidence of anaemia. Estimates suggest that at least 44 per cent of all women in third world countries are anaemic compared with about 12 per cent in developed countries (WHO, 1992, p. 62). In India the figure is as high as 88 per cent (World Bank, 1993, p. 75). This is an important indicator of general health status, suggesting that many women are chronically debilitated, never reaching the levels of good health that most women in the first world take for granted.

In these conditions of poverty, deprivation and disruption, mental distress is clearly a major risk. Though there is little statistical evidence of its prevalence, most community surveys show a pattern similar to that of developed countries, with more women than men reporting feelings of anxiety and depression. However the pattern of treatment is very different, with many more men than women receiving psychiatric help (Paltiel, 1987). Indeed evidence from many third world countries suggests that women receive less medical treatment of all kinds than men, despite their greater need. Rural women in particular are often unable to gain access to modern services, even for obstetric care. Around 75 per cent of all births in South Asia and 62 per cent in Africa still take place without a trained health worker, compared with about 1 per cent in the developed countries (UN, 1991, p. 58). While this reflects very low levels of health spending overall, it also suggests a particular reluctance to invest in the health of women and girls.

Though female life expectancy continues to rise in most third world countries, the 'harsh decade' of the 1980s and the economic rigours of structural adjustment policies have meant deteriorating health for many women (Smyke, 1991; Vickers, 1991). The number of those who are malnourished has risen, resulting in an increased incidence of high-risk pregnancies and low birth-weight babies. Diseases of poverty such as tuberculosis are re-emerging while the so-called 'diseases of affluence' are beginning to proliferate, with cancer already one of the leading causes of death for women between the ages of 25 and 35. Environmental degradation has made many women's lives harder and millions are without access to clean water or sanitation. Yet fewer resources are available to care for them. In recent years a real decline in per capita health spending has been documented in three quarters of the nations in Africa and Latin America and women appear to have been the major losers (UNICEF, 1990).

Does Medicine Have the Answer to Women's Health Problems?

This brief sketch has generated a wide range of questions about women's health. Why do women in most countries have a longer life expectancy than men? Why do women in some countries live nearly twice as long as those in others? Why do rates of morbidity and mortality vary between social classes and ethnic groups? Why do so many women still die in childbirth? Why do women report more sickness than men? How does their race or their culture affect women's experiences of health and health care? As we shall see, medical science can offer only limited resources either for answering these questions or for changing the reality that they represent.

The 'Biomedical Model'

Western medicine offers a powerful framework for describing and classifying much of the sickness afflicting individuals. Using this 'biomedical model' doctors have developed the means to prevent or cure many diseases and to alleviate the symptoms of others. However many other health problems have remained resistant to their ministrations. This has drawn increasing attention to the limitations of the conceptual schema employed by doctors and other health care providers to understand complex human phenomena. Two aspects of medical practice have come under particular scrutiny: its narrowly biological orientation and its separation of individuals from their wider social environment (Busfield, 1986, p. 28).

It is no longer appropriate (if it ever was) to categorise western medicine as a monolithic unified institution devoted only to hard science and high technology. Recent years have been marked by a revival of interest in public health and a 'humanisation' of some areas of research and clinical practice. Yet the natural sciences continue to be seen as the only 'real' basis of medicine, with attention focused predominantly on the internal workings of the human body.

Health and disease are still explained primarily through an engineering metaphor in which the body is seen as a series of separate but interdependent systems (Doyal and Doyal, 1984). Ill health is treated as the mechanical failure of some part of one or more of these systems and the medical task is to repair the damage. Within this model, the complex relationship between mind and body is rarely explored and individuals are separated from both the social and cultural contexts of their lives:

> The notion of disease itself refers to a process that unfolds and develops within the individual and what occurs within the individual and what the individual does is the prime subject of medical interest

and endeavour, rather than the individual's relationship to others or
to the environment or vice versa (Busfield, 1986, p. 25).

This biological and individualistic orientation of modern medicine has
led to enormous successes in our understanding of different types of
disease and their treatment. Indeed it was precisely the concentration of
effort made possible by this explanatory model that led to major
achievements such as anaesthesia, antisepsis, antibiotics, analgesia and
a wide range of other therapies that most people in developed countries
now take for granted. The 'magic bullet' that works is a powerful
weapon indeed. However its obvious success has led to a neglect of
prevention and an over-reliance on this curative model, both in
explaining the causes of disease and in exploring the different ways
in which illness is experienced.

Perils of Reductionism

Attempts to explain the causes of disease primarily by reference to
specific biological hazards are too limited. They rarely examine the
social and economic aspects of the environments within which such
pathogens flourish. Hence they can offer little help in understanding
why some individuals or groups are more likely to become sick than
others. We have also seen that there is more to poor health than
disease. The subjective experience of illness is the product of complex
processes involving the interaction between the whole person and their
social and cultural environments. Because the biomedical model
focuses almost exclusively on the material rather than the mental
dimension of the 'patient', it can offer little help in clarifying and
explaining such experiences. In particular it is often of little use in
understanding psychological distress and disability.

This tendency of modern medicine to reduce the complexity of
sickness and health to matters of specific biological causation has
limited its potential either to understand or to ameliorate the ills of
both sexes. But the interests of women have been especially damaged
by the narrowness of this approach (Birke, 1986). Their higher rates of
depression for instance have often been blamed on hormonal disturbance, leading not only to inappropriate treatment but also to a
mistaken naturalisation of gender divisions that are essentially social in
origin. Too often women's problems have been blamed on their
reproductive systems when it is the social relations of both production
and reproduction that need further examination.

Gendered Research

However it is not just its narrowly biological orientation that limits the capacity of medicine to deal with women's health problems. Even within its own terms there is growing evidence that both the priorities and the techniques of biomedical research reflect the white male domination of the profession (Kirchstein, 1991). Bias has been identified in the choice and the definition of problems to be studied, the methods employed to carry out the research, and the interpretation and application of results (Cotton, 1990; Rosser, 1992, pp. 129–30). While women are in the majority as health care providers, they continue to be in the minority as practising doctors (Doyal, 1994a; Lorber, 1984). They hold few positions of power and therefore have little influence on how funds are allocated or research carried out (Rosser, 1992; US National Institutes of Health, 1992; Witz, 1992).

There has been relatively little basic research into non-reproductive conditions that mainly affect women – incontinence and osteoporosis for instance. In the United States, Congressional Hearings in 1990 showed that only 13 per cent of government research funds were spent on health issues specific to women (US National Institutes of Health, 1992). Even the menstrual cycle itself has not been extensively researched. Hence we have little detailed knowledge about an extremely important aspect of women's bodily functioning that generates a large amount of distress and many medical consultations (Koblinsky *et al.*, 1993). Where health problems affect both men and women, few studies have explored possible differences between the sexes in their development, symptoms and treatment (American Medical Association, 1991).

Researchers working on coronary heart disease, for example, have continued to act as though it were only a 'male' problem, despite the fact that it is the single most important cause of death in post-menopausal women, killing half a million a year in the United States. The Physician Health Study, which demonstrated the effectiveness of daily aspirin consumption in preventing cardiovascular disease, had a sample of 20 000 men but no women, while the sample in the 'Mr. Fit' study of the relationship between heart disease, cholesterol and lifestyle consisted of 15 000 men (Freedman and Maine, 1993, p. 165). AIDS, too, has been treated for research purposes as a predominantly male disease. Though it is now growing faster among women than among men, we still know very little about the differential effects it may have on them (Bell, 1992; Denenberg, 1990b; Kurth, 1993).

As long as most biomedical research continues to be based on male samples there will be significant gaps in our knowledge about women. Even more importantly, treatments tested only on men will continue to be given to women, when they may not be appropriate to their needs (Hamilton, 1985). There have recently been indications, for example, that anti-depressant drugs can have very different effects on men and women and may affect women differently during the various phases of the menstrual cycle. However preliminary testing excluded women, despite the fact that they are the major users of the drugs (ibid.)

It is clear that biomedicine has generated valuable knowledge that has been used to improve the health of individual women. But as we have seen, this understanding is often partial and sometimes erroneous. This is because research has selectively ignored many of the biological differences between the sexes while paying little or no attention to the particularity of women's psychological and social circumstances. Hence it can offer little help in answering the questions posed at the beginning of this section.

In order to remedy these deficiencies we need to move beyond the boundaries of biology. No single discipline will provide an adequate conceptual framework for understanding the complex relationship between women's health and the quality of their daily lives. Instead methods and insights from a variety of disciplines, including history, sociology, psychology, economics, anthropology and cultural studies need to be combined with more traditional biomedical and epidemiological approaches to create an interdisciplinary and interactive framework of analysis (Lupton, 1994, Ch. 1; Turner, 1992:, Ch. 4). The value of bringing the work of natural and social scientists together in this way can be illustrated by a brief history of differences in male and female life expectancy.

Are Women Really the Weaker Sex?

Women have not always been longer lived than men. Indeed what little evidence we have from the pre-industrial period suggests that in most places they had a shorter life expectancy (Shorter, 1984). In Europe and the United States the female advantage over men first became apparent in the latter part of the nineteenth century as the life expectancy of both sexes increased. This gap between the sexes has continued to widen ever since (Hart, 1988, p. 117). In most countries women now experience greater longevity than men, with the size of their advantage being proportional to the life expectancy of the population as a whole. Only in a few countries do men continue to live longer than women. As we shall see, these major historical changes in life expectancy cannot be explained by reference to either biological or social factors alone.

Biological and Social Advantages of Females

Far from being the 'weaker sex', women do seem to begin life with a biological advantage over men (Waldron, 1986a). Around the world, significantly more male than female foetuses are actually conceived but they are more likely to be spontaneously aborted or to be stillborn (Hassold *et al.*, 1983). By the time of birth the ratio is down to about 105 males to every 100 females and in most societies the excess of male mortality continues to be especially marked during the first six months of life (Kynch, 1985; Waldron, 1986a, p. 66).

The reasons for this inherently greater 'robustness' of girl babies are not entirely clear but they seem to include sex differences in chromosomal structures and possibly a slower maturing of boys' lungs due to the effects of testosterone (Waldron, 1986a, p. 66). In adult life too, women may have a biological advantage – at least until menopause – as endogenous hormones protect them from ischaemic heart disease. Thus biological factors do confer an initial advantage on females. However social factors also make a major impact on their longevity. In some societies these factors enhance inherent biological advantage but in others they reduce it or even cancel it out.

European experience suggests that the gap between male and female life expectancy grew as economic development and social change removed two major risks to women's health. As food became more widely available, most women were assured of adequate diets. This improved nutrition contributed in particular to a reduction in female mortality from infectious diseases such as tuberculosis (Hart, 1988). At the same time reduced fertility and safer childbirth combined to lower the maternal mortality rate.

Even before these female hazards began to decline, changes in the sexual division of labour meant that men were taking on new risks. The reasons for this are complex, but two factors are especially significant. The emergence of the male 'breadwinner' in industrial economies led to more men than women taking on potentially life-threatening jobs. At the same time their increased command over resources and their greater freedom contributed to men's more frequent pursuit of dangerous pastimes, including the use of hazardous substances (ibid.)

Young men now run a much greater risk than young women of dying from accidents (especially in motor vehicles) and violence. In the United States in particular, gunshot wounds are now a major cause of male deaths, especially among African Americans. In the United Kingdom, accidents and violence cause 70 per cent of deaths of men under the age of 35, compared with only 35 per cent of female deaths. Later in life men die more often of coronary heart disease and lung cancer. Both of these are influenced by occupational factors but are mainly due to smoking, which has traditionally been heavier among men than among women. According to one estimate, 50 per cent of the entire sex differential in life expectancy in the United States and Sweden can be attributed to (past) gender differences in smoking (Waldron, 1986b). Men's higher rates of alcohol consumption also contribute to their higher mortality rates at all ages.

It would appear therefore, that as many societies have industrialised, a variety of social and cultural factors have combined to allow women's inherent biological advantage to emerge. The hazards of infectious diseases and the dangers of childbearing have been reduced, and certain male risks have increased, giving women longer – though not necessarily healthier – lives. However there are important exceptions to this pattern, showing how biological and social factors may interact in very different ways.

The Impact of Discrimination on Life Expectancy

In certain countries in South Asia, including Bangladesh, men outlive women, while in India and Pakistan the two sexes have almost equal life expectancy (UN, 1991, p. 69). In these societies there is an excess of female deaths both in childhood and in the childbearing years, which most researchers have attributed to material and cultural discrimination against girls and women. In the most extreme cases this sexism leads to female infanticide either during pregnancy or after birth. However it more commonly involves chronic neglect. In childhood, girls may receive less care than boys in a variety of different ways (Sundari Ravindran, 1986; UNICEF, 1990; WHO, 1992, pp. 17–26). They tend to be breastfed less often than boys and for shorter periods, and throughout their childhood receive less food and medical care (Koenig and d'Souza, 1986; Kynch and Sen, 1983; Sen, 1988). In some populations this lifelong discrimination has reached the point where the ratio between men and women has become unbalanced.

In India, for instance, the sex ratio fell from 972 women per thousand men in 1901 to 935 per thousand in 1981, while the ratio of women to men was increasing in most other parts of the world (Kynch and Sen, 1983, p. 377; Sen, 1990b). In these 'classic patriarchies' the biological advantage of most women is therefore cancelled out by their social disadvantage (Kabeer, 1991). This offers a sharp reminder that there is no reason to assume that economic development will necessarily allow women more opportunity to flourish. While discrimination continues, their life chances will be diminished in comparison with those of men:

> Women are biologically stronger, live longer than men and naturally outnumber them. Where they do not it is only because of the effects of war, or if they have been forced to migrate in search of work or because they have suffered severe and systematic discrimination (Seager and Olson, 1986, p. 12).

Redefining Women's Health

If the biological finality of death can only be explained in a wider social context then the complex realities of women's sickness and health must be explored in similar ways. In order to do this, traditional epidemiological methods have to be turned on their head. Instead of identifying diseases and then searching for a cause, we need to begin by identifying the major areas of activity that constitute women's lives. We can then go on to analyse the impact of these activities on their health and well-being.

Any attempt to separate the various parts of women's lives in this way is, of course, fraught with difficulty. The balance of these activities varies both within and between different societies as well as changing over the lifetime of individual women. Moreover, in many social contexts it is precisely the inseparability and co-mingling of their various tasks that tends to differentiate women's lives from those of men:

> Working in production and reproduction are increasingly simultaneous superimposed occupations for women – held in an uneasy tension, misleadingly called the 'double day' because there is never any neat division where one job ends and the other begins (Petchesky, 1979).

It is the cumulative effects of these various labours that are the major determinants of women's states of health. This is true even in old age, when many of these activities will themselves have ceased but their impact on well-being becomes increasingly evident. However, we need to begin by examining each aspect of women's lives separately. This will enable us to identify some important similarities between women, but it will also highlight some of the major differences.

An analysis of this kind offers the opportunity to explore the complex interactions between social, psychological and biological dimensions of health. At the macro-level we can describe the material context within which women's health is formed. We can also identify the cultural constraints within which they can make choices affecting their own well-being. However we need to relate these broader issues to the physical and psychological state of individual women – to their lived experience of health and illness.

At present the conceptual tools for such an analysis remain significantly underdeveloped and continue to be the subject of debate (DiGiacomo, 1992; Scheper-Hughes and Lock, 1987). How, for instance, do we make sense of the complex relationship between the social construction of motherhood in different societies and individual women's experiences of postnatal depression? How do we develop a model of the links between different modes of economic organisation and the 'mindful bodies' of women trying to make ends meet? (Scheper-Hughes and Lock, 1987). The following analysis cannot provide all the answers but it can frame some of the questions more clearly, provide relevant empirical data and indicate important areas for future investigation.

We begin in Chapter 2 with an exploration of women's domestic work. Around the world the most fundamental feature of women's lives is their responsibility for home, family and household labour. Caring for and caring about others is a central feature of these activities wherever in the world they are carried out. However the content of the work itself will vary significantly between rich and poor countries, rural and urban areas and industrialised and non-industrialised modes of production.

In developed countries women are primarily responsible for what is traditionally referred to as 'housework', using a variety of purchased goods to cook, clean and wash for their immediate family group. In other parts of the world they may have to produce the food themselves, as well as acquiring fuel, water and other physical necessities. Home may also be the workplace in which women carry out a variety of economic activities to help their families survive (Young, 1993, Ch. 6). A major theme of our discussion will be the health implications of these cross-cultural similarities and differences in the nature of domestic labour.

Despite its variety of forms in different societies, the household also remains the basic unit within which most women's labour is rewarded – both materially and emotionally (ibid. Ch. 7). Yet there is substantial evidence to show that despite the 'caring' image of the family, resources may not be distributed according to need (Bruce and Dwyer, 1988; Folbre, 1988; Kabeer, 1991). If there are men in the household they usually acquire the greater share of income and wealth as well as emotional support, status and decision-making power. Very importantly they usually monopolise physical power too, putting many women at serious risk of violence. We will therefore examine both the physical and the psychological consequences of the unequal distribution of resources within families. The analysis will place particular emphasis on mental health, since for many women the nature of their labour combined with their limited access to household resources constitute a potential threat to their emotional well-being.

Having opened the door to domestic life, subsequent chapters will look in more detail at the different aspects of sexuality and reproduction that are usually (but not always) contained within the household. Chapter 3 explores the relationship between sex and health. As well as being a significant source of pleasure, sexual activity can also contribute to emotional well-being. However it is increasingly evident that sex with men can sometimes pose a serious threat to women's health. This applies not just to rape and sexual abuse but also to consensual sex. As the AIDS epidemic has spread it has highlighted the continuing constraints both on women's capacity to determine their own sexuality and sexual practices, and on their ability to protect themselves from sexually transmitted diseases. These issues are discussed in more detail in an analysis of the health hazards of heterosex.

For many women the conceiving of a child is a desired outcome of heterosexual intercourse. However others will wish to separate sex and reproduction entirely during their fertile years. They will seek either to prevent conception or, if necessary, to interrupt an established pregnancy, and it is these strategies for birth control that we examine in Chapter 4. An inability to determine her own pattern of procreation will severely limit a woman's capacity to control the rest of her life. Yet as we shall see, many are still constrained in their ability to make informed choices by material, social, cultural and religious pressures. If women do seek medical help in controlling their fertility, doctors may be reluctant to acknowledge their right to choose and the techniques offered may themselves be hazardous to health.

Whatever their circumstances, the vast majority of the world's women do embark, at some point in their lives, on the road to motherhood. In Chapter 5 we discuss the ways in which the social context of this childbearing can have a major impact on their health. Indeed it may determine whether they live or die since for overworked and undernourished women, motherhood can be fatal. It is, of course, this potential for biological reproduction that separates women's health needs most clearly from those of men. But as we have seen, it also separates women most markedly from each other, with the risk of death or disability varying dramatically between rich and poor countries.

Women's relationship with organised medicine is one of the key factors influencing their experiences of pregnancy and childbirth. If a pregnancy goes wrong, lack of access to obstetric care can be fatal and in many third world countries this is the situation many millions of women face each year. In developed countries, on the other hand, doctors are often accused of dominating childbirth to the detriment of mothers and babies. This paradox will be explored as we place contemporary childbearing in its broader social and economic context.

Many millions of women combine motherhood and their domestic responsibilities with economic activities both inside and outside the home. Officially 40 per cent of women around the world are now in the labour force, though this is clearly an underestimate since many are unrecorded, especially in the informal sector or in casualised work (Rowbotham and Mitter, 1994; UN, 1991; Young, 1993). As Chapter 6 will demonstrate, many employed women improve their general well-being through greater access to the basic necessities for physical health, through enhanced social status and through their involvement in wider support networks.

However the circumstances of some women's employment will limit the potential health benefits of waged work. Because they usually retain responsibility for domestic labour, many women workers become physically and emotionally exhausted. This is especially true of those with the least material and social support. The nature of the work itself can also be hazardous. Employment has brought many women into contact with the same hazards that men have faced for generations. Meanwhile there is growing evidence that what is regarded as 'women's work' may involve risks of its own. The impact of women's economic activity on their health therefore needs very careful assessment.

An examination of these different dimensions of women's lives offers a framework for understanding the social context of their health and illness. When these various activities are put alongside each other, it becomes clear that for many women the pressures of demanding work under conditions of inequality and discrimination may lead to considerable distress. During the childbearing years they may have very little time for rest or renewal, always feeling themselves to be carrying a significant burden of responsibility. Later in life, poverty, isolation and poor health may make relative longevity a dubious benefit. In Chapter 7 we explore some of the means by which women have sought to alleviate the negative feelings associated with these experiences.

Psychoactive substances of one kind or another are available in most societies and men have usually been the major users. However the last two decades have seen a marked rise in substance use and misuse by women, often with negative effects on their health. There is evidence of a huge increase in women's consumption of cigarettes and their abuse of alcohol is now becoming visible. In developed countries there has also been an epidemic of tranquilliser use, as some doctors have colluded with women in the creation of a dependency that can have both physical and psychological consequences. This provides us with a further opportunity to assess women's complex relationship with organised medicine and the contradictory effects it may have on their health.

Much of this book will be concerned with women's troubles – with the ways in which their attempts to realise their own potential and that of others can be damaging to their well-being. However its major purpose is to contribute to the process of making their lives healthier. The final chapter will therefore highlight the many strategies adopted by women around the world to promote their own health and that of their families. This will include a discussion of campaigns for reforming medical care. However it will also cover much broader issues, including the fight for reproductive rights and occupational health and safety, the struggle against violence against women, and the role of women in broader environmental and development politics. It will explore the potential contribution of both (reformed) biomedicine and wider social change in promoting women's health.

Further Reading

Fee, E. and Krieger, N. (1994) *Women's Health, Politics and Power: essays on sex/gender, medicine and public policy,* Baywood Publishing Company. A collection of articles that offers a framework for understanding women's struggles for health, topics include women as health workers, women's, occupational health, international reproductive health issues and AIDS.

Koblinsky M., Timyan, J. and Gay, J. (1993) *The Health of Women: a global perspective* (Boulder, Colorado: Westview Press). An interesting collection of articles reviewing the international data on a number of women's health and health care issues, including maternal mortality, violence, nutrition, reproductive rights and mental health. It focuses mainly on third world countries and provides a useful basis for further research.

Martin, E. (1987) *The Woman in the Body: a cultural analysis of reproduction* (Milton Keynes: Open University Press). An important introduction to the use of anthropological methods in exploring women's health issues. Based on interviews with a broad spectrum of women in the United States, it contrasts medical views of the female body with those of women themselves.

Miles, A, (1991) *Women, Health and Medicine* (Milton Keynes: Open University Press). A useful introduction to the sociological literature on women, health and health care in developed countries. It offers a clear account of both the British and American literature and would be of particular value to social science and health studies students.

Smyke, P. (1991) *Women and Health* (London: Zed Books). A campaigning book that explores the relationship between women, health and development. It includes case studies, a resource guide and suggestions for action.

United States National Institutes of Health (1992) *Opportunities for Research on Women's Health* US Department of Health and Human Services (NIH Publication no. 92–3457). A comprehensive review of the health problems facing women in the United States and a research agenda for their resolution. This important publication identifies the key issues that need to be tackled if the male bias in medical research is to be confronted.

White, E. (1990) *Black Women's Health Book: speaking for ourselves* (Seattle: Seal Press). This book offers a broad spectrum of experiences and insights on health issues from African American women. It includes autobiography, history, poetry and interviews as well as a list of organisations in the United States that address black women's health issues.

Worcester, N. and Whatley, M. (1994) *Women's Health: readings on social, economic and political issues,* 2nd edn (Dubuque: Kendall/Hunt). A broad ranging collection of articles covering a wide range of women's health issues. This book is designed particularly for student use and offers valuable material on issues of race, class, gender, sexuality and disability.

World Health Organisation (1992) *Women's Health Across Age and Frontier* (Geneva: WHO). A valuable collection of data on women's health and health care from around the world. It provides useful material for teaching and discussion groups.

2

Hazards of Hearth and Home

Introduction

The private world of the family has traditionally been viewed as the domain of women. Their capacity for mothering has been assumed to tie them to the sphere of domesticity, leaving the public space to be inhabited by men (Moore, 1988, p. 21). The daily lives of most men and women now bear little resemblance to such idealised notions of the male breadwinner and the female nurturer. Yet in most societies women continue to be very closely identified with the world of home and family. As we shall see, these economic and social arrangements can have profound effects on their health.

It is, of course, impossible to generalise about the workings of families between societies or across different communities. Households vary in their composition – in who are defined as members and who are not – and in the dynamics of their internal relationships – in who controls what, who does what tasks, and who receives what benefits. They also vary in their relationship with the wider society. At different extremes, families may be almost entirely self-contained in what they produce and how they utilise it, or they may receive all of their resources from the wage system, from some form of state welfare or from an extended kinship network (Kabeer, 1991; Moore, 1988; Young, 1993, Ch. 7; Young et al., 1981). But despite this variety there are certain commonalities in household operation that we need to understand in order to analyse the significance of domestic life for women's health.

Women's Labour in the Household Economy

Naila Kabeer has defined the household as 'the bundle of relationships in a society through which reproductive activities are organised' (Kabeer, 1991, p. 10). The term 'reproductive' includes not just

27

biological but also social reproduction – the maintenance of the well-being of those individuals located within the boundaries of the household. Thus the activities to be carried out will consist of the production, acquisition and distribution of a variety of valued resources, starting with those essential for survival.

Around the world, households without men are becoming increasingly common, either by choice or through necessity. However the majority of women continue to spend the greater part of their lives cohabiting with men. In most societies their domestic activities are then constrained by a set of principles about how tasks should be allocated between the sexes, and how the resulting resources are to be distributed.

What Do Women Do?

Despite cultural variation between communities, it is usually women who continue to be allocated responsibility for what is regarded as 'domestic work' – the daily tasks of cooking, cleaning and caring for children and other dependants. They may also be responsible for the production of food and other items to meet their families' needs as well as carrying out a variety of economic activities to earn extra income. Even when they take on paid work, most women retain responsibility for domestic labour, and this can lead to an excessive workload, especially during their childbearing years. After the menopause, heavy domestic responsibilities may have to be combined with the care of adult dependants. In the United States, the average woman now spends slightly longer on the care of ageing parents than on raising children.

The most obvious characteristics of domestic work in all countries are probably its open-endedness and its sheer volume. There is no limit to how much can be required in a given period, and no entitlement to holidays or even meal breaks. Very importantly there may be no obvious end to the working day, so that many find it difficult to separate work from rest or 'leisure'. Indeed those with young children may never really be 'off duty' as working hours even extend to periods of snatched sleep. For many this can lead to a punishing burden of both physical and mental labour.

Much of this work has traditionally been invisible. It has been seen as 'natural' and therefore 'good' for women, requiring neither investigation nor regulation. However these assumptions are now being questioned as women themselves have begun to disclose more of the reality of their daily labours. In developed countries the main focus has been on women's mental health in the light of their overrepresentation among those suffering from depression. In the poorest parts of the world it is the physical strains of household labour that have become more visible as women's workload intensifies against the backdrop of social upheaval, economic recession and ecological deterioration.

What Do Women Earn?

The household is not only a workplace for women. It is also the unit through which most receive their allotted share of both material and non-material resources. In most third world countries women have little access to what are, in any case, very small public funds. In developed countries, they form the majority of those dependent on state benefits, but only women living without men receive them directly. For the rest, the benefits come to the family unit through what is usually a male 'head of household'. While an increasing number of women are now involved in paid work, research suggests that many have little control over how their earnings are spent (Bruce and Dwyer, 1988).

Thus many women have the most important components of their health distributed through the family economy. This includes not only essentials such as food, water, income and access to medical care, but also less tangible resources such as time for sleep, reflection and renewal, emotional support, social status, and investment in education to ensure future well-being. Not surprisingly the allocation of these private resources is especially important to women living in societies without public sector health and welfare services. Indeed they may mean the difference between life and death.

Policy makers and academics have traditionally worked within the model of the ideal household, where all activities are designed to maximise the welfare of the unit as a whole (Becker, 1981). Furthermore, individuals within households have been assumed to act altruistically towards each other, ensuring that each member gets if not equal shares, then shares commensurate with their needs. It is assumptions of this kind that have formed the basis of economic and social policies in rich countries, and also the development strategies in much of the third world.

However they have come under increasingly critical scrutiny as concern for women's welfare has led to the opening up of the 'black box' of the family (Dwyer and Bruce, 1988; Kabeer, 1991; Sen, 1990a; Young, 1993, Ch. 7). A growing volume of research has shown systematic variations in the objective interests of different household members, in their capacity to articulate those interests, and in their ability to ensure their needs are met. As we shall see, inequalities in influence and power mean that it is frequently women and girls whose access to resources is most restricted.

This chapter begins by exploring the impact of women's domestic work on their physical health. It then goes on to look at emotional and psychological aspects of household labour and women's access to social support. This is followed by an analysis of what women get in return for their work – the distribution of food, income, time and other valuable resources within the domestic environment. The chapter concludes with a discussion of the health hazards of domestic violence. Physical strength will sometimes be the most powerful weapon a man has, and the nature of domestic life may make it difficult for women to resist. Yet it is often left off the agenda in considerations of the relationship between women's domestic work and their health.

Cross-Cultural Perspectives on Domestic Work

Whatever their cultural differences, most societies give women ultimate responsibility for the well-being of their families, often at considerable cost to their own health. However the implications will vary depending on socio-economic circumstances. Housework and child care are relatively similar in Birmingham England and Birmingham Alabama, but they are very different in the slums of São Paulo or the rural wastes of the Sahel.

No Time for Women

Women in the rich countries work out their survival strategies through their own and sometimes their partner's negotiations with both the labour market and the state. This will often be difficult, time-consuming and exhausting and the impact on the health of poor women should not be underestimated as they cobble together wages, benefits, subsidies or rebates for the purchase of necessities (Blackburn, 1991; Graham, 1993).

The introduction of basic services such as running water, gas and electricity, along with the development of domestic appliances, ameliorated the hard physical labour that exhausted so many working-class women in the nineteenth and early twentieth centuries (Llewellyn Davies, 1978; Oren, 1974; Pember Reeves, 1980). However 'housework' still remains a predominantly female responsibility. In the United States women now spend about 30 hours a week on domestic tasks compared with 15 hours for men, while western European women spend 31 hours and men 11 hours (United Nations, 1991, p. 82). Though this represents a decline for women since 1975, it is more than balanced by an increase in their hours of paid work.

These averages conceal the particularly heavy burden borne by poor women with young children and few resources (Blackburn, 1991; Graham, 1993; Payne, 1991). The number of women on or below the poverty line has increased dramatically in most of the developed countries over the past two decades (Evason, 1991; Glendinning and Millar, 1992; Scott, 1984; Zopf, 1989). The majority are either elderly women dependent on state benefits or single mothers. Many older women have great difficulty in making ends meet and single mothers often lack either the time or the resources to ensure their own well-being (Graham, 1993; Popay and Jones, 1990).

A study in the United Kingdom found that mothers who bring up children alone have consistently worse health than those in two-parent households. According to the women themselves this is due in large part to their money worries combined with heavy caring responsibilities. As one commented: 'It's various stresses you know, little bits and pieces all put together to make a big one' (Popay and Jones, 1990).

Working Themselves to Death

However it is among poor women in third world countries that the rigours of domestic work are at their most severe (Buvinic, Lycette and McGreevey, 1983). Many have little or no money to spend in the cash economy and welfare services are not available to fill the gap. As a result they have to weave their patchwork of survival through the direct production of their own and their family's needs. Many are engaged in subsistence agriculture, growing and then processing the food they can not afford to buy. Fuel is usually collected in the form of firewood rather than purchased from a gas or electricity supply company, and water is collected from a local source rather than flowing to the house through pipes. Thus the physical burdens of domestic labour can be very great.

It is usually women who have to manage the consequences of poverty for the whole family. This often means performing physically heavy work, even during pregnancy and lactation (Dankelman and Davidson, 1988; Momsen and Townsend, 1987; Sen and Grown, 1988). Recent statistics from the African and Asian regions indicate that on average women work at least 12 hours longer each week than men (UN, 1991, p. 82). In many of the poorest countries, between 60 and 90 hours a week of hard labour are required to maintain minimal living standards in the face of economic recession (ibid.) Again the pressures are especially severe for women in the millions of households where they are the sole parent.

According to a study conducted in villages in the Karnataka region of India, the labour of women and children together contributed almost 70 per cent of the total human energy expended on village work, even though strictly domestic tasks such as sweeping, washing clothes and child care were excluded (Kishwar, 1984, p. 4). Work of this intensity can be both exhausting and debilitating. A recent study in Gambia demonstrated that when domestic work is combined with heavy agricultural labour many women use up more calories than they consume. Not surprisingly the resulting weight loss can have serious consequences for their health (Kabeer, 1991, p. 29).

In the richer parts of the world most women can take for granted the existence of a constant supply of clean water. However there are millions of women from the rural areas of Bangladesh to the crowded barrios of Latin America who must face the daily task of acquiring enough water to meet the needs of their families. This is a physically demanding job, which in rural areas will often mean a lengthy journey.

Water is needed not just for drinking but for sanitation and waste disposal, washing, child care, vegetable growing and food processing and also for economic uses such as keeping animals, irrigating crops and brewing beer. The water for all this has to be fetched by women and is usually carried in containers on their heads since few have access to a vehicle of any kind or even a donkey. Many walk miles every day for a few pots of water, and where wells are deep raising the water may be extremely difficult. In urban areas women depend on public taps, which can mean long waits and no privacy for bathing. Research has shown that for some women water collection depletes more than a quarter of the energy gained from their daily food intake (Rodda, 1991, p. 84).

Under these circumstances water will have to be utilised sparingly, making domestic tasks more difficult. Insufficient or polluted water can also result in illness for women or their families. Diarrhoea, for instance, is a major cause of death among young children and is closely correlated with a lack of clean water. Women in particular suffer from inadequate sanitation since religious and moral prohibitions often mean they have to wait until dark to avoid being seen in the act of defecation. This can lead to constipation and strain on the bladder and also exposes them to the risk of assault (Dietrich, 1986).

As well as fetching water, many women are also responsible for procuring an adequate amount of fuel for cooking, boiling water, and heating and lighting the house (Agarwal, 1986). Again this very arduous task is rarely done by men and is a significant factor in the exhaustion suffered by many rural women. Throughout the world women are carrying loads as great as 35 kilograms as far as 10 kilometres. The distance varies but the round trip can take as much as three or four hours per day, and in some areas deforestation means that the time it takes is constantly lengthening (ibid., p. 17).

Many women are also directly involved in the production of food for their families. They grow a variety of crops, either for immediate consumption or to be sold or bartered, as well as raising poultry or small animals. When food for sale or exchange is scarce they may have to scour the countryside for edible matter such as the roots and leaves of plants. Raw food also has to be processed, often by laborious and lengthy methods. Madhu Kishwar's account of food preparation in one region of India gives some indication of the arduousness of the work involved:

> Grain or pulses to be consumed have to be hand-cleaned, little pebbles or pieces of dirt hand-sifted or painstakingly removed, one by one before the cooking of every meal. Many women have to hand-pound the paddy or grind the wheat two or three days a week in order to make it consumable. The paddy first has to be boiled and dried in the sun before it is husked. To husk 20 pounds of paddy, two women can easily spend two to three hours, and it takes much longer if a woman has to do it alone (Kishwar, 1984, pp. 3–4).

In Gambia the hand-pounding of coos – the staple grain – consumes nearly five calories a minute and takes six hours' work (1800 calories) to meet the daily needs of an average family (Kabeer, 1991, p. 27).

The domestic labour of many women is therefore extremely hard. It can be both physically and emotionally strenuous and the hours are long, leaving many exhausted (Popay, 1992). When it is combined with work for pay these pressures are increased, especially for women with few material resources and little social support (Belle, 1990). Caroline White has highlighted the ways in which social and economic deprivation may intensify women's work without reducing the standards achieved. In her study of employed black women in a Johannesburg township she comments:

> Men find their meals as well cooked and their clothes just as beautifully washed and ironed as a man from the Northern suburbs, though they are the product of a primus stove, a flat iron and cold water from a standpipe (White, 1993).

Occupational Hazards of Household Labour

As well as being debilitating, domestic work can also pose more specific threats to women's health. Domestic accidents are relatively common, especially among older women. In Australia half of all accidents suffered by women happen at home, compared with only 21 per cent of those suffered by men, and the pattern appears to be similar in most developed countries (Broom, 1986, p. 20).

In third world countries data on domestic accidents are extremely sparse, but it is clear from the nature of the work that here too they are a major risk. During a recent drought in Madras water was only available at night, and many women had to go without sleep and lift extremely heavy vessels in order to ensure adequate supplies for their families.

> According to doctors, lifting of kodams will lead to a prolapsed uterus. Lakshmi, aged 37, is a victim of this disorder. She is a mother of two, and works as a punching operator, earning about Rs450. For the last five months she has been spending many hours procuring water. She had to go to pumps or taps a couple of streets from her house and each time carried the kodams on her waist. This resulted in a prolapsed uterus and she had to be operated upon. Now supposed to be convalescing, she cannot avoid lifting weights. As she says, 'I have to, what to do?' (Kishwar, 1984, p. 112).

Routine tasks such as wood gathering may also put women at risk, as one report from Burkina Faso indicates:

The women work with energy and considerable courage. Small babies are carried along and shaken at every blow of the machete. Young girls come along to help, the fittest women climb up trees, scramble up steep slopes of sharp scree, often in bare feet, and wrestle with shrubs perched on the edge of cliffs. Falls and injuries from cutting tools and stones are common (Rodda, 1991, p. 49).

The house in which a woman lives will significantly influence her health, both directly and indirectly through its effects on her domestic labour. Of course homeless women are usually at greatest risk, but provision of shelter alone will not suffice. Damp and dilapidated houses require extra labour to keep them clean, and dampness appears to be linked to increased levels of asthma, respiratory disease and chest problems (Hyndman, 1990; McCarthy *et al.*, 1985). While men, women and children will all be affected, it is women who are most vulnerable since their work requires them to spend longer periods at home, sometimes under conditions of physical and mental stress.

Looking after a home and its inhabitants may also bring women into contact with a variety of toxic chemicals that are largely unregulated and often inadequately tested (Dowie *et al.*, 1982; Morton and Ungs, 1979; Rosenberg, 1984). Most of these are products that are in common use in the home and garden, such as cleaning fluids, bleaches, detergents, insecticides. and pesticides. It has been estimated that the average household in the United States contains some 250 chemicals that are toxic enough to necessitate medical attention if ingested. (Rosenberg, 1984, p. 229). A study in Oregon found unexpectedly high levels of cancer among women not employed outside the home (Morton and Ungs, 1979). The authors rightly stress the difficulty of identifying a single cause, but call for further research to investigate potential chemical hazards in what they call the 'cottage industry' of housework (ibid., p. 353).

Few women in poor countries will be at risk from domestic chemicals of the kind found in Britain or the United States. However many are exposed to agro-chemicals, either in use or in storage. The growing shortage of wood in many rural areas has also made cooking more dangerous. In some places wood has been replaced by other flammable substances such as cattle dung and crop residues. These biomass fuels are less convenient for cooking, the fire has to be stoked continuously and the emissions are even more hazardous than woodsmoke (WHO, 1984).

Domestic fuels are major sources of air pollution in the home, forcing some women to inhale more smoke and pollutants than the inhabitants of the dirtiest cities. One study has indicated a daily inhalation of benzopyrene (a known carcinogen) equivalent to that contained in 400 cigarettes (WHO, 1984). Smoke pollution has been identified as a causal factor in the high levels of respiratory and eye disease found among women in some third world countries (Chen *et al.*, 1990; Norboo *et al.*, 1991). As well as respiratory dieseases such as acute bronchitis and pneumonia, it can also cause nasopharyngeal cancer among those exposed from early infancy (WHO, 1984).

Home may be especially hazardous for the millions of women in all parts of the world who do paid work at home to supplement the family income (Allen and Wolkowitz, 1987; Roldàn, 1985). A group of homeworkers in West Yorkshire in the United Kingdom, were asked about the hazards of their labour. As well as reporting eye strain, headaches, backache and tension, they also referred to the dangers of machinery, cutting tools and glues and to the general dirt and 'mess'. Some also commented on the fire hazard from inflammable materials stored in the corridor or kitchen (Allen and Wolkowitz, 1987, p. 141). In India many women work at home making *bidis* (handrolled cigarettes). Their lives are extremely hard, as one of them described:

> My health is now failing me. I am not able to roll more than 700 bidis, my arms are swollen from continuous cutting of the leaves. I resort to massage without effect. My eyes burn, and continual breathing in of the tobacco has made me asthmatic (Womankind Worldwide, n.d.)

Thus the domestic workplace is not free from the hazards found in industrial settings. Toxic substances do not become safe simply because they cross the threshold of the home and more research is needed to identify these dangers as well as more effective regulation to control them. Technical innovation is also required to make cooking and other domestic tasks safer in millions of homes.

Demands, Dilemmas and Distress

In developed countries most attention has been focused not on the physical hazards of domestic labour, but on the psychological risks.

Several studies have shown that full-time 'housewives' are particularly prone to depression, especially if they are at home with young children. Attempts to explain this have focused primarily on the nature of the work itself, on its low social status and on the conditions under which it is performed. The inequalities inherent in many heterosexual relationships have also been identified as causal factors. Though full-time 'housewives' are becoming rarer, these continue to be important issues in explaining women's mental health problems.

Marriage and Marital Status

In a classic investigation, Jessie Bernard found that while American men expressed a considerable degree of dissatisfaction with marriage, they also appeared to have relatively good mental health (Bernard, 1972). Women on the other hand were more likely to say they were happily married but exhibited much poorer mental health than men. This Bernard called the 'paradox of the happy marriage'. The contradiction was especially acute among full-time housewives, many of whom simultaneously expressed high levels of satisfaction with marriage as well as serious psychiatric symptoms. Indeed Bernard describes what she calls the 'housewife syndrome', consisting of nervousness, fainting, insomnia, trembling hands, nightmares, dizziness, heart palpitations, and other anxiety symptoms. She concluded that 'the housewife syndrome is far from a figment of anyone's imagination' and that 'being a housewife makes women sick' (ibid., p. 48).

Depression appears to be an occupational hazard among full-time housewives, especially those with young children. Both clinical experience and community research have shown that many women staying at home experience intense frustration, which is usually expressed in feelings of emptiness, sadness and worthlessness (Brown and Harris, 1978; Nairne and Smith, 1984). Too often these feelings go unacknowledged; women are said to be 'like that' and the front door closes on a great deal of misery and distress.

Brown and Harris, working in South London, found that one third of a random sample of working-class women with children under six who were full-time carers were suffering from what could be classified as 'clinical depression'. Lack of a close confiding relationship and the death of a mother at an early age were both found to be major risk factors, while employment outside the home appeared to offer a significant degree of protection.

In Ann Oakley's study of full-time British housewives few were positively happy with their work and 70 per cent expressed themselves 'dissatisfied' with their lives (Oakley, 1974). The women described most of their household tasks as monotonous, boring and repetitive – the very characteristics that occupational psychologists have shown to be most stressful for waged workers. Although they are not formally supervised, most women doing housework experience very powerful pressures, both from other people and from inside their own heads. Ann Oakley asked one of the women in her study whether she found housework monotonous. Sally Jordan replied:

> Well, I suppose I do really, because it's the same thing every day. You can't sort of say, 'I'm not going to do it', because you've got to do it. Take preparing a meal; it's got to be done, because if you don't do it, the children wouldn't eat. I suppose you get used to it, you do it automatically. When I'm doing housework, half the time I don't know what I'm thinking about. I'm sort of there, and I'm not there . . . I'm always going off into a trance, I don't hear people when they talk to me (Oakley, 1976, p. 147).

Many women get little satisfaction from their routine tasks and this is exacerbated by the lack of value awarded to domestic work by the wider society. Adults in employment receive wages but women working in their homes lack any equivalent rewards. This can limit their self-esteem and promote feelings of worthlessness. Since household work is rarely noticed unless it is neglected, many are deprived of any recognition for their labours, even from those for whom they are caring.

Of course many women do derive a considerable sense of achievement from work done in and for their families, and many develop considerable skills in the process. They learn to deal creatively with challenges and crises throughout their lives and many families would not have survived without women's problem-solving abilities and sheer hard work. Yet the tasks they perform are often not of their own choosing and may offer little in the way of enhanced personal autonomy.

Is Motherhood Maddening?

Mothering appears at first sight to be highly valued work and many find their relationships with their children the most rewarding ones of their lives. Watching them grow can be exhilarating, and the unconditional love of young children is immensely pleasurable. However the reality of daily child care can be both physically and emotionally demanding, especially in societies when there is little support from partner, friends or kin (Boulton, 1983; Graham and McKee, 1980; Oakley, 1981; Stevens and Meleis, 1991). For first-time mothers in particular, the responsibility of a tiny baby can be onerous, and nights without sleep exhausting and demoralising.

Research from a number of countries has suggested that a high proportion of women suffer significant physical problems in the weeks and months after childbirth (Cartwright, 1988; Romito, 1990; Romito and Zalateo, 1992). We know that many also become depressed for varying periods (Romito, 1990; Stein *et al.*, 1989). Precise figures are difficult to obtain but for many women depression seems to continue for long periods and is closely related to the social and economic circumstances in which they are mothering. This would suggest that apparently 'ordinary' motherhood may often be experienced as problematic and that there is a continuum between the experience of mothers who are clinically depressed and those who are not (Romito, 1993, p. 213).

Despite the lip service paid to motherhood as a social duty, few researchers have explored the reality of child care from a woman's perspective. In an attempt to fill this gap the British sociologist Mary Boulton carried out a series of in-depth interviews with young mothers at home (Boulton, 1983). Her aim was to disentangle women's feelings about the labour of child care from their love for their children or their response to the status of motherhood itself. Almost two thirds of women in the study experienced a strong sense of meaning, value and significance in looking after their children. However, over one third did not feel this way (ibid.) Moreover, some 60 per cent of her middle-class respondents and 44 per cent of those who were working class found looking after children to be predominantly an irritating experience. Thus the majority did not find child care 'naturally rewarding'. Yet this was their full-time work.

Many of the women referred to the high levels of stress they experienced in their lives and identified a number of factors contributing to it. The lack of boundaries was a particular problem and many felt themselves to be without physical or mental space. One woman said:

I think that children take away your whole life – your identity really. They are so demanding they take everything from you then come the

evening you're too exhausted to revert back to yourself . . . there's
no doubt about it, that your children just monopolise you, mentally,
physically and emotionally (Boulton, 1983, p. 96).

Many commented on the conflict between child care and housework,
with children constantly undoing what had just been achieved. For
others the major problem was the isolation often imposed by child care
in a nuclear family environment and the lack of opportunity for
significant relationships with other adults. In a study of the maternal
experiences of a group of United States clerical workers many similar
feelings emerged (Stevens and Meleis, 1991). In this case the women
were also employed, adding what were often experienced as further
pressures to their lives.

I have to cook, do errands, clean, grocery shop, visit my sick parents,
commute to work and back, prepare my kid's clothes and lunches for
school every day. My daughter can't participate in activities after
school. I can't take her because I'm at work so I feel bad. I don't
have any time for myself. I can't put aside enough time for just my
husband and me (Stevens and Meleis, 1991, p. 1429).

For some women, the time when their children leave home is a positive
one, offering them the opportunity to move on to new activities. Indeed
in some societies the role of mother-in-law and grandmother is a much
valued one, offering women greater autonomy than at any other point
in their lives. However for others the experience may be devastating, if
their identity has been vested in motherhood and their social and
economic environment offers few options for growth or development.
Under these circumstances depression and other mental health
problems may well result.

Dependants and Dependency

Conflicts and contradictions are also reported by women looking after
other dependants. About 15 per cent of women of working age in the
United Kingdom are caring full-time for someone who is sick, elderly
or disabled (Green, 1988). The need for such work is increasing, and
'community care' policies – now fashionable in much of the industrialised world – are based on the implicit assumption that women will
continue with these unpaid labours (Dalley, 1988; Finch and Groves,

1983). Yet there is growing evidence that they may not be conducive to the promotion of carers' own well-being.

The 'daily grind' of caring has been well documented in a number of British studies (Finch and Groves, 1983; Hicks, 1988). Much of the strain comes from the nature of the job itself – long hours, nightly disturbances and isolation when no substitute care is available. Caring for adults is especially demanding, often causing emotional problems that do not arise in the care of children. The daughter who cares for a parent and the wife who cares for a husband may have to negotiate new relationships under difficult circumstances, often with very little support. A British woman looking after her husband described her experience in the following way:

> The tiredness associated with looking after someone disabled was the hardest thing for me to adjust to . . . the tiredness is, of course, due to different causes for each carer, but the exhaustive effect is the same – for me, the tiredness comes from the physical exertion of caring for someone with severe multiple sclerosis, and from the mental stress of seeing the person you love best in the world suffering from such a disease (Briggs and Oliver, 1985, p. 39).

Many women actively choose to look after dependent relatives and experience great satisfaction in so doing. But for others the 'choice' may be more constrained. Female kin are expected to care for their relatives and moral pressures are often reinforced by the preference of those being cared for (Ungerson, 1987). Since women can rarely command high wages, the opportunity costs of leaving paid employment to become carers are usually less than they would be for a man. As a result many lose much of their independence, sometimes to the detriment of their own health. These problems can be especially acute for women on what has been called the 'caring tricycle' – the lifetime of responsibility that begins with care of children, continues into middle age with the care of an ageing parent and culminates in old age with responsibility for a frail partner.

Evidence from both the United Kingdom and the United States presents a broadly consistent picture. The nature of women's domestic work, the conditions under which it is performed, and the relations of dependency and inequality that often underlie it, can all limit their potential for positive mental health. In order to assess the extent of this problem we need to compare these findings with ethnographic research that explores women's daily lives in different social contexts.

Depression, 'Nervios' or Just Plain 'Bad News'?

Though few studies have looked cross-culturally at women's mental health, interesting similarities are beginning to emerge from very varied domestic environments. We will explore these connections by looking first at women in a southern Indian village and then at a number of studies carried out in Latin America.

An Example from India

In her study of married Brahmin women in an affluent village in southern India, Helen Ulrich found certain parallels with the experiences of United States and British women (Ulrich, 1987). More than half of those interviewed had a history of depressive symptoms. They reported appetite and weight loss, difficulties in sleeping, feelings of worthlessness and lack of interest in their normal activities. When asked about the reasons for such feelings, loss and separation from a loved one were frequently identified.

A number of the women reported early loss of a parent, as did many of the depressed women interviewed by Brown and Harris in South London (Brown and Harris, 1978). However in India these losses were mostly due not to death but to marriage customs, and women's lack of control over their own destinies. For most women in the village, marriage had meant moving to a new household some distance from their parents, making contact difficult. Life with their new families was frequently hard and inhospitable. For the older women, this separation had often occurred before puberty, causing considerable shock and distress.

> Kusuma, age fifty, was married at age twelve. She regarded herself as her father's favourite child. Aware that her father's choice was not her choice, she tried to persuade her father not to choose that person. . . . He came to view her and she reluctantly served him food. She persisted in her opposition. . . .
>
> She confided her despair to her best friend. They did not wish separation. Kusuma did not wish to marry and her friend did not wish to remain single. Twice they tried to drown themselves.
>
> This was the first depression Kusuma had experienced. It lasted two years (Ulrich, 1987, p. 275).

For mothers too, the loss of their daughters will often be a traumatic event, increasing their vulnerability to psychological distress.

The most frequent cause of depressive feelings among women in the village was widowhood. According to Ulrich the most dreaded loss is the death of a husband, and there were few widows who did not appear to be clinically depressed (ibid., pp. 277, 284). The traditional customs of widowhood were greatly feared – removal of jewellery, the wearing of special clothes, the performance of specific rituals and, in the past, the shaving of a widow's head. Some women also reported missing the personal support of their husbands. But the most important losses of widowhood appeared to be status and identity.

Women's existence was defined in relation to that of their husbands, and without them many felt existentially lost and without position in society. In one extreme case, a sixty-year-old woman who became a widow in 1985 'huddled underneath the stairway and indicated her presence only when inquired about' (ibid., p. 280). Tragically, many women reported that their main hope for the future was to die before their husbands.

Ulrich attributes much of the depression she encountered to the cultural devaluation of women and their confinement to the domestic sphere. She points out that in this village at least, circumstances had changed over the past few years, with women gaining a greater say in their lives and more opportunity to be educated and to work outside the home. This has apparently resulted in less depression among younger women.

A Case of 'Nervios'

Medical anthropologists have been concerned for some time with understanding the phenomenon of 'nervios', and studies have now been carried out in a number of countries (Davis and Guarnaccia, 1989; Low, 1989a). *Nevra, nerva, nervios, nevros* or *ataque de nervios* are all terms used to describe a condition experienced by many women and some men across a range of societies. Most of these are Latin cultures, but 'nerves' is also identified as a common problem in some ›Anglo communities.

The nature of the condition – the symptoms – shows some variation between social groups but the general pattern is similar. It includes headache, dizziness, fatigue, weakness and stomach problems as well as feelings of worry, anger and sadness (Davis and Guarnaccia, 1989). The meanings attached to the feelings may vary across cultures, but in most it is predominantly women who experience them, and it is usually the circumstances of their domestic lives that they identify as the main precipitating factor. In some instances the symptoms may be relatively mild but in others they will be disabling and amount to substantial illness.

Most communities in which 'nervios' is a common complaint are poor and occupy a marginal status in the dominant society. This is often a result of migration or some other process of rapid transition. Under these circumstances women often face serious difficulties in holding their family's lives together economically, socially and emotionally. It is the contradictions inherent in their daily lives, and the pressures generated by unrealistic expectations of family and community that appear to be especially distressing, and 'nervios' can best be understood within this context.

In her study of a resettled *colonia* outside Guatemala City, Setha Low identified a number of factors that women themselves associated with the symptoms of 'nervios'. Presented in order of importance, the causes were

> rage and anger (*cólera, se enoja*), grief and sorrow (*pena*), birth control pills, other illness, birth of a child, worries (*preoccupaciones*), problems, fright (*susto*), pregnancy, caring for children, night work, earthquake and death of a child (Low, 1989b, p. 123).

The rural women interviewed by Ruth Finerman in Andean Ecuador gave very similar accounts. Over half of all episodes of 'nervios' were associated with personal or family illness or death and more than a quarter of all women with 'nervios' mentioned domestic disorder, including 'recalcitrance of offspring and *mal compartamiento* (poor comportment) of their spouses (drinking, debauchery, and arguing with wives)' (Finerman, 1989, p. 145).

The complex relationship between domestic 'troubles' and psychological and physical distress is evident in the account of one Ecuadorean woman:

> Sometimes, you know really very often, the children get sick. It is my responsibility to keep them healthy, but with children you are always preparing remedies. When they are all sick they cry, they don't want to eat, and this gives me suffering. When it is really bad I can't think and then I start to shake. . . . Strong headaches hit me, sweat falls from me and I can't eat either . . . the only thing that helps is for the children to eat and recover (Finerman, 1989, p. 146).

Very similar feelings of powerlessness are evident in the account of 44-year-old May, an African American woman who has mothered four children and is now bringing up two grandchildren on her own. She defines her condition as 'bad news'.

> I just worries sometimes about things I don't have no control over. I got a bill and I can't pay that bill. My father is sick, and he never been down sick, cause of my baby born dead. And you know sometimes I have bad headaches and stuff. I have to take medicine for my nerves. I get, you know, just the least little thing tear me to pieces and I just get so nervous cause I just cries and you know and the least little thing just worry me, just worry me (Finkler, 1989, p. 173).

Social Significance of Mental Distress

Thus anthropologists have identified what can be called an 'idiom of distress' that crosses cultural boundaries yet has specific meanings in different social contexts. As we have seen, the feelings are comparable to those described as anxiety and depression within Western medicine, though their particular configuration and the way they are experienced may be very different (Davis and Guarnaccia, 1989, pp. 7–8). The individual and social significance of these 'idioms of distress' can be understood in a variety of different ways.

On the one hand 'nervios' or 'depression' can be seen as a complex physical and psychological response to the contradictory and demanding reality of so many women's daily lives. Indeed some writers have described an *ataque de nervios* as the literal 'embodiment' of women's oppression (Finkler, 1989, p. 174). In some instances they may be a culturally acceptable way of expressing anger and grief when no alternative outlets are permitted. It is also clear that a serious case of 'nervios' is often a cry for help or a means of achieving change when the individual concerned is otherwise powerless.

In her discussion of 'nervios' among menopausal women in Peru, Elyse Ann Barnett illustrates these different dimensions of distress. About 80 per cent of the women she interviewed in Puente Piedre reported feeling 'nervios' to a greater or lesser extent (Barnett, 1989, p. 161). Many reported symptoms of anger (*cólera*), having '*muy mal de humor*' (a very bad temper), as well as '*grita a los hijos*' (yelling at the children) and *fastidio* (finding fault with everything). This suggests that

'nervios' during the menopause may allow th
often suppressed earlier in life.

Significantly 'nervios' in Puente Piedre gave
their homes and to act more independently – g
walks with friends was seen as a potential cure   often
allowed to distance themselves from their husbands, to avoid both
sexual and emotional services that they no longer wished to provide.
Thus in this community, as in many others, it is important to see an
ataque de nervios or other forms of physical or psychological distress as
a negotiating device, a strategy for those with little power to gain some
control over their lives. In some instances these will be successful, but
as we shall see, the circumstances of many women's lives leave little
room for manoeuvre.

Who Cares for the Carers?

Millions of women around the world spend much of their time doing
what could be called 'emotional housework'. This is activity designed
to manage social relationships, to ensure harmony between household
members and to promote the emotional health of others. It is often the
least visible of their labours but may well be a major burden.

> The emotional work of enhancing the status and well-being of others
> is a form of what Ivan Illich has called 'shadow labour'; an unseen
> effort which, like housework, does not quite count as labour but is
> nevertheless crucial in getting things done. As with doing housework
> the trick is to erase any evidence of effort, to offer only the clean
> house and the welcoming smile (Hochschild, 1983).

But who is looking after women's needs while they smile for others?
For many the answer is no-one. Research findings in both the United
Kingdom and the United States suggest that in many families women
do not receive the emotional sustenance they might have expected from
their nearest and dearest. Adult daughters may provide support but
this is much less true of grown-up sons and male partners (Miles, 1988).

In a recent British study Agnes Miles interviewed a group of men
and women who had been diagnosed as suffering from depression.
About half of the women mentioned an unhappy marriage as an
element in their distress, whereas most men referred to work and health
problems (ibid., pp. 28, 42). When asked about the support they had

received, only 24 out of 65 women named their male partner as their main confidante and not all of these were satisfied with the quality of the relationship:

(Iris, 24, no children). 'There is only my husband. I wish there was someone else. Mostly I keep my thoughts to myself. I hoard my thoughts, then I get upset and tell my husband because there is nobody else. I usually regret it afterwards. He is part of the trouble, but who else can I talk to?'

(Bridget, 29, two children 4 and 7). 'I wish I had more people. I wish I had a woman friend. My husband is there but he doesn't want to talk, not like women talk to each other. He doesn't understand. He just says, don't bother me with nonsense (Miles, 1988, pp. 94–5)

Many of the women also expressed their concern about putting too much of a burden on other people. They feared that what little help they had would be withdrawn and saw themselves as fundamentally unworthy of support. Interestingly, the men in the sample did not report the same problems in getting help from their wives. As Miles expressed it, 'both took it for granted that this was the natural order of things' (ibid., p. 113).

Susannah Ginsberg and George Brown uncovered a similar pattern in their study of women in the North London suburb of Islington (Ginsberg and Brown, 1982). Again they were interviewing women who fitted the clinical diagnosis of depression, in an attempt to see how relatives, friends and doctors responded to them. This research repeated the common finding that signs of depression (such as inexplicable crying) are often given little attention since they are regarded as 'normal' for women, especially when they are young mothers or menopausal. Three quarters of those interviewed who were living with their husbands felt that he had given 'little or no support'. Mrs Thomas, for instance, said:

'I told my husband how depressed I've been feeling. He just sits in silence. If he could just talk things out and suggest something – but he doesn't.'
    'Has he suggested you should go to the doctor?'
    'No, he doesn't realise anything is wrong. He doesn't notice that I haven't been getting on with things.' (Ginsberg and Brown, 1982, p. 93)

The majority who were living with their husbands said they did try to talk about their depression but most were unsuccessful. Many apparently responded with such comments as 'You're imagining it all', 'Stop being silly', or 'You mustn't talk like that, there's the baby' (ibid., p. 95).

American psychotherapists Luise Eichenbaum and Susie Orbach have used psychoanalytic insights to explore these sexual divisions in caring. Most men, they say, are looked after by women all their lives, from their mothers and other female relatives through female teachers to their wives or female partners in adulthood. A girl on the other hand is brought up to assume that she will marry a man and provide nurture, care and emotional support for him and his children. While she is expected to *appear* 'dependent, incompetent and somewhat fragile', the internal reality is rather different:

> behind this outward façade is someone who, whatever the inner state, will have to deal with the emotional problems met in family relationships, a person who knows that others will expect to rely and lean on her, a person who fears that she will never really be able to depend on others or never feels content about her dependency (Eichenbaum and Orbach, 1985, p. 21).

Thus many adult women cannot fulfil their own basic need for nurture and emotional fulfilment, despite – or because of – their position at the hub of what is widely regarded as the most caring institution in modern society.

Of course families vary greatly in the amount of social support they are willing and able to give to their female members, and cross-cultural generalisations are difficult to make. We know for instance that in many Afro-Caribbean and African American families the relationship between mothers and daughters is especially strong, with each supporting the other in times of need. In other communities, where extended kinship networks are still the norm, relatives may offer a supportive network and continuing source of validation. In Ulrich's study of Brahmin women, for instance, about a third of those who were depressed had received significant support from within their families (Ulrich, 1987, p. 281). Similarly, many studies in Latin America and elsewhere have shown that considerable help may be mobilised by signs of 'nervios' (Finerman, 1989).

However there is growing evidence that for millions of women emotional support is rarely available. And it is not just in developed countries that women may find their homes heartless. Even in societies where extended families continue to be the norm, relationships may be competitive rather than supportive. Indeed in many cultures antagonism between mothers and daughters-in-law is endemic. In some parts of the world the dramatic upheavals associated with economic migration and urbanisation are putting women under greater domestic strain, while at the same time destroying traditional sources of support. For one Ecuadorian woman no comfort was available in her old age:

It has been 11 years now since my husband died. . . . When this happened it was like a knife cut into me. My heart beat, I shook like an earthquake. I cried for months. . . . Everyone said I would recover but this wasn't the case. . . . I have no-one to take care of me. They are all married and live [far away] in the Oriente. Two of my children died; a son and a daughter. I have no-one to talk to; family, friends, no-one. So I sit alone in the house and cry and stare at the wall (Finerman, 1989, p. 153).

We know that social support is an essential element in the promotion and maintenance of physical and mental health. Women play a central part in providing that support to those around them, but too often they are denied it themselves. Those who can afford it may turn instead to doctors to cure the 'illness' of depression or remove the distress associated with 'nervios'. However they rarely obtain what they are seeking. The experiences of two African American women can speak for many:

I told them up at the hospital about my nerves. They told me to let my problems out, to talk to other people. Onliest thing is there is no-one to talk to.

I told my doctor – doctor gave me pills all the time and said to stop worrying. He says that but he never tells me how (Camino, 1989, p. 307).

To Each According To Her Needs?

Thus far we have painted a picture of domestic environments in which women (and girls) often work extremely hard, their labours sometimes more intensive than their male partner's. This presents a striking contrast with the low levels of investment many families make in girl children, and the limited material rewards allocated to their mothers.

The pattern of resource allocation within households remains a largely private affair. However recent research in both rich and poor countries has identified gender inequalities in access to income, wealth and other material requirements for a healthy life (Dwyer and Bruce, 1988; Pahl, 1989). Of course the degree of such inequalities varies markedly between societies, reflecting both cultural values and women's perceived contribution to the family and to the wider economy (Papanek, 1990; Sen, 1990a). Inequality is greater for instance in 'classic patriarchies' such as Bangladesh, where women are socially constructed as passive and vulnerable, and less in many parts of Sub-Saharan Africa, where women tend to have greater economic independence (Kabeer, 1991, pp. 20–5). Generally speaking however, women get less than men and are often the poorest of the poor.

Further research is needed to identify both the processes by which these inequalities are generated and the effects they have on women's health and well-being. However we can begin to unravel the complexity by looking at the growing evidence of gender differences in access to nutrition and health care. Although women are usually responsible for the purchase and preparation of food, and sometimes for its production too, it is clear that in many countries they do not get enough to eat. The pattern of food distribution within families commonly has an age and sex bias, and this is especially true in some of the poorest third world economies (Sen, 1990a). While both sexes may be damaged by lack of food, women are especially vulnerable. This is due in large part to special needs associated with biological processes of reproduction (Hamilton *et al.*, 1984). However in some communities these needs are increased by the socially constructed burden of household and agricultural labour (Mebrahtu, 1991).

Menstruation, pregnancy and lactation all increase women's need for protein, vitamins and minerals. This is difficult to measure precisely, but it has been estimated that pregnant women need 350 extra calories per day, while those feeding their babies need 550 extra calories, as well as three times the normal intake of calcium and double the amount of vitamin A (Protein-Calorie Advisory Group, 1977). Research in both developed and third world countries has shown that many pregnant women do not get enough of the right food to meet these needs.

A study carried out in 1988 by the London-based Maternity Alliance showed that despite the existence of a welfare state some British women were still not able to feed themselves adequately during pregnancy. The average cost of the diet recommended for pregnant women by the Department of Health was equivalent to nearly half the weekly benefit payable to a single person and a third of that for a couple (Durward, 1988). As a result the many pregnant women on state benefit could not afford to eat what was officially defined as necessary to sustain their own health and that of their unborn children.

In many third world countries the nutritional problems of poor women are of course much greater. While this is partly due to the greater scarcity of food for both sexes, discrimination is also a contributory factor. There is abundant anecdotal evidence to suggest that even when food is plentiful, male 'breadwinners' are given entitlement to the best. In conditions of scarcity women are even more likely to lose out:

'And if very rarely we get fish, only the head is left for me', a village woman from Sri Lanka explained laughingly. Another woman in Sri Lanka who had just given birth and was afraid of not having enough milk told me not laughingly but in tears: 'I bought lula [a variety of fish] from the money I earned myself because it is good for breast milk. When I had just prepared it my brother entered. He smelled the fish and wanted me to dish up food. When I told him it was my fish and that I needed it myself to have enough milk for the baby he got terribly angry. He grabbed the pot and threw all the fish to the dogs' (Schrijvers, 1988, p. 32).

It is significant that this discrimination affects not only adult women but young girls, who may receive less than their brothers throughout their lives (Sundari Ravindran, 1986). In societies where 'son preference' is strongest, selective infanticide may be tolerated, with female babies not surviving long after birth. Such cases often reflect the real desperation of poor parents with several daughters who cannot afford the dowries that will be expected of them (Venkatramani, 1986). But whatever the immediate circumstances, the killing of girls provides striking evidence of both the cultural and economic strength of sexism in some of the world's most intensely patriarchal societies (Miller, 1981).

If they survive gestation and birth, girls may then be breastfed for shorter periods than boys and subsequently receive a less adequate diet. A classic study in Matlab, Bangladesh found that the calorific intake of girls under five was lower than that of boys, both in terms of absolute intake and when adjusted for estimated nutritional requirement (Chen *et al.*, 1981). Young girls also received less protein and less vitamin A than boys. As a result more than 14 per cent of female children in the sample were found to be severely malnourished, compared with only 5 per cent of males. When sick, boys also benefited from more frequent hospital visits, a finding replicated in studies in a number of other countries in Asia, Africa and the Middle East (Sundari Ravindran, 1986; Waldron 1987, pp. 201–2).

The effects of discrimination of this kind on health are difficult to assess. However it seems to have a significant effect on mortality rates. In one study in the Punjab, girls born to families who already had one or more surviving daughters were much more likely to die in childhood than their siblings (das Gupta, 1987, p. 93). In most countries with an overall life expectancy of less than 60 years, girls have a higher mortality rate than boys and discriminatory practices make a contribution to this pattern (Waldron, 1987, p. 196). While there are about 106 women per 100 men in Europe and the United States, there are only 95 in Asia (Sen, 1990b, p. 124). In Pakistan there are only 90 women for every hundred men and in China too, 'son preference' appears to be persistent, with only 0.94 women to every male (ibid., p. 124).

We have seen that the allocation of resources within families can seriously damage the physical well-being of their female members. However it is also important to recognise the psychological effects of these practices. As Papanek points out, women and girls get messages about their own value from the way in which they are treated by others. Consistent experiences of discrimination are likely to lead to diminished self-worth and a 'culture of female sacrifice' that continuously reproduces preferential treatment for males (Papanek, 1990, p. 173).

Adding Injury to Insult

The home is commonly represented as a haven from the threats lurking in the outside world. Indeed it is in part the assumption of male protection that is used to justify inequalities in resource allocation. However the reality is often very different. Millions of women and girls are physically and sexually abused every year in what should be a safe place by men who are supposed to care for them and about them.

The Scope of the Problem

Physical violence inflicted on partners in intimate relationships is a common phenomenon and some 90 per cent of such attacks are

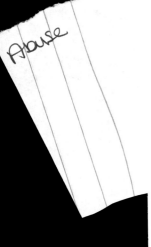

>etrated by men on women (Campbell, 1992; Dobash and Dobash,
); Levinson, 1989). Research in the 1970s and early 1980s was
:entrated mainly in developed countries, where violence was a
>r issue for the reemergent feminist movement. However it is now
that domestic violence is a public health issue on a global scale
:e, 1993; United Nations, 1989b). The 1993 *World Development*
rt indicated that rape and domestic violence together account for
.....i 5 per cent of the total disease burden of women aged 15–44 in
developing countries and 19 per cent in developed countries (World
Bank, 1993, p. 50). Domestic violence is more common in some
societies than in others and its legal status varies, as do levels of
public acceptance. However there appear to be none in which women
can feel entirely safe (Brown, 1992).

Precise estimates of the number of women battered each year are
hard to obtain, since many are both ashamed and afraid to reveal their
private suffering. Indeed one British study indicated that only about 2
per cent of such assaults are ever reported to the police (Dobash and
Dobash, 1980). However research in a number of developed countries
has suggested that the levels of domestic violence women experience are
broadly similar (United Nations, 1989, p. 20). Several studies in the
United States have indicated that at least 20 per cent of women have
been physically abused by a man with whom they have an intimate
relationship (Stark and Flitcraft, 1991, p. 123). Between 22 per cent
and 35 per cent of women visiting emergency rooms in United States
hospitals are there because of battering (World Bank, 1993, p. 50). In
the United Kingdom, too, a recent study suggested that one in four
women has been similarly attacked, while Norwegian figures present a
comparable picture (Andrews and Brown, 1988; Schei and Bakketeig,
1989).

Evidence now emerging from third world countries suggests that in
some the incidence may be even higher (Cox, 1994; Heise, 1993). A
comprehensive survey by the Papua New Guinea Law Commission
revealed that in certain areas more than two thirds of wives had
experienced marital violence (Gillet, 1990, p. 36). This appears to have
been intensified by the urbanisation and rapid social change, which has
loosened traditional constraints. Similar processes can be seen at work
in South Africa, where conflict during the years of apartheid has
intensified male domination in all racial groups (Armstrong, 1994). A
recent study estimated that around 60 per cent of cohabiting relationships now involve physical abuse (Motsei, 1993, p. 1). There is also
evidence of increasing violence against women among Afghanis forced

by civil war to live as refugees in Pakistan (Bradley, 1994, p. 18). Around the world, refugee women are particularly vulnerable to male attack (Cox, 1994).

In India the ending of domestic violence has been a major focus of the new feminist movements (Gandhi and Shah, 1992, Ch. 3; Mies, 1986). Wife beating was not defined as a crime until 1983 and thus far the law has had relatively little impact on male practices (Das, 1988). Urban and rural women, working class and middle class, young and old are all the potential objects of male abuse, but the most widely publicised attacks have been the so-called 'dowry murders' carried out in both India and Bangladesh. In these cases young women have been abused and eventually killed because husbands and their families were not satisfied with the money and goods their wives brought to the marriage. Many are deliberately burned to death, but a cooking accident with a kerosene stove is blamed. In 1990 the police officially recorded 4835 dowry deaths throughout India but the Ahmedabad Women's Action Group estimates that 1000 women may be burned annually in Gujurat state alone (Heise, 1993, p. 175). One out of four of all Bombay women dying between the ages of fifteen and twenty-four are officially said to have been killed by 'accidental burns' (Karkal, 1985).

It is clear that a significant proportion of the women who live with men have their health diminished or even destroyed by violence. Despite cultural differences the experience of being battered is shared by millions of women and it is often their performance as wives or mothers that provides the immediate excuse. The paradox of violence perpetrated on women in the apparent sanctity of their own homes is highlighted by the fact that pregnancy often appears to be a precipitating factor. In the United States women are significantly more likely to be battered by their partners if they are expecting a child (McFarlane *et al.*, 1992; Stark and Flitcraft, 1991, p. 135).

The Reality of Domestic Violence

A physical battering can include pushing, punching, kicking, hair pulling, clubbing, stabbing, shooting or throwing acid or boiling water, and the damage inflicted may be severe. Moreover coercive sex is often a significant component of an abusive relationship. In Papua New Guinea research has shown that a husband forcing his wife to have sex is one of the main elements of wife beating (Bradley, 1994, p. 17). In studies of battered women in Latin America, between 30 per cent and

58 per cent say that they are raped by their husbands (Cox, 1994, p. 135).

In one British study of the survivors of violence, nearly 80 per cent reported visiting their doctor at least once for injuries inflicted by their husbands (Dobash and Dobash, 1980). Nearly 40 per cent said they had sought medical care on five or more occasions and many had been prevented by their husbands from getting help when they needed it. Another study of women in British refuges found that about three quarters had put up with violence for three or more years, and a third had suffered life-threatening attacks or had been hospitalised for serious injuries such as fractured bones (Binney *et al.*, 1981). In many cases the violence proves to be chronic and some women report 'serial victimisation'. A chilling story of long-term abuse was given in a report from the Alexandra Township Clinic in Johannesburg:

> Ms. B was assaulted in October 1989 with fists and a brick. She sustained multiple injuries and a swollen jaw. She was given analgesics and discharged. Four months later she was stabbed with a knife on the shoulder region. She was sutured, given analgesics and discharged.
>
> In addition to the above physical injuries Ms. B reported three times at the clinic with sexually transmitted disease. On all these occasions she was asked to urge her husband to come for treatment and he refused.
>
> In the last visit, she had been assaulted with a bottle. She had a laceration on her lower lip and a broken tooth. Her laceration was sutured, and she was referred to a dentist (Motsei, 1993, p. 20).

In some cases a woman's injuries will be fatal; in most countries she is more likely to be killed by her male partner than by any other assailant.

The Psychological Effects of Battering

As well as causing physical damage, domestic violence also involves psychological distress and trauma. Emotional violence is much more common than physical abuse and probably has the longest lasting effects. At least two thirds of British women interviewed in refuges identified mental cruelty as one of the main reasons for leaving home (Binney *et al.*, 1981). Most battered women are debilitated by anxiety about the next attack and feel shocked, upset, angry and bitter about being damaged – often by someone who allegedly loves them. For many it produces what has been termed post-traumatic stress disorder (PTSD). Indeed women who have been sexually abused and physically assaulted constitute one of the largest groups of PTSD sufferers in the United States (Koss, 1990, p. 375).

A number of studies have indicated that women who have suffered domestic violence have increased rates of depression and substance abuse (Andrews and Brown, 1988; Koss, 1990, p. 376; Plichta, 1992; Stark and Flitcraft, 1991, p. 123). Years of violence may leave them in a state where alternatives are difficult even to visualise, much less to carry out. Economic dependency may be reinforced by physical intimidation, creating a condition of 'learned helplessness' from which women can find it difficult to extricate themselves (Walker, 1979). Too often, attempts to obtain support from social workers, police and other authorities lead only to further humiliation (Stark and Flitcraft, 1991). Women therefore remain without sanctuary or sanctions, tied into a set of familial relationships that ultimately condone male violence (Counts *et al.*, 1992).

For some, suicide may appear to be the only way out. According to one analysis some 30–40 per cent of all battered women in the United States attempt to kill themselves at some point in their lives (Stark and Flitcraft, 1991, p. 141). In a number of societies this is a recognised cultural phenomenon that gives the powerless some (paradoxical) feeling of control over their lives (Counts, 1987). In one New Guinea province in 1985, about two thirds of all suicide attempts and eight out of nine successful ones were carried out by women and most followed a beating.

> A woman who is struck repeatedly when she attempts to speak is said to have *ailolo sasi* – a 'bad stomach' – a condition that is a mixture of anger, shame and despair that may cause a person to kill herself (Counts, 1987, p. 200).

Conclusion

This chapter has explored some of the key characteristics of the domestic environment. It has shown that most women are engaged in complex processes of cooperation and conflict with male partners and other family members over resources, rights and responsibilities

(Sen, 1990). Deniz Kandiyoti has described this process of negotiation as 'patriarchal bargaining' (Kandiyoti, 1988; Kabeer, 1991). We have seen that the outcome is often detrimental to women's well-being, with an asymmetry between the responsibilities they are given and the resources allocated to meet their needs.

This paradox will be explored further in the chapters that follow. Sexuality, fertility control and child bearing are all areas for negotiation and conflict within households and, as we shall see, women's room for manoeuvre is often severely limited. Entry into waged work may also require complex bargaining processes both inside and outside the family. In the final chapter we will focus on the ways in which many women are challenging the rules of the 'patriarchal game' in an attempt to increase their influence over the domestic decisions that can have such a profound effect on their health.

Further Reading

Bruce, J. and Dwyer, D. (1988) *A Home Divided: women and income in the third world* (Stanford, CA: Stanford University Press). A collection of articles addressing the issue of resource allocation within households. Though not specifically focused on health it offers a valuable introduction to the social and economic context within which many women struggle to sustain their well-being.

Davis, M. (1994) *Women and Violence: responses and realities worldwide* (London: Zed Press). An outstanding collection of articles on violence against women around the world. It also provides the most comprehensive account of women's responses in a variety of social contexts.

Graham, H. (1993) *Hardship and Health in Women's Lives* (Brighton: Harvester Wheatsheaf). An important study exploring the impact of poverty on the daily lives of women looking after children in the United Kingdom. It places great emphasis on the diversity found among these women but also stresses the health risks they all face in caring for others.

Ravindran, Sundari (1986) *Health Implications of Sex Discrimination in Childhood: a review paper and an annotated bibliography* (Geneva: WHO/ UNICEF). Reviews much of the recent evidence of the bias against girls found in many societies. As well as summarising the literature, it offers a list of suggestions for preventive action.

Russo, N. (1990) 'Overview: forging research priorities for women's mental health', *American Psychologist*, vol. 45, no. 3, pp. 368–73. A summary of key research issues relating to women and mental health in the United States. It includes a useful bibliography covering major aspects of the relationship between women's mental health and their domestic environments.

United Nations (1989) *Violence Against Women in the Family* (Vienna: Centre for Social Development and Humanitarian Affairs). The first international summary of information on domestic violence against women. It discusses the volume, the results and the causes of violence and examines the range of possible responses.

3

Safe Sex?

Introduction

This chapter will examine the largely unexplored relationship between women's (hetero)sexual lives and their well-being. Put bluntly, it will ask whether sex with men is good for women's health. Too often feminists and non-feminists alike have buried the health implications of women's sexual activity in a discussion of issues related to birth control and childbearing. This chapter will put the spotlight on sexual activity itself as an important factor that can either enhance or reduce women's well-being.

The subject of the chapter will be the sexual intercourse most women have with men over the greater part of their lives. This narrowing of focus to heterosex does not imply a denial of the validity of lesbian sexuality or of its centrality in many women's lives. Rather it reflects the reality that most of the sexual hazards women face relate to experiences with male partners. A lesbian sexual identity can, of course, be damaging to a woman's health because of the stigma and discrimination it may engender in many areas of social and economic life (Stevens, 1992). However sex is still immeasurably safer between women than between women and men.

Is Heterosex Good for Women?

The emergence of human sexuality from the shadows of Victorian prudery has been a notable feature of modern medical, psychological and social discourse. In some parts of the world this liberalisation has given women the opportunity to experience a greater variety of sexual relationships than those experienced by their mothers or their grand-mothers.

> There is no doubt that many millions of women now expect sexual pleasure in their lives and many are willing to struggle to obtain it . . . large numbers of men have begun to alter age-old sexual practices in order to fulfil these new expectations of female pleasure. They may do so grudgingly, half-heartedly, or without ever directly asking women what they want. But there is an expectation that sex is supposed to produce pleasure for women as well as men, and this is a very significant historical change (Valverde, 1985, p. 36).

However we should not overestimate the scope of these developments. In many societies, attitudes towards women and their sexuality have changed little over generations, and women have often lacked the social or economic autonomy to underpin sexual choices. The recent rise of the 'New Right' in the United States, along with the resurgence of fundamentalism in Islam, Hinduism and a number of other religions, has meant a return to earlier, less enlightened attitudes. Thus the traditional heterosexual couple continues to be the main arena in which the majority of women experience their own sexuality.

Even to ask questions about heterosexuality – and certainly to contest its 'naturalness' – is, of course, deeply threatening. As Maria Valverde has commented, heterosexuality is so pervasive in today's society that 'it resembles the proverbial water of which fish are unaware' (ibid., p. 83). Most women live much of their adult lives in relationships that involve heterosex. Most have apparently consented to them, whether in the individual context of 'romantic love' or as part of a more collectively determined contract negotiated with family or kin group. Indeed many have learned to see marriage and motherhood as the main reasons for their existence. So what sense could it make to suggest that the sexual activity embedded in such relationships might damage women's health?

Clearly 'sex' between men and women is not always the same. It varies between historical periods, in different societies, between classes and racial groups, and between individuals with different biographies. It may also be different for the same individual on different occasions and at different stages in their life (Weeks, 1986). It is not merely a spontaneous and instinctive biological act but is socially constructed in complex and highly symbolic ways (Foucault, 1979). But despite such differences of time and place, we can identify certain core elements in the discourses and hence the practices of sexual behaviour across most cultures.

There is widespread promotion of the 'normality' of heterosexuality, while other sexual identities and practices are defined as deviant. The essence of heterosex is assumed to be penetration of the vagina by the penis followed by ejaculation, which of course coincides with male orgasm. Though women may be seen as 'temptresses', sex is defined primarily in terms of men's desire, with women seen as the passive recipients of male passions. As many feminists have pointed out, it remains to be established how far this mode of sexual intercourse will ever be compatible with women's sexual pleasure (Holland, Ramaza-noglou and Scott, 1990, p. 508). It is perhaps even more pertinent to ask how far it is compatible with their health.

For some women it is a fundamental principle that heterosex can never contribute positively to their well-being. They argue that the essence of all heterosexual intercourse is male domination, both physical and psychological. The sex act itself they see as intrinsically violating, as the inevitable result of uncontrolled male lust. Women are advised to avoid it both for the sake of their own well-being and for that of other women since all are said to be damaged by any strengthening of male power (Daly, 1979; Dworkin, 1981; Rich, 1980). Thus heterosexuality is identified as the key to the male domination of women, and celibacy, autoeroticism and/or lesbianism are seen as preferred – or healthier – sexual choices for women.

However other feminists take a different view, arguing that heterosex need not necessarily put women at risk (Segal, 1987; Snitow *et al.*, 1984; Vance, 1984). They emphasise the fact that many women find it extremely pleasurable and capable of meeting deeply felt emotional needs. While recognising the threats it can pose, they do not agree that the experience must inevitably be negative, or that women who have intercourse with men are always putting others at risk. Rather they see heterosexual activities as necessarily ambiguous for women:

> The tension between sexual danger and sexual pleasure is a powerful one in women's lives. Sexuality is simultaneously a domain of restriction, repression and danger as well as a domain of explora-tion, pleasure and agency (Vance, 1984, p. 1).

There is no doubt that sex with men gives pleasure to many women as well as providing a means to motherhood. It is clear that it can also be both distressing and damaging to health, especially if it is not desired. But whatever their feelings, relatively few women around the world are in a position to determine the nature of their sexual lives. It is important, therefore, to identify the potential hazards of heterosex more clearly in order to determine how it could be made both healthier and more satisfying.

The differential power of men and women is evident in most sexual intercourse as it is in the wider context of male–female relations. Of course individual men may not feel powerful or confident in their sexual interactions with women, as Lyn Segal points out in her discussion of the 'psychic casualties produced by phallic failure' (Segal, 1990, p. 218). However the broad picture is one where men's sexual coerciveness towards women has not merely been tolerated but expected and even encouraged. Indeed there is a widespread belief that male dominance can satisfy women sexually – in and of itself. This socially sanctioned male control of heterosex can affect women's health on a number of different levels.

We begin by examining the implications for women's mental health of sex that is expected or required rather than being jointly desired. Psychological distress is often reported by women in relationships involving 'compulsory' heterosexual intercourse. This will involve little intimacy and is sometimes an expression of downright hostility, which can have serious effects on women's emotional well-being. For millions of women and girls this unwanted sex becomes rape or abuse when they have not consented to sexual acts performed on and in their bodies or when they are forced to participate in such acts in front of others. As we shall see, the physical and psychological damage caused by such attacks can be profound. We then go on to investigate the ways in which women may be harmed not by the immediate act of intercourse itself but by the diseases it can transmit. Many of these affect both sexes, but as we shall see biological characteristics and social inequalities often combine to enhance women's vulnerability. The chapter concludes with a discussion of the 'unkindest cut of all'. Genital mutilation provides a potent symbol of both the internal and the external influences that continue to inhibit so many women's capacity to realise their own sexual potential.

Mad with Desire

It is often claimed that 'sex is good for you' but there is little formal evidence linking particular patterns of sexual activity (or lack of it) with mental health or illness. Moreover, most claims of this kind utilise ungendered notions of 'sex' that ignore the differences in the material reality and the phenomenology of intercourse as it is experienced by people of different sexes and sexual orientations. Not surprisingly, these ideas are of little help in understanding the impact of heterosex on women's psychological health.

In developed countries women are heavily over-represented among those seeking help for what is defined as the 'illness of inhibited desire' (Richgels, 1992). The reasons for this are complex and reflect in part a tendency for all problems in sexual relations to be blamed on women. However it is also significant that many women derive little pleasure from heterosexual practices that prioritise male wants. Lack of desire can itself be a source of distress and low self-esteem, especially in cultures where sexual satisfaction is highly prized. Such damage is likely to be even greater when women feel compelled to engage in sexual activities against their own wishes.

What doctors call 'loss of libido' is frequently cited as evidence of depression. Thus it is seen as a symptom but not a cause of mental health problems. However it is equally possible that withdrawal from sex may be a rational response to an unhealthy situation in which unwanted sexual activity may be playing an active part in the creation of mental distress. It is clear that coercive sex can be a significant cause of anxiety or depression. 'Routine' sex too may be an important but largely unrecognised element in the complex of factors that leave so many women with little sense of autonomy or self worth.

Women's own accounts of sex they neither refuse nor desire are scarce, especially in those societies where female sexuality is least visible. However the words of those who have spoken, say a great deal. Many report feelings of alienation, powerlessness and lack of emotion in relation to sexuality to a degree incompatible with standard definitions of mental health.

In a recent study, young British women reported a wide range of pressures in their early experiences of sex and many felt coerced by men whose main objective was penetrative sex. Nearly one quarter of the sample had engaged in unwanted sexual intercourse in response to pressure from a man. These pressures varied from mild insistence on giving way to intercourse or to intercourse on his terms, to threats, assault and rape. According to the authors, 'Only a handful of young women managed to develop relationships in which their needs could be asserted and given importance, including the need to refuse intercourse at times (Holland *et al.*, 1990).

Other research has produced similar results. In Liz Kelly's study of 60 English women from a variety of social backgrounds, less than a third felt that they had freely consented in any positive sense to their first intercourse (Kelly, 1988, p. 82). Another young English woman described what appears to be a very common experience in the following, joyless terms: 'I was seventeen. My boyfriend persuaded me to go upstairs at a party. It was all over very quickly and I got no satisfaction – I wasn't even that willing (Hamblin, 1983, p. 110).

Clearly such responses are not universal; there are women who enjoy their early heterosexual encounters and experience them as an important step on the road to an emotionally healthy and sexually fulfilled adulthood. However most studies suggest that such women are currently in the minority. This is especially true in cultures where marriage involves the social ritual of 'deflowering' a virgin bride, which can be both physically and psychologically traumatic.

It appears that many women continue to have similar experiences in adulthood, often feeling obliged by economic or other domestic pressures to remain in relationships where regular sex, which they neither enjoy nor desire, is expected as part of the heterosexual 'contract'. In some instances the sexual pressures may be relatively insidious, as one British woman described to sociologist Liz Kelly:

> When I was living with Mark, I'd come home from work and I'd be shattered. I'd just want to go to bed and sleep. He'd start cuddling up and touching me and I'd think 'oh here we go again'. It was like a duty, that was sort of paying the rent. I had a roof over my head and that was what I was expected to pay (Kelly, 1988, p. 110).

A New Zealand woman told Nicola Gavey:

> Like always when I used to stay the night a couple of times a week, he'd always wanted to have sexual intercourse in the morning and that's just how it was. Like, you know you had a fuck when you get up and you had a cup of tea then you had your breakfast (laughs) and I never really enjoyed sex. And I mean I just thought, you know, like I didn't even question it. . . . I guess I just wasn't tuned into my own feelings or I couldn't have gone through with it (Gavey, 1993, p. 102).

This pressure women feel to subordinate their own needs to give sexual pleasure to men has been widely documented in different social contexts. After living for several years in a village in Southern Italy Ann Cornelisen described her perception of the women around her:

There is no way to avoid it: peasant women are not universally plagued by irresistible fiery longings, but the men need to think so and the women let them. Peasant women are by instinct pragmatic enough to let the illusion stand: they may even sense its importance to men who have nothing else. When they are alone, talking, a wife who boasts of her husband's sexual charms always says the same thing with pride: 'He's valente, valente' – he's very, very quick (Cornelisen, 1977, p. 20).

The American anthropologist Dooley Worth encountered similar experiences among a group of women with whom she worked in an AIDS prevention clinic in downtown New York:

All the women participating in the center sessions expressed the desire to be loved. 'Love', one heroin addicted woman in the Montefiore program said, 'means being understood, not just wanted sexually'. The women complained repeatedly that men confuse sexual desire with affection: this feeling was particularly strong among the Puerto Rican women who were very vocal in expressing dissatisfaction with their sex lives, speaking in a derogatory way about their partner's sexual behaviour and skills (Worth, 1989, pp. 302–3).

In some societies the rights of husbands to sexual intercourse (and the appropriate female responses) are not merely assumed but overt and publicly codified. A recent study of the lives of young Indian wives (bahū) in a village in Uttar Pradesh reported that:

Conjugal sexual activity is expected and enjoyed: but a bahū's demeanour should not imply that she is sexually active. While the young couple share a chūlhà (household) with his parents, his mother may regulate when they sleep together (at least at home at night). Otherwise however, the husband has the right of sexual access to his wife at times when he decrees: she should neither take the initiative nor refuse him. . . . An essential component of a husband's rule is sexual power over his wife (Jeffery *et al.*, 1989, p. 29).

To say that women often have sex with men when they do not desire it is both to state the obvious and to speak the unspeakable (Gavey, 1993, p. 93). They may do this because it is expected of them, because it is their duty and/or their wish to conceive a child, because the consequences of not complying would be worse than the reality of the sex itself or because they feel affection or guilt because a partner's wishes are not being fulfilled (Kelly, 1988, Ch. 5). Under these circumstances a woman's own sexual desires will be of little concern, and may not be clear even to the woman herself. Indeed sex may serve merely to reinforce the negative feelings she has learned to have about herself and her body from an early age. A Lebanese woman described the anger she felt at the suffering caused to many women by the internalised oppression they bring to the marriage bed.

> We were brought up to think that sex was very dirty. I was not even 12 when I had my first period. My aunt used to say: 'Don't touch yourself; if you ever touch yourself you'd get tuberculosis'. That was really frightening. It was very difficult for me to shake all that off and look at sex as something enjoyable, beautiful and clean. Thousands of Arab women spend their lives with their husbands and breed children without being able to enjoy sex as a good thing to have, and without ever enjoying it. . . . They are relieved when it is all finished. I find that very sad (Shaaban, 1988, pp. 125–6).

The psychological effects of such experiences repeated on a regular basis are not easy to assess, and more research is needed to explore them. However the negative consequences of being used as a means to the end of someone else's pleasure should not be underestimated, particularly when it is achieved through the very intimate act of bodily penetration. Morcover many women also feel obliged to simulate sexual pleasure, thus exacerbating still further the alienation they may feel from their own body and their own senses.

It is important for our mental health that we experience ourselves as both autonomous and dependent, as subject and object. For some women sex with a man or with another woman can be the most important means of achieving this, providing an arena in which both partners can recognise and express their own needs and have them acknowledged by a significant other. However for the majority of women heterosex offers little opportunity to be dominant or in control, or even to share their feelings. Paradoxically perhaps, psychoanalytic theory suggests that much male aggression towards women and the refusal of many men to acknowledge emotional dependence reflects their fear of women's psychic or procreative powers (Hollway, 1983). However few women are able to feel such power in themselves and their experience of heterosex merely confirms the lack of autonomy and low self-esteem they feel in other areas of their lives.

Sex and Violence

We have seen that heterosex can damage women's health even when they have not refused it. The risks are of course much greater if they actively withhold consent – if they are forced by men to take part in sexual acts. Forced sex is a demonstration of power and control and should not be confused with mutually loving sexual expression. Its negative consequences can be extensive, causing both physical and psychological damage and even death. Indeed it is significant that much of the violence directed against women takes place in the institutional context of heterosex.

Problems of Measurement

It is extremely difficult to quantify the number of women who are raped, much less to assess the extent of the damage it does to their health. In the first place, the legal definition of rape varies. Forcible intercourse is widely tolerated in private if not in public discourse, and it continues to be legal in marriage in most societies around the world. Even the inadequate data currently available show that a large proportion of rapes are committed not by 'sexually frustrated prowlers' but by husbands or partners at home. The majority of sexual assaults are inflicted on women by men they know ('date rape' or 'acquaintance rape') and this makes it especially difficult to report them.

There is also a widely held belief that those who are raped are somehow responsible for their own fate – that they 'asked for it'. Under these circumstances many women find it extremely difficult either to reveal what has happened, or to avoid feeling guilty. This is especially true in societies where the 'honour' of the family is measured by the purity of its female members (Douglas, 1966; Goddard, 1987). Defilement, even through rape, may destroy the rest of a woman's life. Indeed in a few cultures the only way out is to marry the rapist.

These problems are compounded by the response of many law enforcement agencies. Too often rape complaints are not taken seriously and even when they are accepted and processed, convictions are hard to achieve. In the United States estimates of the percentage of rapes reported to the police vary from 4 per cent to 40 per cent. Less than 15 per cent of reported rapes reach trial, and only 1 per cent result in conviction, meaning that only one rapist in 250–2500 is convicted (Kelly, 1988, pp. 51–2). Rape is one of the most under-reported and least convicted crimes in the world, and the damage it causes to women's health is correspondingly invisible.

In recent years a number of victimisation studies have been carried out in the United Kingdom and the United States, where rape has been high on the feminist agenda. Methodological problems mean that they have produced a range of estimated prevalence rates, but all show an astonishingly large number of women reporting sexual violence. In Ruth Hall's study, 17 per cent of a broad sample of women in London reported having been raped and 20 per cent reported attempted rape (Hall, 1985). More than 40 per cent of battered wives in a United States study as well as 14 per cent of a random sample of a thousand married women reported having been raped by their partner (Russell, 1982). A recent prevalence study in the United States suggested that at least 20 per cent of adult women, 15 per cent of college women and 12 per cent of adolescent girls had experienced sexual abuse or assault at some time in their lives (Koss, 1988).

Men of all ages, races and classes rape women and girls from all social and economic backgrounds. Hence the potential damage to health is a universal one. However it is significant that some women's circumstances put them at greater risk than others, those with the fewest resources to protect themselves being most vulnerable. Work by the anthropologist Peggy Sanday has also shown that women are most at risk in what she calls 'rape prone' societies (Sanday, 1981). This suggests that the extent of violence against women is closely linked not to male hormones but to the lack of female power and influence in the wider society.

Sexual Abuse and Male Power

Historically men's abuse of their power is strikingly demonstrated in the treatment received by many black women at the hands of white slave owners. One example is particularly evocative of the psychological as well as the physical damage involved:

> When Linda first entered the service of her owner Dr. Flint, she was thirteen years old. He did not rape her but began to constantly torment and persecute her by verbally announcing his intention to take her sexually. At the onset of their encounter he informed her that if she would not willingly submit, he would use force. Describing herself at fifteen Linda wrote: 'I was compelled to live under the same roof with him – where I saw a man forty years my senior daily

violating the most sacred commandment of nature. He told me I was his property, that I must be subjected to his will in all things' (hooks, 1982, p. 25).

Hooks goes on to argue that this rape of enslaved women has had long-term significance, contributing to a widespread perception that African American women are particularly 'rapeable', that they are 'the 'fallen' woman, the whore, the slut, the prostitute' (hooks, 1982, p. 52).

Similar abuses of male power have become a focus of feminist concern in India, where an increasing number of rapes by policemen have been reported. Most of these have been inflicted on landless labourers and poor tribal women, but one well-publicised case showed that no woman is safe from the guardians of law and order:

> Maya, a 23 year old woman from a well to do farmers' family, was travelling with her husband by car to attend the wedding of her niece. Maya was pregnant. When one of the tyres got a puncture they stopped near a police station at Baghpat. A policeman in civilian dress came up to the car and started to molest Maya. Her husband gave him a beating. The man went to the police station and came back with a whole police force which started firing at them. . . . After this Maya was dragged out of the car, beaten, robbed of her ornaments, stripped naked and paraded through the market place. She was then brought to the police station where she was raped by seven policemen and arrested. She was also offered their urine to drink (Mies, 1986, p. 155).

In a growing number of countries, these rapes do not appear to be isolated incidents perpetrated by rogue officials. Instead government agents use rape and sexual abuse as deliberate policies to coerce, humiliate, punish and intimidate women. Such cases have been reported from places as far apart as Peru, the Philippines, Uganda, Guatemala, Greece, Palestine, Turkey and Northern Ireland (Amnesty International, 1991). In the former Yugoslavia this use of rape as a political weapon reached new depths as part of the policy of what has been called 'ethnic cleansing'.

We have seen that all women are at risk of rape and that the powerless are most vulnerable. Yet there have been very few studies exploring the long-term health consequences of such experiences. Even fewer have compared these effects for women in different social, economic and cultural contexts. Work done in the United States in the 1980s has been valuable in drawing attention to problems that had previously been ignored. The identification of a 'rape trauma syndrome' for instance, highlighted the variation in women's responses to sexual assault (Burgess and Holmstrom, 1979). However serious gaps in our knowledge and understanding of the global impact of rape still remain.

Physical Effects of Rape

Rape is a complex and multifaceted experience, which the women involved (and therefore researchers) need to understand as a totality (Kelly, 1988, pp. 186–9). After such an experience many women will, quite literally, never be the same again. It is therefore important to explore not just the damage done by rape but also the means by which women cope with the experience and learn to survive – to live without being dominated by the attack (Kelly, 1988). This means listening very carefully to survivors' own accounts of the impact of sexual abuse on their health and well-being.

Most research has concentrated on the psychological, sexual and emotional effects of rape, but it is also an act of violence. In one US study of women whose rape had led them to a hospital emergency room, 63 per cent of adult women and 73 per cent of young women had at least one sign of general trauma noted on their records, while 43 per cent of adult and 59 per cent of young women had at least one sign of gynaecological injury (Burgess and Holmstrom, 1979, p. 88). The physical damage inflicted may be severe or even fatal. A letter written by a Philadelphia rape survivor to *The Village Voice* makes this point with devastating clarity:

> Forcible rape is not in any normal sense intercourse. In most cases the lubrication of the vagina required for normal completed intercourse does not exist, since petting has, more often than not, not occurred. As a result of this crucial aspect, as well as the fact that the victim is usually in a traumatized state immediately preceding the rape, and thus the muscles at the entrance to the vagina are not relaxed, penetration cannot either easily or immediately occur. . . . As can be imagined forcible rape is traumatically painful. When I was being raped I felt as though I was being repeatedly stabbed with a knife in one of the most sensitive areas of my body (Stanko, 1985, p. 35).

As well as injuries to the genital or anal areas, many women also suffer additional beatings on other parts of their body, with weapons being used in a significant number of cases. Often the fear of death is paramount. Chris was accosted while on her way home from a peace demonstration in Chicago:

> He grabbed her and pulled her off the sidewalk; he had one hand over her mouth. . . . He leaned down toward her ear and said softly that in the last three months he had killed three people along these very blocks, that if she screamed he would kill her. She did not see a weapon, she did not know whether to believe him, but she was too terrified to challenge him. She nodded and he let her mouth go (Stanko, 1985, p. 45).

Of course not all attempted rapes succeed. Women may be able to avoid penetration, but few escape without violence and terror.

> I went on fighting and there was this really terrifying bit where he'd got me pinned against the wall, and I'd banged my head slightly. So I was feeling kind of woozy and I thought for a minute I was going to faint. I was absolutely terrified: but I managed to get a hand free and I started scratching his face. I think at that point he started giving up and realised it was going to be too difficult to overpower me. . . . He – I think in total anger – punched me in the mouth and in doing that he had to let go of me and I managed to get away (Kelly, 1988, p. 165).

Many women who have been raped also have to face the possibility of pregnancy. Fear of having conceived often becomes a major cause for concern, and despite the 'morning after' pill many worry until their next period. If a woman has been impregnated, ambivalence about abortion may well cause further suffering, and women who might have already conceived with their partner during the same cycle can face serious dilemmas.

> Mary Ellen was composed until the physician came back in and told her what to do if her period did not come – namely to make an appointment at the clinic. At this point it dawned on her that she could be pregnant as a result of what had happened. She faltered, lost her composure a little. She asked with great distress, almost a kind of panic, 'what am I going to *do*?' (Burgess and Holmstrom, 1979, p. 84).

The possibility of venereal disease has always been a major concern for women who have been raped, and since the spread of HIV/AIDS such fear can be extremely severe. There are no preventive strategies available and no immediate test can offer reassurance (Berer and Ray, 1993, pp. 125–6). We have little evidence concerning the extent of HIV transmitted during rape, but Mere Kisekka has highlighted the plight of women in Northern Uganda who have experienced incessant guerilla warfare:

> the North of the country was free from AIDS until after the battleground shifted following President Museveni's victory in May 1986. The high rate of AIDS among the soldiers, reportedly at the rate of one in three, combined with their habitual harassment of women, leaves no doubt of their role in the epidemiology of the disease (Kisekka, 1990, p. 45).

Emotional Effects of Abuse

One study in the United Kingdom found that of all serious crimes, rape was the one from which women took longest to recover (Stanko, 1985, p. 46). Recent research in Detroit found that 80 per cent of women who had been raped went on to develop Post Traumatic Stress Disorder (PTSD) (Breslau *et al.*, 1991). Not surprisingly, most studies report a negative impact on sexual satisfaction and increased feelings of fear and vulnerability as well as depression, loss of trust, nightmares, phobic reactions and loss of self respect.

In her attempt to make sense of women's psychological responses to sexual attack, Liz Kelly has emphasised the losses involved (Kelly, 1988, pp. 189–214). Many lose their memory of the attack(s) in an attempt to suppress unpleasant emotions. Many of the women also reported the loss of their sense of security and safety. This was especially true of women who had been assaulted by men they knew. Home no longer seemed safe and the men often continued to harass them. More generally, many women began to fear their vulnerability, knowing they could never properly protect themselves. One British woman reported: 'I think my attitudes have changed permanently – I will never feel safe walking down the street by myself ever again. I will never feel safe in a situation where I'm alone with a man I don't know very well' (Kelly, 1988, p. 198). The experiences of an Indian survivor were very similar: 'I used to fearlessly go and lie under a tree and sleep in the shade. Then an incident happened . . . today I have fear, disturbance . . . what bloody right does anyone have to do this to me? To take away my sense of security?' (Forum Against the Oppression of

Women, 1994, p. 77). Many women lose any desire for heterosexual intercourse for some period of time. Nearly half of the women interviewed by Liz Kelly chose a period of celibacy after being attacked, while 50 per cent reported that they were determined to avoid any form of coercive sex in the future (Kelly, 1988, p. 205).

This section has focused primarily on the rape and sexual abuse of adult women. However it is evident that young girls are also at serious risk. The extent of sexual abuse of girls by (usually male) members of their families or other caretakers is difficult to measure. However the last decade or so has seen a marked increase in the number of cases identified. Surveys in both the United Kingdom and the United States suggest that between 25 per cent and 40 per cent of women have experienced sexual abuse of some kind by the age of 16 (Finkelhor, 1991, p. 84).

The effects of such experiences may be severe. Those caring for abused children have noted a wide range of symptoms, including hyperactivity, depression, mood swings, disturbances in sleeping and eating patterns, inappropriately sexualised behaviour and problems at school (Browne and Finkelhor, 1986). In adult life, women who have been sexually abused as children report more mental health problems than those who have not had such experiences, especially depression and drug and alcohol abuse (Finkelhor, 1991; Russell, 1986). One British study found that half of all women who see a psychiatrist have been sexually abused as children (Palmer *et al.*, 1992). Thus the psychological effects of non-consensual sex can be far reaching both in childhood and in later life.

Dying for Sex

Whether or not women desire a particular sexual encounter, and whether or not they have consented to it, intercourse can also be a direct cause of physical illness. The most widely publicised of these potential hazards is HIV infection, but this is not the only sexually related disease. Reproductive tract infections of all kinds are common in many third world countries, causing a great deal of suffering and sometimes death (Germain *et al.*, 1992; Wasserheit, 1989; Wasserheit and Holmes, 1992). Though rates are generally lower in the developed countries they are still a significant cause of morbidity, especially in the inner cities of the United States where gonorrhea, syphilis and chancroid are increasing at epidemic rates (Aral and Holmes, 1991).

There is also a close connection between heterosexual activity and cancer of the cervix. As we shall see, women's capacity to protect themselves from these diseases can be severely limited first by their inability to control the terms on which they do (or do not) have sex with men, and second by their lack of access to effective medical care.

Sex and Cervical Cancer

Worldwide the incidence of cancer of the cervix is second only to that of breast cancer among the malignancies most closely associated with women. Nearly half a million new cases are reported each year and about three quarters of these occur in the third world, with a peak age of between 30 and 40 (WHO, 1986c, p. 607). In developed countries the number of deaths caused is much lower and the peak age higher – between 50 and 60. But here too it is the poorest women who are most at risk. In the United Kingdom, women married to unskilled workers are about four times more likely to die of cancer of the cervix than those married to professional men (Whitehead, 1988). In the United States it is disadvantaged women from ethnic minorities who have the highest mortality rates (Devesa and Diamond, 1980).

Cancer of the cervix is extremely rare in women who have had little or no heterosexual intercourse. It is highest in women who begin intercourse early and is positively related to the number of male sexual partners a woman has. Research during the early nineteenth century suggested that nuns were much less susceptible than married women or prostitutes to cancer of the cervix, leading to the identification of female 'promiscuity' as a major cause (Robinson, 1982; Saffron, 1983). As a result, many women, already distressed by a diagnosis of cancer, have been additionally humiliated by insensitive questions about the numbers of sexual partners they have had. In reality the increased risk facing heterosexually active women is related not only to the number of relationships a woman herself has, but also the sexual habits of her male partner(s). In one British study the relative risk of a woman contracting the disease was nearly eight times greater if her husband had had 15 or more partners outside marriage (Buckley *et al.*, 1981).

Barrier methods of contraception offer the single most effective means for preventing cervical cancer (WHO, 1986c, p. 608). They can protect the cervix from infection as well as shielding it from other potentially carcinogenic substances such as dusts and oils picked up by either partner in their workplace (Robinson, 1982). However the obvious benefits of barrier methods for women's health have received little publicity and have so far made little impact on the patterns of contraceptive use.

A Smear in Time

Most public health strategies have focused instead on secondary prevention. This involves screening healthy women through the use of cervical smears to detect and treat abnormal cells before they progress to become cancerous. In some countries this has been extremely successful, showing that falls of 50–60 per cent in both morbidity and mortality can be achieved (WHO, 1986c, p. 610). Canada, Iceland, Norway, Finland, Sweden, Denmark and some parts of Scotland have all reported significant reductions in deaths. Other countries, including England and Wales, have given less priority to both screening and treatment. As a result they show a much smaller decline in deaths, with continuing regional and class inequalities (Davey, 1986).

It is in third world countries that the incidence of cervical cancer is greatest. Though the scope of services varies widely, few countries can afford even minimal coverage of the female population. In India facilities for both screening and treatment are restricted to large urban centres and even a twelvefold increase in trained technicians would permit screening for only 25 per cent of women at risk by the year 2000 (WHO, 1986c, p. 610). In 1989 55 per cent of cervical cancer cases in the South African state of Transvaal were diagnosed when the disease was already invasive, and in the country as a whole the mortality rate is nearly two and a half times greater among African women than among white women (Fonn *et al.*, 1993). Worldwide only about half of adult women in developed countries and less than 5 per cent of those in third world countries have been screened for cancer of the cervix in the past five years (WHO, 1986c, p. 610).

A Culture of Silence: The Female Burden of Reproductive Tract Infections

Lack of medical care is also a major factor in explaining the burden of reproductive tract infections (RTIs) in women in many parts of the world. Many diseases can be transmitted through sexual intercourse, including viral infections (genital herpes and warts), those related to bacteria or similar organisms (syphilis, gonorrhoea, chlamydia, vaginosis), or fungal or protozeal infections (candiasis or trichomonas). Women can also be infected by the insertion of unclean materials into the vagina to prevent pregnancy or induce abortion, by unsafe childbirth techniques and by female circumcision.

Worldwide, gonorrhoea is probably the most common of the reproductive tract infections. It is prevalent in most of the developed countries and hyperendemic in parts of Central Africa (Dixon-Mueller and Wasserheit, 1991, p. 5). It can cause abdominal pain and menstrual problems, spontaneous abortion, prematurity and eye infections in newborn infants. It is also a major cause of pelvic inflammatory disease (PID), which can lead to inflammation and scarring of the fallopian tubes and ovaries. Acute cases may need hospital care (if it is available) and the disease can become chronic, leading to infertility or even potentially fatal tubal pregnancy. Between 15 per cent and 25 per cent of women who develop PID become permanently infertile (ibid., p. 9).

Statistical data on the incidence of RTIs and other gynaecological diseases are difficult to obtain. However a recent study of two rural villages in the Indian state of Maharashtra found that an astonishing 92 per cent of women had gynaecological or sexually transmitted diseases, with an average of 3.6 diseases each. Infections constituted 50 per cent of this enormous burden of suffering, and the authors suggest that the figure would have been even higher, had more refined diagnostic tests been available (Bang *et al.*, 1989).

Only 8 per cent of the women had ever had a gynaecological examination, though 55 per cent were aware of having gynaecological disorders. When 30 men and 32 women were asked to list women's health problems in order of importance, 95 per cent put 'white discharge' at the top of the list. One woman said 'like every tree has flowers, every woman has a white discharge. Except that it's not soothing like a flower' (Bang and Bang, 1992, p. 27).

Most sexually transmitted diseases are potentially more damaging to women than to men, since women are more likely to develop chronic infections or become infertile. Loss of fertility can lead to divorce – the abandoned woman will then lose emotional and financial support and is likely to be heavily stigmatised. However the same consequences rarely follow for men. Indeed their symptoms may well be taken as an indication of virility or sexual potency. As Bassett and Mhloyi have reported from Zimbabwe, 'Having an STD is almost a rite of passage into manhood, proof of sexual activity: a bull is not a bull without his scars' (Bassett and Mhloyi, 1991, p. 151).

Huge amounts of distress are caused by reproductive tract infections yet there are few services available to deal with them. As a result many women spend years suffering in silence (Khattab, 1992). However pressure to provide effective diagnosis and treatment is now mounting. This can be explained in part by the discovery that reproductive tract infections are not just disabling but also increase the risk of HIV transmission (Laga, 1992).

Sex, Gender and Aids

HIV and AIDS are now a major threat to women around the world and heterosex is the most common route by which they are acquired (Berer and Ray, 1993). By early 1992 best estimates suggested that about 12.9 million people in the world were HIV positive, of whom 1.1 million were children, 4.7 million women and 7.1 million men. Thus about 40 per cent of seropositive adults in the world are female (Mann *et al.*, 1992, p. 29). About one fifth of these already have AIDS and about 2.5 million have died.

The proportion of male:female among those known to be infected by HIV is estimated to be 10:1 in Eastern Europe, 8.5:1 in North America and 2:1 in South-East Asia (ibid., p. 31). In a number of African countries the proportion of men and women who are HIV positive has equalised, and in Uganda women are now said to be in the majority (Berer and Ray, 1993, p. 46; Mann *et al.*, 1992, p. 31). In the United States about 13 per cent of people with AIDS are women and most come from disadvantaged social groups. Black and Latina women are significantly more likely than white women to be infected (Kurth, 1993, p. 3). Thus AIDS can no longer be represented as an epidemic among gay men. By the end of the twentieth century it is estimated that there will be as many women as men with AIDS worldwide (ibid., p. 7).

Why are Women at Risk?

It is now clear that women are at greater risk than men of contracting the HIV virus from an individual act of intercourse and from each sexual partnership. This 'biological sexism' also applies to most other sexually transmitted diseases. A woman has a 50 per cent chance of acquiring gonorrhoea from an infected male partner while a man has a 25 per cent chance if he has sex with an infected woman. In the case of HIV there is still considerable debate about the precise size of this differential, but it is clear that women's risk is greater (Kurth, 1993, p. 7).

The reasons for this are complex but they derive partly from the fluid dynamics of unprotected sex, in which the male deposits several millilitres of potentially infectious semen over the surface of his partner's vagina, where it is likely to remain for some time. The risk is further increased by the fact that the virus is more heavily concentrated in semen than in vaginal secretions, and by the greater permeability and greater surface area of the mucous membranes of the vagina compared with those of the penis. Thus all women bring greater biological vulnerability than men to a potentially dangerous sexual encounter. As we shall see, this is frequently reinforced by cultural, social and economic factors that place major constraints on their ability to avoid infection.

The male domination of most heterosexual encounters provides the cultural context within which women have to negotiate strategies to protect their health. Not surprisingly, many feel they have no right to assert their own needs and desires in a situation where society defines the male partner's wants as paramount. They feel unable to assert their wish for safe sex, for fidelity or for no sex at all. These beliefs may not simply kill a woman's desire, they may also lead to her contracting HIV.

Economics of HIV Transmission

This cultural domination of heterosex is reinforced by broader gender inequalities in income and wealth. For many women economic security – sometimes their very survival – is dependent on the support of their male partner. Sexual intercourse done in the way that he desires may well be the price they pay for that support. Hence many women's ability to control their exposure to HIV will be limited by their financial dependence. Requests for safer sex can be made, but if they are ignored most women will have few options, as Ugandan MP Miria Matembe reports:

> The women tell us they see their husbands with the wives of men who have died of AIDS. And they ask 'What can we do? If we say no, they'll say pack up and go. But if we do where do we go to?' They are dependent on the men and they have nowhere to go. What advice can you give these women? (Panos Institute, 1990, p. vi).

These links between economic support and heterosex can take very different forms. Some sexual relationships have no financial implications at all while in commercial sex specific acts are performed solely for money. In most societies sex is implicitly assumed to be a husband's right in return for supporting his family, and there is usually a clear dichotomy between marriage and other forms of social and economic exchange. However in some communities there is a continuum of different types of sexual services (Seidel, 1993, p. 188). In parts of Africa for instance, women may have long-term 'sugar daddies' on the explicit understanding that they will receive money in return, and some young girls use such arrangements as the only means of funding their education (Bassett and Mhloyi, 1991, p. 150; de Bruyn, 1992, p. 255). Whenever sex is part of an economic exchange women will be constrained in their attempts to protect themselves from sexually transmitted diseases – the greater the degree of financial dependence, the greater the constraint.

In many countries, social pressures are now pushing an increasing number of women towards selling sex for subsistence, under circumstances that may seriously damage their health. A recent study of women in mining towns in South Africa emphasised that the decision to provide sexual services is usually an economic one:

> Women talk of 'spanning donkeys' (hopana dipokola) or 'spanning oxen' (hopana dikhomo) when describing prostitution. In other words, women harness men's desires to work for and support them. Taking sexual partners is a way to supplement meagre salaries or replace them (Jochelson *et al.*, 1991, p. 167).

As one woman described it:

> I worked for six months and saw that it's better to span. I could send home money for my children to get something to eat, just think what it's like if you have no place, no money, no husband (Jochelson *et al.*, 1991, p. 167).

In parts of Asia, too, many more women are beginning to sell sex and the rate of spread of HIV among commercial sex workers is extremely rapid. Recent figures indicate that infection is spreading rapidly in India's urban slums. In the red light district of Bombay the rate of seropositivity rose from 0 per cent to 25 per cent between 1986 and 1989 and about 20 per cent of the 100–300 000 women sex workers are now HIV positive (Panos Institute, 1992, p. 15). Similar increases have been noted among female sex workers in Thailand, where the earning potential of international 'sex tourism' draws many young women in from the countryside. Selling sex is likely to pay as much as 25 times more than other jobs open to uneducated young women, and many are under considerable pressure to help their families pay off growing debts (Ford and Koetsawang, 1991, pp. 408–9). In the northern region, around Chiang Mai more than 40 per cent of women working in brothels are already HIV positive (ibid., p. 406).

As well as economic and social insecurity, many women also have to face the threat of physical violence. Reports from around the world suggest that some men respond with a beating to women's attempts to protect themselves from HIV infection. Not surprisingly, many prefer to risk unsafe sex in the face of more immediate threats to their physical well-being. The Ugandan sociologist Mere Kisekka has illustrated the problem with a case from Kampala:

> Recently on the outskirts of the city centre a husband allegedly assaulted his wife because she refused to have sex with him. She was fearful that his former philandering ways might have inflicted him with the disease. For almost two years he had totally ignored her until now. But she wanted no part of him. His reaction was to viciously beat her up. Few would condone such behaviour. But then again, as one sympathetic man noted on the incident: 'She was his wife. He had every right to sleep with her if he so wished' (Kisekka, 1990, p. 46).

For some women refusal to consent to intercourse may also be the trigger for rape or other sexual abuse. Tragically, this may heighten the danger of infection because lacerations or bleeding make it easier for the HIV virus to enter a woman's bloodstream.

Poverty and Seropositivity

Thus women's sexual behaviour is the outcome of a complex set of internal calculations and interpersonal negotiations that cannot be understood outside the context of their cultural, social and economic environment. Not surprisingly it is the poorest women who have the least autonomy, run the most frequent risks and are most likely to be infected. As Bassett and Mhloyi have observed in Zimbabwe: 'For many women faced with divorce or dire poverty on the one hand and the risk of HIV infection on the other, the choice becomes one of 'social death' or biological death' (Bassett and Mhloyi, 1991, p. 146).

The growing numbers of women with HIV and AIDS are concentrated in the world's poorest countries. At present the majority are in Sub-Saharan Africa, where the migrant labour system, rapid urbanisation and frequent 'low intensity' wars have combined with growing landlessness and poverty to create an environment that is ripe for the spread of all sexually transmitted diseases, and of HIV in particular (Bassett and Mhloyi, 1991; Jochelson *et al.*, 1991; Zwi and Cabral, 1991). Latest estimates suggest that nearly four million African women are now HIV positive – 83 per cent of HIV infections among women worldwide (Mann *et al.*, 1992, pp. 89–90).

The interrelationship between these various factors is, of course, complex and has to be understood in relation to the detailed history of individual countries or regions. Broadly speaking however, the pattern is one where colonial policies of land expropriation, rural impoverishment and the forcible introduction of male migrant labour have led to changing patterns of family and sexual relations, often involving long separations and multiple partners. These developments have left many in situations of increasing poverty as world economic trends erode the limited gains made by independent African countries (Bassett and Mhloyi, 1991; Jochelson *et al.*, 1991; Kisekka, 1990). The effects of this social upheaval and disorganisation are exacerbated by lack of access to adequate food and water supplies or to medical care, leaving both men and women without treatment for sexually transmitted (and other) diseases and an increased susceptibility to HIV/AIDS.

But HIV-positive women are not confined to the poorest parts of the world. In the United States, the richest country of all, some 130 000 women are now thought to be infected with the virus (Mann *et al.*, 1992, p. 83). Again it is the poor who are most at risk with women of colour accounting for about three quarters of all women with AIDS in the United States (Banzhaf, 1990, p. 81; Kurth, 1993, p. 5). As one US activist has put it:

When you're talking about women and AIDS think women of color. Whenever you hear about women and AIDS think women of color. That should be your first image, because that gets lost. I have seen it get lost repeatedly on the part of people who are making policy for us (Smith, B., 1992, p. 85).

Many of these women are intravenous drug users or the partners of intravenous drug users. They may have little chance of achieving social equality, and sex may be the only commodity they can sell to support themselves and their families (Worth, 1989). For many this means unsafe sex with multiple partners, making the crackhouses of the 1990s as dangerous for women as the bath-houses of the early 1980s were for gay men (Anastos and Marte, 1991, p. 193). Drug use or sex with potentially infected men may be the only means of escape from the impoverishment and marginality of their daily lives. As a counsellor working in inner-city New York put it:

> If the only ways of escape people have are through drugs and sex – which offer a rare chance to feel like a complete human being – and both of these are closely linked with AIDS then what hope is there of addressing the issue of AIDS prevention without addressing the underlying issue of what people are trying to escape from? (Panos Institute, 1990, p. 35).

Prevention and Power

We have seen that women are biologically more vulnerable than men to HIV infection. In most societies their own freedom of sexual choice is limited. Most have little power in sexual negotiations and can make only a limited impact on their partners' sexual activities. Under these circumstances HIV and AIDS prevention strategies have often failed to meet their needs. Such policies are based on the assumption that given accurate knowledge men and women will make rational decisions to practise safer sex and will act on those decisions. However a condom is only as useful as the capacity to negotiate its use and many women are unable to achieve this (Worth, 1989).

Recent research among Latina women in New York has shown that many are becoming increasingly assertive in their interaction with sexual partners. One woman said of her boyfriend: 'Mine doesn't have a choice. Like it or not he has to use a condom with me. Or else nothing can happen. He will suffer for months.' An African American woman reported: 'I insist that he use protection. And if he doesn't want to, then he don't get the goodies. That's all' (Kline *et al.*, 1992, p. 453). But others feel unable to make such demands, and some men resist all attempts to change them (Carovano, 1991; Stein, 1990, p. 460; Ulin, 1992; Worth, 1989).

In one piece of action research in Zaire, 60 married women in a church group attempted to persuade their husbands to use condoms. One third refused without discussion and many of these were angry and hostile; one refused his wife 'housekeeping' and suggested she go out and 'hustle for money'. One third of the men convinced their wives that there was no risk (perhaps correctly). Only one third agreed in principle to use the condom (Grundfest Schoepf *et al.*, 1991, p. 199). In a national survey of Zimbabwean men, over 65 per cent said they had never used condoms and most saw them as appropriate only for use with prostitutes (Mbivso and Adamchak, 1989).

Reports from many countries have documented women's fears of family conflict, violence and economic loss if they try to enforce condom use. Young girls in particular may also fear that they will be accused of mistrust, of 'not loving him enough', or of being too sexually assertive (Holland *et al.*, 1990). For them, the problem may be not so much economic or social dependence as a fear of challenging dominant ideas about heterosex – of asserting their own needs and putting male pleasure in second place. After Holland and her co-researchers had studied the sexual behaviour of teenage girls in the United Kingdom, they suggested that the main thing standing between young women and safe sex was the men they were with (ibid.)

Many prevention strategies also recommend faithfulness within a sexual relationship as a means of ensuring that sex is safe. In Uganda, for instance, government education campaigns have promoted mono-gamy or 'zero grazing' as the key to prevention of HIV (Kisekka, 1990). However this will mean little to the millions of women who already confine their sexual activity to their husband or long-term partner. It has been estimated that between 50 per cent and 80 per cent of all HIV infected women in Africa have had no sexual partners other than their husbands (Reid, 1992, p. 659).

In a recent study carried out in an HIV/AIDS clinic in Harare, in almost all cases it was the male partner who had been responsible for bringing HIV infection into the family unit. Among 75 couples there were only two in which the wife was seropositive and the husband negative. In both these instances the wife had an identifiable risk factor (blood transfusion and first marriage to a partner who died of an AIDS-like illness) (Latif, 1989). Though women themselves are not always monogamous, economic, social and cultural factors often combine to make them more likely than men to limit their sexual contacts. Yet this does not prevent them from being at serious risk from infections picked up by their partners.

Motherhood or Safer Sex?

Of course women as well as men may ignore calls for safer sex. Some reject the 'aesthetics' of sex with a condom or the meanings associated with it. A black woman from New York with an HIV positive partner reported: 'I don't like them. Because it's some kind of chemical, the stuff it's made from, the stuff they have on those Trojans. And it rubs off into the woman by being rubber, and it causes a lot of problems too' (Kline *et al.*, 1992, p. 452). A Hispanic woman in the same study commented: 'You get embarrassed going to the store. When you go to the store you tell the person at the counter you want a pack of condoms and then he'll shout it where everyone in the store will know what you are there for' (Kline *et al.*, 1992, p. 452).

However the desire for pregnancy is often a more fundamental obstacle to safer sex. Most women wish to become mothers at some point in their lives and most will want to have more than one child. Unless male fidelity can be assured, conception cannot be combined with HIV prevention. Noerine Kaleeba, director of TASO, the AIDS Support Organisation in Uganda, has reported the feelings of one young woman who came to her for counselling. She could not protect herself from HIV, the woman said, because: 'Babies and condoms don't go together, non-penetrative sex is no sex at all for a man, and it is a woman's responsibility to bear a child' (Carovano, 1991, p. 135).

Of course many men also wish to become parents and the number of children a man fathers may be seen as an important measure of his potency. But for women the need for children is usually more profound. In many societies motherhood represents the only route to status, identity and personhood, and ultimately to security and support in old age. Indeed, it may be the only way a woman can keep a husband or partner, since in many communities a man is expected to leave a wife who does not 'give' him children. As a result many women feel forced to choose between motherhood and unsafe sex – to put their own life at risk in order to bring another one into the world. As one Ugandan woman put it, 'I don't mind dying but to die without a child means that I will have perished without trace. God will have cheated me' (de Bruyn, 1992, p. 255)

Equal Opportunities in Treatment?

If a woman becomes infected, gender inequalities also affect her survival chances and the quality of care she receives. AIDS cannot be cured but survival after diagnosis, as well as quality of life, are directly affected by the availability of medical services. Though the anti-viral drugs currently available are not proving to be as effective as many had hoped, AZT does seem to reduce the rate of transmission of the virus from mother to child. Certain other drugs are valuable in treating opportunistic infections such as pneumocystis carinii pneumonia (PCP), and in providing symptom relief. Yet women often experience great difficulty in gaining access to these treatments.

In those parts of the world where AIDS is commonest, health care budgets are often so small that neither sex can expect sophisticated treatment. But even here resources appear to be spent disproportionately on men. According to a recent survey none of the new care and support programmes either operating or being planned in Uganda, Rwanda, Zambia and Zimbabwe were designed to meet the particular needs of women (Seidel, 1993).

In the United States, too, a variety of factors – including gender and race – have been shown to influence quality of care. As long as a disease has no known cure, clinical trials of new drugs may represent the only hope for survival. Hence participation in trials of new AIDS drugs has been keenly sought (Denenberg, 1990a; Korvick, 1993). However women have often been excluded, usually on the grounds that their numbers are too small to give an adequate sample, or that any potential pregnancy could be endangered and the foetus harmed. Possible damage to an unborn child is clearly a matter for concern, but it is not an insurmountable problem and entry to trials is now being opened up (Korvick, 1993). This will give women early access to potentially valuable drugs as well as identifying any sex differences in their safety and efficacy (Berer and Ray, 1993, p. 31; Korvick, 1993; Rosser, 1992).

Male bias in clinical medicine is not of course confined to HIV and AIDS, but it is particularly noticeable in this context. In the United States gay men have been heavily involved in the organisation and funding of both research and treatment facilities, and concentration on their needs and priorities was entirely appropriate in the early stages of the epidemic. But as more women become infected, lack of knowledge about their clinical and psychosocial needs is posing serious problems (World Health Organisation, 1990). The percentage of scientific articles containing references to women and HIV/AIDS between 1985 and 1991 averaged 4.4 per cent though women made up 11 per cent of people with AIDS in the United States and a much higher proportion worldwide. Two thirds of US funds earmarked for research on AIDS in women and children have been used for research on children though infected women outnumber infected children by six to one (Kurth, 1993, p. 4).

We still know very little about sex differences in the transmission, symptoms and progression of HIV and AIDS – differences in its 'natural history' (Anastos and Vermund, 1993; Denenberg, 1990b). Data derived from the experiences of men cannot simply be extrapolated to women and a number of important questions remain unanswered. Very little is known about the specifics of HIV transmission to women or its biological consequences, and we need to explore both the social and the biological factors that lead to women becoming infected at a younger age than men (Reid, 1992).

Another area of particular ignorance is the relationship between HIV/AIDS and pregnancy (Brettle and Leen, 1991). Existing studies offer contradictory results, and despite the completion of a large number of at-risk pregnancies we still know very little either about the influence of pregnancy on the progression of HIV/AIDS or about the impact of HIV/AIDS on the reproductive outcome. The vertical transmission of the virus between mother and baby is also little understood, though the woman's state of health and the stage of her illness do appear to be significant factors in determining whether or not the child becomes infected. The proportion of children of HIV-positive women who are themselves infected varies between about 15 per cent and 40 per cent, with the children of poor mothers being most at risk (Berer and Ray, 1993, p. 74).

Thus women who contract HIV may face even greater uncertainty than infected men. This often begins with the problems they face in getting a correct diagnosis. Until recently diagnostic guidelines paid little attention to symptoms such as yeast infections, PID, herpes, menstrual problems and cervical cell abnormalities that seem to characterise the early stages of the disease process in many women (Berer and Ray, 1993, pp. 15–18; Brettle and Leen, 1991; Denenberg, 1990b; Kurth, 1993, pp. 9–10; Marte, 1992). Indeed a significant number are diagnosed only during pregnancy or when their child is found to be HIV positive.

At present the combination of unequal or delayed access to care and the male bias in existing knowledge means that women in both rich and poor countries have a shorter life expectancy than men after a diagnosis of AIDS (Anastos and Vermund, 1993). In Brazil for instance the average woman survives only 5.8 months while a man survives about three times as long (de Bruyn, 1992, p. 250). In New

York City a similar gap has been reported, with men surviving an average of 374 days after diagnosis compared with 298 for women (Rothenberg *et al.*, 1987, p. 1298). Since 1991 US studies have suggested that this gender difference is reducing as women get better access to care (Anastos and Vermund, 1993, p. 156). However social inequalities continue to influence clinical outcome. The survival rate for black and Hispanic women is shorter than that for white women, and women using intravenous drugs have a particularly poor prognosis. As one observer has commented, 'Black women who contract AIDS do not live as long or die as well as their white or male counterparts' (Richie, 1990, p. 182).

As well as the differences in clinical needs between men and women, their different psychosocial circumstances may also require a specialised response that male-oriented services are ill-equipped to provide. HIV-positive women who become pregnant or who consider doing so have to make major choices and face potentially traumatic emotional experiences, often without appropriate help or support (Kass, 1991; Walker, 1990). The possibility of giving birth to a terminally ill child is daunting, as is the threat of one's own death when the child is still small. Yet many decide to go ahead and almost one in eighty births in New York City now involve HIV-positive mothers (Faden *et al.*, 1991, p. 309).

We have seen that women are increasingly vulnerable to contracting the HIV virus and often succumb to it more rapidly than their male counterparts. Evidence from around the world indicates that women have frequently been the focus of attention as potential transmitters of the disease, or as the moral guardians of their male partners. Yet many are denied access to appropriate preventive and curative services, especially in those parts of the world where their need is greatest. As the epidemic has progressed, women have taken increasing responsibility for those who are made sick or orphaned by AIDS. However they have been allowed little influence over the relevant policy and planning decisions and are only beginning to have their own needs as people affected by HIV and AIDS taken seriously.

The Unkindest Cut

This final section addresses what is sometimes called female circumcision but is in fact genital mutilation. Though it directly affects only a minority of the world's women, it has long had symbolic importance as one of the most visible examples of patriarchal control over female sexuality. In those communities where it is practised, there can be no doubt that women's health and well-being is put at risk by the mutilation of their sexual organs. In other cultures the processes of control may be more subtle, but 'circumcision' offers an important point of comparison for some of these less visible forms of heterosexism. In particular the social reality of genital mutilation is an important illustration of the complex ways in which many women participate in the recreation of their own inequality in heterosexual relationships.

Female genital mutilation is a major health hazard affecting between 85 and 140 million women (World Bank, 1993, p. 50). It is still carried out in around 25 African countries, in Malaysia, Yemen and Indonesia, and in parts of Brazil, Mexico and Peru. It also occurs occasionally in European countries among migrants from geographical areas where it is normally practised. Genital mutilation is related to particular cultural beliefs and its distribution does not correspond to modern political boundaries. It is not tied to one particular religion, and is practised by Moslems, Catholics, Protestants, Copts and others in the areas where it is prevalent. Despite its frequent association with Islam, it is not recommended in the Koran or in any other religious texts (Hicks, 1993, pp. 23–5; Smyke, 1991, p. 78; Thiam, 1986, p. 58).

There are three types of mutilation, of varying degrees of severity, all of which involve the removal of parts of the external female genitalia. Clitoridectomy, also known as *sunna*, is the mildest form and involves removing only the skin over the clitoris or the tip of the clitoris. Excision means cutting and removing the entire clitoris and the labia minora but without closing up the vulva. Infibulation, or Pharaonic circumcision, is the most extreme. It involves the removal of the clitoris, the labia minora and parts of the labia majora, stitching together the sides, and leaving just a small opening for urine and menstrual fluid to pass through. As Susan Kenyon has described the practice in Sudan,

> Together with the removal of all bodily hair, the total effect is a sort of neutering one. There is no outward sign of a woman's sexual parts other than a faint scar where the genital slit should be, and a small opening at the vaginal entrance (Kenyon, 1991).

Age at circumcision varies between cultures. It is sometimes done at a few days old (by the Nomads of Sudan for instance), sometimes at around seven (in Egypt and many countries in Central Africa) or sometimes at adolescence (among the Ibo in Nigeria for example) (Minority Rights Group, 1980). These operations will be carried out by traditional practitioners (usually female) sometimes by western trained midwives or occasionally by doctors. In non-medical settings they may be done with a razor blade, a knife or a piece of broken glass. In many cultures thorns are traditionally used to sew together the torn edges. Anaesthetics are rarely available and the child is held down by other women during the process. In the case of infibulation, the girl's legs are usually bound together after the operation and she is immobilised to permit the formation of scar tissue.

PK, a woman from Mali, still remembers her excision – a relatively mild form of circumcision, which was carried out when she was twelve:

> My throat was dry and I was perspiring though it was early morning and not yet hot.
> No sooner had I lain down than I felt my thin frail legs tightly grasped by heavy hands and pulled wide apart. I lifted my head. Two women on each side of me pinned me to the ground. . . . A hand had grasped a part of my genital organs. My heart seemed to miss a beat. I would have given anything at that moment to be a thousand miles away; then a shooting pain brought me back to reality from my thoughts of flight. . . . The operation seemed to go on forever as it had to be performed 'to perfection'. I was in the throes of endless agony, torn apart both physically and psychologically. . . . I felt wet, I was bleeding. . . . Never had I felt such excruciating pain.
> Afterwards the most terrible moments were when I had to defecate. It was a month before I was completely healed, as I continually had to scratch where the genital wound itched (Thiam, 1986, pp. 61–2).

For girls undergoing the more extensive infibulation the operation is correspondingly worse, and recovery often more difficult. Moreover the process can be almost never-ending, since such women must be 'disinfibulated' on their marriage and before childbirth, and are usually 'reinfibulated' after each child. Disinfibulation at marriage is sometimes achieved by the penetration of the husband's penis alone, sometimes by a cut where stitching had previously been done and sometimes by both. Whatever the means, the process is inevitably painful.

Hanny Lightfoot-Klein investigated women's experiences of circumcision in Sudan, where over 90 per cent of those she interviewed had undergone the more severe Pharaonic circumcision (Lightfoot-Klein, 1989, p. 58). All the women, without exception, reported a great deal of suffering during the process of gradual penetration, which lasted on average two to three months after marriage (ibid.) About 15 per cent reported that their husbands were unable to achieve penetration of their infibulation and that they had to be opened surgically under conditions of great secrecy. A study by Asma el Dareer, a Sudanese doctor, produced very similar findings, with the average time required for full penetration being two to twelve weeks with a Pharaonic circumcision (el Dareer, 1982).

The complications resulting from genital mutilation are many. One West African study showed that 83 per cent of circumcised women had received medical attention at least once in their life for a problem related to their mutilation (Koso-Thomas, 1987, p. 19). Immediate complications include haemorrhage, post-operative shock, urine retention and infection, particularly tetanus. There can be no doubt that some young girls die as a result of circumcision but there are no statistics, since few cases reach hospital, and the cause of death is likely to be concealed.

Once the immediate crisis is over, many circumcised women continue to experience related health problems. Infections of the urinary tract, uterus and vagina are common, and menstruation is often extremely difficult since the vagina has become a semi-sealed organ. The hole left after infibulation is often so small that clots of menstrual blood cannot escape freely, causing severe pain and very long periods that may need surgical intervention. Dr Ollivier, working in Djibouti, reported the case of a sixteen-year-old girl brought to the hospital with extreme abdominal pain. She had not menstruated for several months and had not had intercourse, but her abdomen was swollen and sensitive and she appeared to be in labour. She was infibulated, with a very small opening. A surgical disinfibulation was performed and released 3.4 litres of blackish, foul-smelling blood. Paradoxically this young woman was relatively lucky since others have been killed if absence of menstruation leads their family to believe they are pregnant before marriage (Minority Rights Group, 1980).

When they do become pregnant infibulated women risk serious complications during childbirth, since scar tissue and fibrosis often mean the tissue will not stretch easily, leading to more painful labour and an increased incidence of obstruction and stillbirth. The baby's head may be pushed through the perineum, which tears more easily than the infibulation scar, causing serious pain and blood loss, and other organs — including the urethra, bladder and rectum damaged, with long-term consequences. Again there is a ser infection, especially since most women are even up again child. Women may therefore undergo this process as many times during their reproductive lives.

Not surprisingly, little research has been undertaken on the qualitative effects of genital mutilation, particularly its im sexuality. However it is clear that the amputation of the clit have a profoundly deleterious effect on a woman's orgasmic po seriously impeding her ability to achieve sexual gratification. As the Sudanese doctor Nahid Toubia has put it, 'Female circumcision unlike male circumcision is an act of ablating the sensory organs of a woman's genitals as a means of removing her sexuality while retaining her reproductive functions' (Toubia, 1985, p. 135).

The contradiction between the obvious health hazards of female genital mutilation and the widespread support for its continuation among both men and women has made it an extremely sensitive political issue. It is clearly part of a patriarchal system for controlling female sexuality, safeguarding a woman's virginity until marriage, protecting family honour and enhancing men's pleasure in intercourse (Hicks, 1993, pp. 73–8). As such it is part of the wider process of subordination that defines women as being of less value than men. Yet many women have themselves learned to see mutilation as normal, necessary and even desirable if they are to fulfil their potential as wives and mothers, and to be accepted as members of their community (ibid., pp. 79–81). Hence many have internalised their oppression and continue to be implicated in the reproduction both of their own inferiority and that of their daughters.

Conclusion

We have seen that most sexual encounters between men and women involve a process of negotiation that may be either implicit or explicit. Many women are compelled to conduct these negotiations from a position of weakness and as a result heterosex may be neither a happy nor healthy experience for them. Instead the potentially pleasurable and life-enhancing effects of sex between men and women may be limited or even destroyed by the fundamentally unequal nature of their relationship. As we shall see in the next two chapters, these inequalities are often reinforced as a result of bargaining over fertility control, pregnancy and childbearing.

Further Reading

Berer, M. and Ray, S. (1993) *Women and HIV/AIDS: an international resource book* (London: Pandora). A unique and invaluable book for anyone interested and/or involved in women and HIV/AIDS issues. It brings together material from a wide range of both published and unpublished sources providing a world view of both problems and potential in this very difficult area. The guide to groups and resources is excellent.

Germain, A., Holmes, K., Piot, P. and Wasserheit, J. (1992) *Reproductive Tract Infections: global report and priorities for women's reproductive health* (New York: Plenum Press). An outstanding collection of articles on a much ignored topic. This book includes clinical, epidemiological, social and economic observations on reproductive tract infections and provides valuable case studies from a number of third world countries.

Kelly, L. (1988) *Surviving Sexual Violence* (Oxford: Polity Press). A study that aims to 'give voice' to a group of British women who have survived sexual violence. It also includes an illuminating discussion of some of the theoretical and methodological problems of research of this kind.

Kurth, A. (ed.) (1993) *Until the Cure: caring for women with HIV* (London and New Haven: Yale University Press). Based on the US experience, this is an important reference book for people working on the front lines with women living with HIV disease. It offers succinct and valuable information as well as a vision of best practice in helping women to cope in the absence of a cure.

4

Regulating Reproduction

Introduction

If women are to maximise their health and their autonomy, they must be able to determine the nature of their reproductive lives (Correa and Petchesky, 1994; Dixon-Mueller, 1993). If they have sex with men, they must have the means to enjoy it without fear of infection or unwanted pregnancy, they must be able to control their own fertility without risking unpleasant or dangerous side effects, and they must be able to pass safely through pregnancy and childbirth to raise healthy children. Men can control their bodies and maintain their health without controlling their fertility. Since women cannot do the same, they have always sought the most effective means of enhancing their reproductive self-determination (Gordon, 1976; Petchesky, 1986).

Health and Reproduction

Pregnancy and childbirth have profound effects on both mind and body. In the best of circumstances motherhood is actively chosen, and constitutes one of the most fulfilling experiences of women's lives. Indeed many will be prepared to undergo considerable hardship to ensure a successful conception and the live birth of a healthy child. However such experiences are by no means universal. Instead many women's lives continue to be severely constrained because they are denied the opportunity to make real choices about their own procreation. This inability to influence one of the most fundamental aspects of biological functioning can have profound effects on both physical and mental health.

Protracted childbearing with inadequate spacing between pregnancies is not conducive to physical well-being and an interval of at least two years is generally recommended to allow a woman's body to recover from pregnancy and lactation. Shorter gaps can cause what has been called 'maternal depletion syndrome' as women who are overworked and undernourished become chronically debilitated. Maximising a woman's ability to control her fertility is therefore a prerequisite for promoting her physical health.

We know much less about the psychological consequences of unwanted childbearing. The emotional effects of pregnancy and birth are always complicated for a woman. While she may describe a 'pregnancy' as unwanted, the baby itself and the reality of motherhood will inevitably engender more complicated feelings. However there can be little doubt that for many women the involuntary use of their body to nurture a child they have not actively chosen to bear will induce profound feelings of fatalism, making it difficult to maintain a sense of identity or self-worth. Such feelings are likely to be exacerbated if they have not consented in any positive way to the sexual intercourse that led to the initial conception.

But uncontrolled childbearing causes more than physical and psychological harm. Women who cannot limit their family size will also be socially damaged since they usually bear responsibility for the care of any children they produce. As a result the option of engaging in activities outside the family will effectively be denied to them. The greatest harm will result if the woman is denied access to education since literacy – 'medication against fatalism' – is strongly associated with declining fertility and improved health status (Royston and Armstrong, 1989, pp. 56–62).

The importance most women place upon the capacity to limit their fertility is evident from the almost universal existence of practices designed to prevent unwanted conceptions and to terminate unsought pregnancies. However many continue to face major obstacles in achieving these goals. This is because women's capacity to conceive and give birth to children is not only important to them as individuals. It also has much wider material and cultural significance affecting their partners, families and communities. In many societies women's sexual lives are highly contested arenas over which a variety of individuals and groups fight to maintain control. Hence any attempt to understand the determination of their fertility must begin not with biological or technological questions but with the complex web that constitutes the social relations of reproduction.

Who Controls Whose Fertility?

At the centre of this web is the woman herself, whose reproductive deliberations take place within a particular set of beliefs and values about the nature of men and women, the purposes of sexuality and the meaning of parenthood and family life.

Family Ties

In most cultures women experience powerful pressures to 'prove' their 'femaleness' by becoming a mother. At the same time women and their partners will also be influenced by the social and economic reality of the world around them: 'A woman does not simply "get pregnant" and "give birth" like the flowing tides and seasons. She does so under the constraint of material conditions that set limits on "natural" reproductive processes' (Petchesky, 1986). For many couples this will result in the decision to have a large family not, as is often assumed, out of ignorance or religious obscurantism, but because children represent an important supply of labour and a sign of social status as well as a source of material security.

High infant mortality means that parents cannot be sure their children will survive to contribute to the family economy and to take care of them in their old age. The poor are thus caught in a death trap. They have to keep producing children in order that some will survive (Hartmann, 1987, p. 9).

Decisions of this kind are usually represented as belonging to 'couples' or households, but it is significant that most are made in the context of gender inequality. As we have seen, the institution of heterosexuality legitimates men's claims to control women's sexual and reproductive lives. Under such circumstances women may find it difficult to articulate – or sometimes even to perceive – their own interests, and the jointness of decisions made by individual couples may be more apparent than real. It is women who may have to pay with their health for high levels of fertility. Yet many find themselves in the paradoxical situation of choosing – or feeling unable to refuse – to risk their own well-being as part of a survival strategy for themselves and their families (Kabeer, 1985).

The Power of Religion

Beyond the immediate family – though often working through it – other social institutions exert direct or indirect power over women's reproductive choices. Organised religion is clearly one of the most important of these. The last hundred years have been marked by a decline in the popularity of religious observances and a general secularisation of social life in most of the developed countries and in some parts of the third world. However religious institutions still wield considerable power over women's sexual lives. The Catholic Church, for instance, continues to be an important opponent of the legalisation of abortion in Latin America and led the recent campaign that succeeded in enshrining the rights of the unborn child in the Irish constitution (Barry, 1988). In Poland, too, it was a reemergent Catholicism that played a significant part in the passing of a 1993 law to protect the foetus and recriminalise abortion (Jankowska, 1993).

This reflects a more general trend in which the revival of religious fundamentalism has led to attempts to take back those freedoms that some women had gained over reproductive decision making (Yuval Davis, 1989). In the United States, for instance, 'born again' Protestantism forms an important element in the New Right coalition to restrict reproductive rights not just in America but on a global scale. Similar pressures can be seen at work in other countries, especially where religious fundamentalism is allied with nationalism, as it is in many parts of the Islamic world. Under such circumstances many women are forced to make extremely difficult choices, balancing their own health needs and their religious beliefs with the interests of their families and the pressures of the wider community.

Nationalism and Natalism

For most women, access to fertility control is also determined by the priorities of their governments. These are reflected in basic health care and other social programmes and more particularly in policies designed to effect demographic change. Since very few women hold positions of influence in national governments, this often means that the reproductive health needs of women are subordinated to what is defined as the collective good. Broadly speaking, governments will adopt either pro-natalist or anti-natalist policies depending on their economic and social priorities and what they perceive to be in their political interests. In either case the policies will be directed largely at women, profoundly influencing some of the most intimate areas of their lives. We can illustrate this through an examination of the very different policies found in two countries defining themselves as socialist (Davin, 1992).

The best known example of anti-natalism is probably the 'one child policy' adopted in 1979 by the People's Republic of China. This was an attempt to boost economic growth and maintain living standards for a rapidly expanding population, but its effects on women's health and well-being have been mixed at best (Davin, 1987; Hardee-Cleaveland and Banister, 1988; Hartmann, 1987, Ch. 8; Hillier, 1988). Couples have been put under enormous moral pressure to comply and are offered economic and social incentives to do so. However the pressure falls disproportionately on women. After 1982 all women with one child were expected to accept an IUD, for couples with two children one partner was supposed to be sterilised (in the majority of cases this was the woman) and those conceiving unauthorised children were expected to abort them.

Despite some regional variations, the policy was vigorously implemented across the country and there have been consistent reports of coercive sterilisations and abortions, with some of the latter done at a very late stage (Davin, 1987, p. 121). The many problems engendered by this one child policy have been exacerbated by the continuing 'son preference', which has deep cultural and material roots in Chinese society. If a couple's only authorised child is a girl, the mother in particular has often come under extreme pressure and cases of female infanticide have been documented (ibid., p. 117).

In Romania, too, women's reproductive health has been threatened by government policies. In this case pro-natalist policies were introduced by former president Ceaucescu in order to increase the size of the Romanian population. Abortion was made illegal in 1966, with very few exceptions, and contraception was available only on prescription to women whose health would be endangered by pregnancy. All imports of contraceptive drugs and devices were banned and only condoms and spermicides were produced within Romania itself. The inevitable result of these policies was a marked rise in the maternal mortality rate and a huge burden of ill health borne by women.

Thus government policies designed to effect dramatic changes in the birth rate have historically impinged most severely on women. Though the Chinese and Romanian cases are very different, both illustrate the dangers involved in putting what is perceived as the collective good before the interests of individual women. This is not to suggest that it is never appropriate for societies to have demographic policies. There are clearly circumstances under which family size needs to be subject to some element of social negotiation. However it is essential that women participate at least equally with men in the formulation and implementation of appropriate strategies (Berer, 1993).

Social Eugenics and Social Control

A further danger inherent in existing population policies is that they rarely target all women equally. Most national governments have more complex agendas, often involving attempts to maintain or restructure existing social divisions. Hence women's access to or exclusion from fertility control will be influenced by their social class, their race and their national or ethnic identification.

The importance of social class as a factor in birth control policies was evident in both the United Kingdom and the United States at the turn of the century. In both countries powerful interests were pushing for eugenic policies designed to control the 'breeding' of working-class women, especially in the slum areas of the big cities (Gordon, 1976; Petchesky, 1986). There were widespread fears that the resulting degeneration of the population would make it unfit for economic or military competition, and proponents of these neo-Malthusian views vied with those whose religious beliefs led them to oppose birth control on moral grounds. The interests of the women themselves were largely ignored in the resulting battle.

The racial politics inherent in many demographic policies are particularly clear in South Africa. Despite the need for labour, the official birth-control programme has historically been targeted primarily at black women (Klugman, 1993). Moreover different racial groups have been encouraged to use very different contraceptive techniques. A recent survey in Transvaal indicated that while African women were usually offered injectable forms of contraceptive and very little else, many white women did not even know of their existence (ibid., p. 52). 'Family planning' has been the only free health care available to black women and Depo Provera the most widely used contraceptive. In some instances black mothers have had to present family planning cards when applying for a job while white women have been encouraged to have large families (Hartmann, 1987, p. 193). Thus family planning issues are difficult to separate from wider social control policies and black women have been offered few opportunities to make informed choices.

Discrimination is also evident in Israel. Until recently only Palestinian women were able to obtain free contraceptives. Jewish women on the other hand were recruited into a 'demographic war' to bear more children as their national duty to the Jewish people in general and the Israeli Jewish people in particular (Salzberger *et al.*, 1991; Yuval Davis, 1989, p. 100). In the early 1950s David Ben Gurion called upon women to ensure a Jewish majority in the new state, suggesting a quota of at least four or five children per family. This pro-birth policy was backed with cash incentives for women having their tenth child. However the majority of women awarded the prize were Palestinian, and it was eventually discontinued in 1959 (Salzberger *et al.*, 1991, p. 6). It seems that reproduction has now become a weapon for Palestinian nationalists too. Hence there are conflicting pressures on demographic decision making for all Israeli women – both Palestinian and Jewish (Yuval Davis, 1989, p. 5).

During the postwar period the impact of these national policies on women's lives has been increasingly shaped by international influences. In the 1970s the United States government, in collaboration with a variety of international organisations, was heavily involved in attempts to restrict the growth of populations in the third world (Hartmann, 1987; LaCheen, 1986). The agenda was clear and the methods often draconian, especially in India where collaboration with the government produced a national 'push' against pregnancy (Sundari Ravindran, 1993). For millions of women these 'population controllers' did open up access to contraception. However the services were usually applied with little sensitivity to different cultural contexts, and frequently abused the rights of both women and men. Success was evaluated only in terms of numbers accepting contraception, with little concern for users' satisfaction or for the long-term effects on their health.

The intense pressure of the 1970s has now relented in most countries. However women seeking to regulate their fertility continue to be reliant on medical workers to achieve these goals. As we shall see, the effects of this 'medicalisation' of reproduction have been paradoxical. On the one hand medical scientists, in conjunction with the pharmaceutical industry, have developed a range of new methods – both conceptive and contraceptive – that potentially offer women greater control over their fertility. On the other hand these techniques have made women more dependent on the medical profession for access and continuing care and doctors have not always responded with either the competence or the respect that women could reasonably expect.

A Contraceptive Revolution?

Throughout history both men and women have employed a variety of drugs, devices and practices designed to break the biological connection between sex and pregnancy. However it was not until the late nineteenth century that high levels of contraceptive efficacy could be reliably achieved by men using a rubber condom and by women using a diaphragm. Women in developed countries began to benefit from these techniques during the first half of the twentieth century, but it was the 'contraceptive era' of the 1960s that saw a dramatic increase in access to fertility control. During this period a range of new techniques were developed and made available to women around the world – though rarely on their own terms.

Expanding Contraceptive Technologies

In developed countries the entry of women into the labour market combined with more liberal attitudes towards female sexuality to create a growing demand for a wider range of contraceptive methods. This coincided with an increasing fear of population growth in the underdeveloped world, providing an incentive for the US government to work with the pharmaceutical industry in the development and marketing of what became known as 'the pill'. The pill and the intrauterine device, or IUD, together provided the basis for the global spread of contraception – a massive international exercise that had a major impact on the lives of many women. By 1962 the pill was being used by some two million women in the United States alone and the use of modern family planning methods increased by as much as 500 per cent in many parts of the third world during the 1960s and 1970s.

It is significant that these developments were initially marked by a convergence of interest between three of the major groups involved. Feminists were anxious to improve women's ability to control their own fertility; a range of interest groups in the first world felt threatened by population growth among some of the world's poorest nations, while pharmaceutical companies saw the pill in particular as a potential source of spectacular profit. However this apparent consensus has gradually broken down in response to a variety of national and international pressures.

Women's health activists have been increasingly critical of the risks attached to most contraceptive technologies and of the scant regard paid by too many providers to women's own needs and desires.

Population controllers have curtailed a number of their activities in response to the international 'right to life' movement as well as to the growing criticisms of their policies by some third world governments. At the same time, most US drug companies are now ceasing to research, develop and manufacture contraceptive drugs and devices in the face of the escalating cost of testing new products under the rigorous protocols now required in the United States, as well as the insurance needed to protect them against law suits from women and children already damaged by their products (Lincoln and Kaeser, 1988).

The advent of the 1990s has therefore witnessed a reassessment of the benefits of modern contraceptive technologies and the social relations that have created them. There can be no doubt that the wider availability of contraception has freed many women from anxiety, improving their physical and mental health through the avoidance of unwanted and possibly dangerous pregnancies. However too many women still do not have access to the most basic knowledge or supplies. Moreover those who can obtain services are often unhappy with the methods or the terms upon which they are provided. Individual women in the developed countries and in the third world are increasingly critical of the range of choices offered to them and many are reluctant to pay the social, economic and health costs associated with the more widely promoted methods. A woman at a village meeting in Java stated the problem plainly:

> We would gladly accept family planning provided that it doesn't interfere with our work, do us any permanent harm or be against our religion. It should also be explained to us by a woman who will examine us if necessary and keep it secret. It should also cost very little money' (Warren, 1987, p. 22).

At present such options are available to only a small minority of women, most of them living in developed countries, and it is unclear whether the means will be found to develop and fund improved techniques and services on a global scale. If the 'contraceptive revolution' was born in the 1960s it now seems to have run aground and, as we shall see, one of the most basic health needs of millions of women remains unmet (Lincoln and Kaeser, 1988).

Contraception as 'Women's Business'

As Judith Bruce has pointed out, 'women's bodies are usually the vehicles through which modern contraceptive services are delivered to communities' (Bruce, 1987, p. 362). Until the early 1960s male methods of fertility control were used more frequently than female methods, but the 'contraceptive revolution' shifted the emphasis dramatically in the direction of women, with the ratio of female to male contraceptive use rising to 2.7:1 in the mid 1980s (ibid., p. 343). Worldwide, about 340 million out of 880 million married couples of reproductive age now use a modern method of contraception (Mauldin and Segal, 1988, p. 341). In the vast majority of those cases it is the woman who contracepts. 155 million rely on sterilisation but it is the woman who has been sterilised in two thirds of these; 80 million use the IUD and 61 million use hormonal methods. Only about 38 million men use condoms, despite their acknowledged safety, efficacy and potential for preventing sexually transmitted diseases.

Relatively few attempts have been made to develop new methods of contraception for men and less than 5 per cent of research budgets are currently devoted to this task (Bruce, 1987, p. 362; Hartmann, 1987, p. 100). The reasons for this bias in development activities are complex. They reflect in part our relative lack of knowledge about the male reproductive system compared with that of women who have long been the objects of a more intense 'clinical gaze'. Moreover women are fertile for only a short period, and there are more possible points of intervention during their reproductive cycle. However it would also appear that male researchers have been particularly sensitive to the possible side effects of any contraceptive for men, especially as it might affect their potency or libido: 'One senses that where sex as opposed to reproduction is at issue, the male of the species is still regarded by a patriarchal culture and medicine as the delicate and vulnerable one' (Petchesky, 1986, p. 173).

The implications for women of this shift in responsibility for contraception are, of course, contradictory. On the one hand they have potentially gained more control over their own lives. This is especially important for young women in transient relationships and for those who cannot trust their partners to respect their decision to avoid pregnancy. However it also places the health risks of contraception firmly on women's shoulders. This is an important consideration both because of the potentially hazardous nature of these new female techniques but also because a man's failure to use a condom will greatly increase his partner's chances of contracting a variety of sexually transmitted diseases, including AIDS: 'Women should perhaps be suspicious of the fact that while in every other sphere men are very reluctant to give responsibility to women, in this case they appear only too eager to do so' (Rose and Hanmer, 1976).

Barriers to Birth Control

Although the rate of contraceptive use has increased worldwide, it still varies markedly between countries and regions, from 70 per cent in developed countries, to 49 per cent in Asia and the Pacific and only 12 per cent in Africa (United Nations, 1989a). The reasons for low rates of contraceptive use are varied. Sometimes they simply reflect a continuing desire for large families. However it is clear that in many instances they represent a major failure to meet women's demand for family planning services.

Evidence of Unmet Need

One index of this demand is the 50 million abortions performed around the world each year. Further evidence is contained in the results of research undertaken by the World Fertility Survey, which investigated the relationship between contraceptive use and desired family size. Recent data suggest that in most Latin American countries women want to have only two or three children but average family size is still five or six (Royston and Armstrong, 1989, p. 191). In Bangladesh too the fertility rate is twice what women say they desire, though in Sub-Saharan Africa fertility broadly reflects desired family size. Globally some 300 million couples say they want no more children but are not practising contraception, while many millions more wish to space their children more effectively (ibid., p. 184).

At their starkest, these statistics represent unnecessary deaths. Recent estimates suggest that if women were able to have only the number of children they wanted, this would result in a reduction of 35 per cent in the maternal mortality rate in Latin America, 33 per cent in Asia and 17 per cent in Africa (ibid., p. 192).

Dynamics of Demographic Decision Making

The barriers women face in meeting their desire for safe and effective contraception are many. For some the struggle begins at home if their partners are resistant. Thus far there have been few formal studies of demographic decision making within families, but it is clear that many men play a dominant role. Recent research in rural Peru concluded that partners often have the last word in choices about reproduction and contraception (Maynard-Tucker, 1989). A similar study in Khartoum found that 54 per cent of Sudanese men believed that family planning should be the husband's decision alone (Khalifa, 1988).

In some countries a husband's power over his wife's ability to contracept is formalised in laws or regulations. The Family Guidance Association of Ethiopia had a requirement until 1982 that a husband's signed consent was required for his wife to obtain contraceptives. As a result 16 per cent of the women who requested them were turned away because they did not have such an authorisation (Cook and Maine, 1987). When the requirement for spousal consent was removed, clinic utilisation increased by 26 per cent within a few months. In Papua New Guinea the law bans the sale of contraceptives to a married woman without her husband's authorisation, while in Niger too government clinics give women contraceptives only with spousal consent (ibid., p. 340).

When men do consent to their partner's use of contraceptives, they may still have the final say on the method to be used. In a British survey of female university students, many commented on the reluctance of their partners to have their pleasure interfered with by contraception. The 'invisibility' of the pill made it especially popular with men, though many of the women were more ambivalent. One reported:

> I'm not happy about taking the pill. It's the simplest, but I thought the cap was quite safe. I've been thinking of taking a break but my husband said 'Oh no, the smell of the cream was revolting', so I guess I won't go back even though I was quite satisfied really with the cap (Pollack, 1985, p. 71).

Another said,

> He didn't like it one bit when I was having him use the sheath. He prefers me to damage my health with pills. He doesn't have to worry about that. He reckons it [the sheath] spoils all the fun (Pollack, 1985, p. 72).

Thus even women with relatively high levels of social status and economic power felt constrained by the desires of their male partners to the point of risking their own health.

Similar findings were obtained from a study in a very different social context. In a nationwide survey in Mexico the majority of female respondents expressed strong concern that their chosen method should meet their husbands' requirements for sexual gratification. While the men themselves identified lack of interference in their own feelings as a major factor influencing their choice of method, the women did not (Folch-Lyon *et al.*, 1981, pp. 418–19). Significantly contraceptive methods that interfere least with men's sexual pleasures are those most likely to interfere with women's health.

Shortage of Services

Whatever their partners' attitudes to birth control many women still find advice and supplies difficult to obtain. For some rural women, clinics are too far from home, while young women are often excluded by their age, by their unmarried status or by their lack of knowledge about how to obtain the appropriate care. Many more live in countries where contraceptives are still illegal or formally restricted.

Family planning supplies have been difficult to obtain in much of Eastern Europe, with no hard currency to import them and central planners failing to meet the need through domestic production (Davin, 1992). Behind what Jodi Jacobson has called the 'contraceptive iron curtain' some 70 million women of childbearing age live in the countries of the former Soviet Union. Yet they do not have a single factory producing modern contraceptives. The few condoms available are poor in quality and widely referred to as 'galoshes' (Jacobson, 1991, p. 30). While recent political developments have opened up a 'reproductive glasnost', the unmet need for contraceptive supplies remains high.

Similar shortages exist elsewhere. Though more than half the population have easy access to at least one method of contraception in 86 per cent of countries in Latin America, the same is true in only 44 per cent of countries in Asia and Oceania and 12 per cent in Africa (United Nations, 1989a, p. 65). Thus many women wishing to control their own fertility still face serious obstacles in both private and public arenas. But what of those who have benefited from the 'contraceptive revolution'? As we shall see, major problems remain for them too. Access to a method of birth control does not, in itself, meet women's reproductive health needs and the technologies and the organisations that provide them continue to have serious limitations.

Mrs Hobson's Choice: Picking a Contraceptive

There cannot be a single, perfect contraceptive suitable for all biological, social and cultural circumstances. However many women still cannot find a method that is more than minimally acceptable. While the number using contraception has risen dramatically, the 'drop-out' rate for individual methods remains high and many women feel obliged to adopt techniques that prevent pregnancy but do not meet their wider needs. Boxed into a no-win situation between unwanted childbirth and less than perfect contraception, they choose to endure 'side effects' that seriously threaten their well-being (Hardon, 1992).

Sexism and Sterilisation

Sterilisation is now the most popular method worldwide for preventing pregnancy. Male sterilisation is both cheaper and easier than its female equivalent since the surgery required is less invasive and can be done easily under local anaesthetic. However about 70 per cent of all sterilisations are performed on women. Though the newer minilaparotomy has a relatively low complication rate, the problems associated with female sterilisation continue to be significant, especially under the less than ideal surgical conditions found in many parts of the third world (Khan, 1989, p. 262). In Bangladesh one in every five thousand women who undergoes sterilisation dies as a result of the procedure (Editorial, *The Lancet*, 1989).

The differences in the health risks of male and female sterilisation are very marked (Smith *et al.*, 1985). The mortality rate for women is about five times greater than that for men and the risk of long-term morbidity is also much higher for women. Yet the Netherlands is now the only country in the world where more men than women have been sterilised and around the world the gap between male and female sterilisation is widening (United Nations, 1989, p. 56). Thus the health hazards of permanent contraception are borne disproportionately by women, though both sexes benefit from the results.

Sterilisation can of course be a major boon for those women who have decided not to have children in the future, and have easy access to good surgical care. But because it is irreversible, effective arrangements to ensure freedom of choice and informed consent are of the utmost importance. Evidence from a number of countries suggests that the quality of such arrangements is extremely variable and that many women's capacity to determine their fate is seriously impaired.

Sterilisation and Abuse

In the United States there has been a lengthy history of the use of sterilisation for eugenic purposes among poor, immigrant and ethnic minority women (Davis, 1981; Petchesky, 1986; Shapiro, 1985). A survey in 1970 found that 20 per cent of all married black women had been sterilised, and that 43 per cent of all women sterilised through federal programmes were black (Gerber Fried, 1990a, p. 159). This trend continued during the 1970s and 1980s. While free abortions under Medicaid are now denied in most states, sterilisation receives 90 per cent funding, giving women a major incentive to 'choose' the latter. By 1982 some 15 per cent of white women in the United States were sterilised compared with 24 per cent of black women, 35 per cent of Puerto Rican women and 42 per cent of native American women (ibid., p. 259).

Many women are unable to comprehend the complex issues involved in sterilisation because they are given inadequate explanations, sometimes in a language they cannot understand. Some realise too late what has happened to them. A Latina woman, Maria Figueroa, described her experience in a California hospital:

> A doctor asked me if I wanted to have a tubal ligation. I told the doctor I did not want to be sterilised since my husband and I planned to have another child. . . . I was groggy from the drugs, exhausted from the labour, as well as from the doctor's constant pressuring. Finally I told the doctor, 'Okay if it's a boy, go ahead and do it'. . . . My daughter Elizabeth was born by caesarean section. While my husband was visiting me in the medical center, the doctor came to my bed and informed me he had performed a tubal ligation on me (Dreifus, 1978).

In Puerto Rico sterilisation and immigration control were the major planks of population policy in the early 1960s. Huge numbers of women had *la operacion*, often without understanding the consequences and many have tried unsuccessfully to get the process reversed. Today the proportion of women in Puerto Rico who are sterilised is said to be 45 per cent – the highest in the world (Fuentes, 1987, p. 14). In recent years more rigorous guidelines have been introduced in clinics in Puerto Rico and the United States in an attempt to prevent abuses. But because of their circumstances many Puerto Rican women still opt for sterilisation. According to Digma Sanchez of the New York Committee on Hispanic Children and Families, 'Sterilisation is an easier solution than finding jobs, better education, affordable housing. Women feel life is so difficult why not get sterilised? (Fuentes, 1987, p. 15).

Since the 1970s sterilisation abuses have been documented in many other countries, including Bangladesh, Bolivia, Colombia, El Salvador, Guatemala, India, Indonesia and Mexico. In India and Bangladesh in particular, extensive programmes were initiated in the 1970s offering both men and women a variety of inducements to be sterilised (Hartmann, 1987; Shiva, 1992). Despite widespread criticism both nationally and internationally, the practice continues in some areas:

> Desperate to feed their families, women in the arid, West Indian state of Rajasthan have been agreeing to sterilisation – often without telling their husbands – in return for 2,000 rupees of famine relief . . . it was the women who trooped in for the operation because they were desperate for money to feed their children – and for any opportunity to halt the endless cycle of childbearing. Now, many have been sterilised but few have received the promised cash (Asian and Pacific Women's Resource Collection Network, 1989, p. 75).

In Brazil, too, many women have been pushed into sterilisation. Every year more than 300 000 have a tubal ligation, according to Ministry of Health statistics (Christensen, 1991, p. 11). In parts of the Amazon and in poor states in the north-east, as many as 75 per cent of women of childbearing age are said to have been sterilised. Here there are no formal incentives or coercive policies like those found in India. However poverty has had the same effect, according to Carmen Barosso, a feminist health researcher in São Paulo.

> Women cannot feed their children because of the policies of the IMF and that leads them to limit their births with desperate moves. . . . Coercion is institutionalised. It is not done against women's will. But their will has no choice (Christensen, 1991, p. 12).

Recent reports have drawn attention to major abuses of women's human rights in Tibet (Campaign Free Tibet, 1994). Forced abortions and sterilisations have been a dominant feature of Chinese policies designed to maintain control over the Tibetan population. An English nurse described her experiences in Lhasa:

> Once, in August 1987 I heard a commotion at dusk. Looking out of my window I saw a truck with its back open and three wicker baskets inside. Two contained Tibetan women. Caged like animals. A large crowd of protesting Tibetans and a lot of Chinese soldiers were milling around. I imagined the women had committed some crime but were told they were being taken away for 'having too many children'. They must have been pregnant for I heard people say that 'soon they won't be pregnant any longer' (Free Tibet, 1994, p. 157).

Are IUDs the Answer?

For those not wishing permanent contraception, the intrauterine device or IUD works by preventing the implantation of a fertilised ovum. Worldwide it is the next most popular method after sterilisation, but about 50 million out of a total of 80 million users live in China where central control over contraceptive supplies has made individual choice extremely limited. In developed countries, particularly the United States, use of the IUD has declined in recent years and it is now the least popular method. Insurance companies refuse to cover IUDs and the pharmaceutical companies withdrew most devices from the US market after 1986 as a result of the huge losses incurred from legal suits.

IUDs do have the clear advantage of offering a high level of reliability and necessitating only one action to ensure a long period of protection. This can be especially valuable for women who need to conceal their contraception or who live in circumstances where it is difficult to store and use contraceptive supplies. However they can also have major health risks, which too many women are unaware of when the device is inserted.

These include heavy or prolonged bleeding and painful cramps. Studies done on menstrual blood loss have shown that plain plastic devices cause a 100–150 per cent increase in blood loss and copper IUDs a 30–60 per cent increase (Khan, 1989, p. 253). Heavy bleeding of this kind is obviously uncomfortable for all women, but for some it will have additional social or cultural significance. In many societies menstruating women are regarded as unclean or impure and may have to restrict activities such as hair or clothes washing, praying or visiting new mothers. In one WHO study three quarters of Hindu women said that they avoided cooking meals when menstruating and many said that they needed to rest more often (WHO, 1981). Seventy-nine per cent of women in a Brazilian study reported that excessive bleeding discouraged sexual intercourse, often causing difficulties in family relationships (Bruce, 1987, p. 373).

Menstruation is relatively rare in societies where women do not use modern methods of contraception. A woman who bears four children, breastfeeds for eight months and then uses a temporary contraceptive will have more than three times as many menstrual periods as her mother who bore seven children and achieved three-year birth intervals through extended breast feeding (ibid.) When even greater bleeding is induced by an IUD many women will experience both physical and psychological distress, especially if they are poorly nourished and doing hard physical work. It will increase their risk of iron-deficiency anaemia and may pose a serious threat to health.

There is a one in a thousand risk of the IUD causing perforation of the uterus, either when it is inserted or subsequently. For women who conceive while using an IUD there is also a high risk of ectopic pregnancy. Although the method has a low failure rate (3–5 pregnancies per 100 users) about one in twenty of those who do conceive will have an embryo that implants in one of their fallopian tubes – a potentially life threatening problem without immediate surgery. Not surprisingly, therefore, the mortality rate from IUDs is twice as high in the third world as it is in developed countries (Hartmann, 1987, p. 206).

A more common complication of IUD use is pelvic infection (PID). Concern about such risks has led many women's health advocates to suggest that it should never be prescribed in the 'infertility belt' of central and southern Africa. It has also led individual women to request the removal of their IUD and many others to be afraid of trying one – even if there are no alternatives. One Bangladeshi woman gave voice to the dilemma of many others in describing the death of her sister-in-law, who had had an IUD inserted and suffered severe bleeding and infection. Although the device was removed, the bleeding did not stop and she died.

This is why women won't use it. Don't we understand that we are poor? Don't we understand that we have too many children and can't feed them? We understand. But what can we do? Whatever caused this woman's death we had no facilities for helping her (Abdullah and Zeidenstein, 1982, p. 195).

Benefits and Hazards of Hormonal Methods

The contraceptive techniques that affect women's bodies most profoundly are those involving the ingestion of hormones to prevent
ovulation. When 'the pill' was first introduced in the 1960s it was hailed
by many women in developed countries as the answer to their prayers,
separating sexuality entirely from procreation and giving them control
over their reproductive destinies. As early as 1965 it had become the
major method of contraception in the United States but its popularity
soon began to wane. On the one hand the sexual and social revolution
which it seemed to herald was quickly shown to be largely illusory as
far as women were concerned. At the same time there was a growing
realisation that the pill might have unexpected side effects that could be
seriously damaging to women's health.

Preliminary testing of the pill was carried out mainly on women in
Haiti and Puerto Rico (Petchesky, 1986). The major emphasis was on
its efficacy in preventing pregnancy and relatively little attention was
paid to its impact on the well-being of users. Indeed the long-term
effects over a woman's reproductive lifetime could not be known, given
the short period of testing involved. The relationship between
hormonal contraception and the incidence of different types of
cancer, for instance, has been especially difficult to assess, given the
long latency period before the cancers could be expected to develop
(Holck, 1987). However some health effects of the 'pill' began to
emerge very quickly.

By the late 1960s oral contraceptives were being implicated in the
causation of circulatory disease. These fears were confirmed by a study
of some 46 000 British women in the early 1970s, which showed that the
risk of dying from circulatory disease was five times greater among oral
contraceptive users than among non-users (UK Royal College of
General Practitioners, 1974). The risk was shown to be greatest
among women over 35, women who had taken the pill for at least
five years, and women who smoked. While new products have reduced
these hazards, the use of oral contraceptives still involves an increased
risk of myocardial infarction, venous blood clots and elevated blood
pressure (Khan, 1989, p. 256).

Hormonal contraceptives have also been shown to affect women in
ways that are not life-threatening but can nevertheless be detrimental
to their health. As in the case of the IUD, these are often written off by
researchers and doctors as mere side effects, but they can have a
significant impact on a woman's well-being. Extensively reported

effects of this kind include depression, loss of sexual desire, nausea and excessive weight gain. Lack of periods too can cause great anxiety to those women who welcome their bleeding as a normal cleansing process and a sign of health.

An interesting contrast in perspective can be seen in the views of Gregory Pincus, one of the pill's inventors, and those of a village woman using the drug in Bangladesh. Pincus had few concerns about the pill, and claimed that reported side effects were 'all in the mind'. Weight gain, for instance, he explained as 'loss of anxiety about accidental pregnancy with consequent weight improvement' (Petchesky, 1986, p. 174). The village woman on the other hand had tried the pill but menstruated two or three times a month and felt continually dizzy. She said: 'We are unable to get medicine. We have to spend money to alleviate discomfort. Can we afford to pay? I don't want to increase my diseases by taking the pill'. She subsequently became pregnant with her eighth child (Abdullah and Zeidenstein, 1982, p. 193).

Experiences of this kind have led to widespread fears among women about the potential hazards of the pill. While these fears may not always be congruent with current scientific evidence, they have made many women reluctant to put their psychological and physical health at risk, as Fatima Mernissi found in her study of Moroccan women:

> Deeply ingrained beliefs in Maadid held that the pill attacks the heart, causing palpitations, affecting blood pressure, weakening the entire body and causing dizzy spells. The majority of women, many actually on the pill, stated that it is really suited only to the rich who can afford a balanced diet (Mernissi, 1975, p. 422).

In recent years many countries have seen a decline in the use of the pill, either absolutely or as a proportion of contraceptive methods used. The most dramatic drops have been recorded in the United States, where pill use declined from 25 per cent of married women aged 15–44 in 1973 to only 14 per cent in 1982, and in Puerto Rico, where it declined from 20 per cent to 8 per cent between 1974 and 1982 (UN, 1989, p. 57).

Introducing Injectables

Despite these concerns about the pill, the past decade has seen the development of a number of new techniques designed to deliver hormonal contraception by a different route. One of the first of these was the long-lasting injectable Depo Provera (DP) or medroxy progesterone acetate, developed and manufactured by the US company Upjohn. It has been followed by a range of products, including long-acting progestin injections, plastic IUDs filled with progestin, vaginal rings and postcoital oral pills (Hardon and Achthoven, 1991). These new devices have maintained contraceptive efficacy while reducing some of the health risks through including progestin alone, rather than the combined oestrogen and progesterone used in most oral contraceptives. However many of the side effects remain and additional concerns have been raised by the form in which these contraceptive hormones are delivered.

The introduction of Depo Provera met with considerable opposition from women's groups concerned both with its safety and with the potential threat it posed to women's freedom of choice. Campaigns by American feminists contributed to a refusal by the US Food and Drug Administration in the 1970s and 1980s to license domestic use of DP, though in 1992 permission was finally granted. Meanwhile the drug has been used by about four million women in 90 countries, most of them in the third world (Duggan, 1986; Hardon, 1992, p. 12; Hartmann, 1987, pp. 186–96).

Many of those who were initially concerned about the drug would now accept that the potential health risks are probably no worse than those associated with other hormonal methods or with the IUD (Women's Health Matters, 1993). However menstrual disorders are reported by about two thirds of women in the first year of use (Hardon, 1992, p. 12). If the woman is pregnant when it is injected, the drug may harm the foetus and it may also get into breast milk. These unpleasant and potentially dangerous 'side effects' are reinforced by women's lack of control over its mode of delivery.

The introduction of Norplant has crystallised the concerns many women feel about the latest phase of contraceptive innovation (Mintzes, 1993). This device consists of six hormone-releasing rods implanted under a woman's skin, the effects lasting up to five years. Like DP it allows a woman to limit her fertility even if her partner is opposed to contraception. For many this invisibility is extremely important. Paradoxically, however, in order to achieve this control a woman must put herself totally in the hands of health workers since an implant cannot be removed without professional help.

Under these circumstances it is essential that all users have a clear understanding of the risks and benefits involved and can exercise their right to informed consent. They also need access to effective help should problems arise. However it is evident that in many parts of the world such conditions do not apply. Indeed in the United States the characteristics of Norplant have led some courts to order its use on low-income women as a condition of more lenient sentencing (Scott, 1993). This has contributed to serious doubts among many women's health advocates about whether these new methods can responsibly be promoted, especially when health services are inadequate (Garcia and Dacach, 1992; Mintzes, 1993). Similar concerns have been expressed about the safety and acceptability of the new generation of fertility regulating vaccines (WHO, 1993).

Contraceptive Providers: Care or Control?

For too many women, their visit to a family planning clinic is not an empowering experience that helps them to plan their lives more effectively. Instead they are demeaned and inconvenienced by a health worker of higher social status than themselves (usually a man) who may not even speak their own language. One of Fatima Mernissi's respondents in Rabat offered a telling account:

> The nurse asks you precise, brisk questions that you are supposed to answer like a book. If you take time to think, if you hesitate she will shout at you 'Can't you speak Arabic? In what language do you want me to address you?'. . . . When we are waiting to get into a gynaecological service they will shout at us, 'Take your pants off in the hall and sit there waiting'. There are draughts of cold air, people walking by, you feel inhuman (Mernissi, 1975, p. 424).

The inequality inherent in social relationships of this kind is reinforced by the 'provider dependence' of the new methods and also by the ideology of population control prevailing in many clinics. Health workers may be primarily concerned with getting a woman to 'accept' a method and to continue to use it – whatever her circumstances and her feelings. Indeed acceptance will sometimes mean financial rewards for the workers concerned. Few clinics offer a range of methods and women are encouraged to take 'high tech' options requiring little voluntary compliance. In Mexico, for instance, the largest national health system (Instituto Medico de Seguro Social) adopted a policy that 90 per cent of women leaving its hospitals after delivery should have an IUD inserted (Rogow, 1986, p. 77).

Thus major problems remain for the millions of women wishing to separate heterosexual intercourse from procreation while also protecting their own health and that of their families. Such problems are often dismissed on the grounds that all modern contraceptives are safer than uncontrolled childbearing. However the risks of a particular method need to be measured not against childbearing but against those of other contraceptives. Barrier methods are much safer than the pill for example. If she is given the choice a woman using contraceptives for child spacing may prefer to risk an unplanned pregnancy with the condom rather than risking her life on the pill (Hartmann, 1987, p. 174).

Even more importantly, while the health risks of childbearing are unavoidably borne by women, the risks of contraception can – in theory – be assumed by either partner. Thus unhealthy contraceptive use by women is not the only option. Greater condom use by men as well as the development of safer methods for both sexes could constitute a real 'contraceptive revolution'. In the meantime millions of women continue to seek abortions each year in an attempt to end unwanted pregnancies.

Abortion – A Global Epidemic

The universal significance of abortion can be summed up in the experience of one American woman:

> As I rode in the back seat of the car through Maryland countryside on my way to have an illegal abortion that day in May 1968, I came to a shocking realisation. For the first time in my life, I understood that I was a woman, not a human being but a woman (Cerullo, 1990, p. 89).

A safe termination can be both a metaphorical and a literal life saver. However abortions can also be fatal. At least 200 000 women die each year because they can see no option but to risk an unsafe termination of pregnancy and many thousands of others suffer serious damage to their physical and mental health. Thus the right to abortion may – for a woman – be the right to life. Millions more feel they have little option but to carry unwanted pregnancies to term, often with negative effects on their own well-being and sometimes that of their children. This 'invisible plague' is entirely preventable, arising as it does from a complex mixture of 'social intransigence, religious intolerance, economic self interest and political apathy' (Jacobson, 1990, p. 39).

Counting the Cost

It is difficult to obtain an accurate estimate of the number of abortions performed each year. Though most of the developed countries now have reasonably accurate statistics, information is sketchy elsewhere, especially in those countries where termination is illegal. We know relatively little about the women who undergo abortions, and we know even less about the effects on their health. Thus a 'moral smokescreen' continues to cover the massive human cost of restrictive abortion policies (Coeytaux, 1988; Jacobson, 1990, p. 7).

In an attempt to fill this information gap, the Alan Guttmacher Institute regularly publishes its own estimates of the global incidence of abortion. The most recent of these puts the number of abortions performed in 1987 at between 36 and 53 million. Between 26 and 34 million of these were legal and between 10 and 22 million illegal (Henshaw, 1990, p. 81). Not surprisingly, different countries have very different rates, reflecting a wide range of cultural, social and political factors.

In 1987 the countries of the former Soviet Union had the world's highest annual rate at an estimated 112 abortions per thousand women of reproductive age, compared with a low of five per thousand in Holland. Independent observers put the number of abortions in the USSR in 1987 as high as eleven million compared with less than six million live births (Henshaw, 1990, p. 78; Remennick, 1991). The numbers are also considerable in Latin America, the Caribbean and South Asia, with more than ten million Chinese women undergoing terminations each year. African and Middle Eastern rates appear to be lower, reflecting in part a continuing desire for large families, though demographic data suggest that the numbers may be seriously underestimated (Coeytaux, 1988). In most of the developed countries the abortion rate is now between five and twenty per thousand women of reproductive age, though the United States remains slightly higher at twenty-eight per thousand (Henshaw, 1990, p. 78).

These figures suggest that there is one abortion for every two to three births worldwide and that abortion ranks fourth after female sterilisation, IUDs and oral contraception as a method of family planning. Though a growing number of terminations are performed on young women, it is clear that the majority of recipients are in stable relationships and already have children. Thus abortion is not a deviant act perpetrated by a tiny promiscuous minority as its opponents often claim.

Between a third and a half of all women of reproductive age decide to have at least one abortion but many are forced as a result into criminality and may have to risk their health and even their lives. The experience of a Colombian woman can be used to illustrate the fate of so many who die as a result of clandestine abortions:

Esperanza, 30 years old, had already borne five children, including one who had died at the age of ten months. Neither she nor her husband was happy when she became pregnant again . . . Esperanza had recently found work as a housemaid in the city and her wages were much needed by the family. She made the decision alone to visit an abortionist in town. She was frightened and unsure about what was actually done to her.

After three days of bleeding Esperanza developed severe abdominal pain and began to vomit. Her husband took her to a hospital where she was diagnosed as suffering from incomplete septic abortion. She was treated and sent home after forty-eight hours. The pain returned but Esperanza did nothing about it at first, fearing she would lose her job if she took any more time off. Then she developed a high fever and started vomiting. She was admitted to the intensive care unit of the hospital. Abdominal surgery was performed for peritonitis, but her condition deteriorated, her heartbeat became irregular, and she died five days later (Starrs, 1987).

Abortion: Public or Private Choice?

In most countries it was not until the nineteenth century that abortion was made illegal. Indeed the distinction between contraception and abortion was often unclear, with termination being widely accepted if it was done before 'quickening'. However, from the early 1800s onwards religious and medical pressures combined to ensure that abortion was increasingly regulated. The first penalties for abortion were enacted in the United Kingdom in 1803 while in France the Napoleonic Code of 1810 stipulated 5–10 year prison terms both for women having abortions and for those procuring them. By 1868 almost all US states had passed laws restricting abortion, as had most European countries. This regulatory fervour then spread to much of the rest of the world through the export of metropolitan legal systems as part of the process of colonialism (Cook, 1989).

Despite sporadic attempts at reform, it was not until after the Second World War that these restrictive laws began to be liberalised. In response to a variety of social, economic and political forces, abortion was made easier in most parts of Eastern Europe in the 1950s, in Western Europe, Canada, Australia and New Zealand in the 1960s and 1970s, and in many parts of the third world in the late 1970s and 1980s (Cook, 1989). Some 40 per cent of the world's women now live in countries where abortion is available on request, half of them in China and the former Soviet Union; 23 per cent live in countries where it is allowed on 'social grounds' (which may in practice mean on request), and 12 per cent live in countries where it is allowed on medical grounds. This leaves 25 per cent in countries where abortion is allowed only if the woman's life is in immediate danger. Most are in Africa, Muslim parts of Asia, and in Latin America, but several million also live in Ireland, the only developed country where abortion remains illegal (Barry, 1988).

The legal status of abortion is the single most important factor determining its impact on women's health. In the United States its legalisation led to a decline in mortality from thirty to five per thousand terminations between 1970 and 1976. In contrast mortality in Romania rose from 21 to 128 per 100 000 live births between 1965, when abortion was made illegal, and 1984 (Henshaw, 1990, p. 82). Thus the criminalisation of abortions does not stop them from happening. It simply ensures that more women will damage their health in attempts to end unsupportable and often unsupported pregnancies.

However the legal status of abortion is by no means the only factor influencing health outcomes. Interpretation of the law, levels of public funding and modes of professional practice can all exert a powerful influence. Despite state pressure on Russian women to use abortion as a family planning method, too few resources have been allocated to provide the necessary services. Abortion has frequently been a degrading as well as a dangerous experience, and many women still choose a private procedure despite the very high cost (Henshaw, 1990; Remennick, 1991, pp. 846–7). In the United States, too, many women face financial problems in obtaining a termination. Federal funding for abortions is prohibited, affecting young, poor, black and minority ethnic women in particular (Gerber Fried, 1990a; Jacobson, 1990). Thus legal, economic and social factors combine to ensure that many millions of women are unable to obtain easy access to a safe abortion. What implications does this have for their health?

Risks of Termination

Legal abortions are regarded by many women as the method of last resort for birth control. The experience may well be distressing and is rarely taken lightly, as the African American Judy Simmons has eloquently described:

> Abortion is a great equaliser of women. Whatever their age, class or race women tend to walk the same way after ending a pregnancy. They sort of hunch their shoulders, fold their arms rather protectively across their upper bodies and take small steps (Simmons, 1990, p. 120).

However these feelings are often accompanied by enormous relief, and the procedure itself is usually trouble-free. When performed by qualified health workers, termination of pregnancy is an extremely safe surgical procedure. Evidence from the United States suggests that it is eleven times safer than a tonsillectomy and a great deal safer than pregnancy and childbearing, though it will of course be more dangerous in countries where surgical facilities are inferior. Only 0.7 per cent of legal abortions performed in the United States lead to complications, and there is little evidence of long-term emotional or physical health risks (Adler *et al.*, 1990; Henshaw, 1990, pp. 83–4).

Clandestine abortion, on the other hand, can be extremely dangerous. Half a million maternal deaths occur each year and between 115 000 and 204 000 of these are due to illegal abortions performed by unqualified practitioners. About 50 per cent occur in South and South-East Asia with the highest reported mortality rate being 2400 deaths per 100 000 abortions in Bangladesh (Henshaw, 1990, p. 81). In Latin America and southern Africa, too, complications of illegal abortion are now among the main causes of death in women aged 15–39. Thus hundreds of thousands of women die each year – often in appalling circumstances – not because there is no technical means of saving them, but because they are denied access to those means. They are forced instead to choose between compulsory motherhood and a painful surgical procedure performed under hazardous conditions. 'What consigns so many women around the world to death or physical impairment is not a deficiency in technology but a deficiency in the value placed on women's lives' (Jacobson, 1990, p. 39).

Worldwide, the most frequent complication of any termination is incomplete abortion or retained products of conception, requiring evacuation of the uterus. However illegal abortions and those performed under clandestine conditions can also cause excessive blood loss, shock, pelvic infection and subsequent infertility (Mtimavalye and Belsey, 1987). There is frequently trauma to the reproductive organs, particularly cervical lacerations, uterine perforations and damage to the bladder and intestines, and in Sub-Saharan Africa and India tetanus too is a common and often fatal complication.

The method used for inducing abortion influences the nature and severity of any complications. Damage to the uterus and other internal organs is particularly common in India where abortions are often induced with twigs or sticks, sometimes dipped in substances such as arsenic or phosphorous (Population Information Programme, 1980, p. 136). The resulting tears usually require immediate surgery and sometimes hysterectomy. Internal bleeding and organ damage can also be caused by abdominal massage as practised in parts of South-East Asia, Africa and the Middle East, while potassium permanganate tablets and other chemical substances inserted into the cervix can cause burns, bleeding and even the formation of bladder or rectal fistulas. Eating and drinking certain herbs or drugs such as quinine can cause serious toxic reactions, including liver and renal failure or damage to the central nervous system (Ladipo, 1989, pp. 25–6).

Not surprisingly, public accounts of women's experiences of clandestine abortions are rare, but examples from around the world illustrate the universality of the experience. In an attempt to get the law changed the Muvman Liberasyon Fam of Mauritius have spoken out about methods employed in their own country:

The medium priced abortion in Mauritius is not used as much as it would otherwise be, because it is painful. The abortionist inserts a flexible rubber catheter into the woman's uterus and leaves it in place. Its end sticks out palpably. The woman then goes home, goes about her usual activities and then 24 hours later tugs on the catheter, quite violently, and this provokes a spontaneous abortion. She gets painful cramps and starts bleeding. She then returns the catheter to the abortionist, who returns her 'catheter deposit money'. If she gets any complications, as she may well do, having used a very secondhand catheter, she is advised to go quickly to the hospital (Muvman Liberasyon Fam of Mauritius, 1989).

Pregnant women often have to bear not just the emotional but also the financial costs of abortion, as the experiences of Margarita, a Bolivian woman, testify:

I got pregnant again at the beginning of this year. My husband came by and I thought maybe there was a chance of getting back together again. Well we didn't get back together but I did get pregnant. . . .

So I decided to get an abortion. I just can't afford any more children. It was hard because I am a Catholic and I think it is wrong. But I just couldn't see any other way. I went to a private doctor who I heard will get rid of pregnancy for you, but the office was so crowded I had to come back another day. It cost 80 bolivianos ($40) which I borrowed from my aunt who runs a little store and has some money saved. The doctor treated me politely. But when I came home I felt bad like I had done something wrong, against God. And after about three days I was in terrible pain and started to bleed a lot.

My aunt took me to hospital in a taxi. They cleaned up whatever was still there, but before they did, the doctors told me I was evil for having an abortion, and I felt even worse. I was there for three days and they charged me 50 bolivianos ($25) which I also had to borrow from my aunt. I have no idea how I will ever pay her back (McDonnell, 1987).

Finally, as the story of a Bangladeshi woman shows, the results of clandestine abortion can affect the entire family:

Zarina, who is thirty three, has had eight children. Six have survived – one died at birth and the other died of measles. Desperate to avoid another birth, Zarina recently turned to the local, traditional midwife for an abortion. She haemorrhaged and nearly died; now she is unable to perform the hard labour required for her own and her family's sustenance (Germain and Ordway, 1989).

Wider Costs of the Abortion Epidemic

The cost of abortion complications falls on the wider community through the drain it imposes on health care budgets. Estimates suggest that at least 30 per cent of the beds in gynaecological and obstetric wards in most urban hospitals in Latin America are filled with women suffering abortion complications, caused by illegal procedures. At University College Hospital, Ibadan, over 80 per cent of women with septic abortions have undergone induced terminations outside a medical setting (Ladipo, 1989, p. 24). Women admitted under such circumstances usually require complex and expensive treatment and abortion complications are said to consume at least half of the available blood in many hospitals in Africa and Latin America (ibid., p. 25). In Brazil, estimates suggest that neary half the obstetric budget is spent on treating women who have had unsafe terminations (Jacobson, 1990, pp. 42–3).

The financial and health costs of limiting women's access to safe abortion are now clear and unambiguous. Though considerable progress has been made in the liberalisation of abortion legislation, there is evidence that in some countries this progress may now be reversed. Across the world, anti-abortion campaigners are attempting to reinstate restrictive laws (Gerber Fried, 1990a). As a result many American women have had new obstacles placed in their path as they seek safe and affordable terminations. Funding has increasingly been withdrawn, and many have had to face serious violence as abortion facilities are picketed, vandalised and fire-bombed (ibid.)

Even more seriously, these restrictive policies have not been confined to home territory. The internationalisation of the 'right to life' movement means that organisations such as Operation Rescue have been active in many parts of the world in an attempt to limit the number of women obtaining abortions in their own countries. The growing power of this movement was evident in the 1984 Mexico City Policy, which cut off US funds to international organisations providing or promoting abortion services (Cook, 1989). As a result many of the world's poorest women were thrown back onto the services of unqualified practitioners.

Politics of Innovation

The political significance of the abortion issue has recently been highlighted by the development of an important new drug, RU 486 (Clarke and Montini, 1993). This is a hormonal method of inducing termination – or preventing the implantation of a fertilised egg – without the need for surgery. Not surprisingly, feminist health activists have been extremely wary of yet another hormonal preparation for controlling reproduction and the realities of drug distribution in many third world countries have again caused particular concern (Hardon, 1992, p. 14; Kabir and Germain, 1992; Raymond *et al.*, 1991). However most agree that potentially at least, RU 486 offers a valuable means of extending some women's access to abortion if appropriate back-up services are available. Anti-abortion activists on the other hand have fought extremely hard to prevent its introduction, both through political pressure in France (where it was developed) and the United States, and through a consumer boycott of the manufacturers Roussel and Hoechst. As a result very few women currently have the choice to interrupt a pregnancy in this way.

Conclusion

In this chapter we have explored the complex influences on women's capacity to control their fertility. We have seen that very often they have to make difficult choices in circumstances not of their own choosing. Many face particular dilemmas in attempting to reconcile their own health with that of their children – both born and unborn. We take this analysis a stage further in the next chapter by looking at contemporary experiences of pregnancy and childbirth.

Further Reading

Hartman, B. (1987) *Reproductive Rights and Wrongs: the global politics of population control and contraceptive choice* (New York: Harper and Row). An exploration of the relationship between population control and reproductive choice in the third world. This book puts population problems and population policies into a wider social and economic framework in order to assess how health and family planning programmes could better meet the needs of the poor.

Jacobson, J. (1990) *The Global Politics of Abortion* (Worldwatch Paper 97) and Jacobson, J. (1991) *Women's Reproductive Health: the silent emergency* (Worldwatch Paper 102). Taken together these pamphlets provide an excellent introduction to current trends and debates in the area of reproductive health.

Mintzes, B. (ed.) (1992) *A Question of Control: women's perspectives on the development and use of contraceptive technologies* (Amsterdam: Women and Pharmaceuticals Project, Health Action International and WEMOS). Available from Women's Health Action Foundation, PO Box 4263, 1009 Amsterdam, The Netherlands. A collection of papers from a conference of reproductive rights activists held in the Netherlands in 1991. A number of contributors discuss the new hormonal contraceptives and there are case studies from Asia, Africa and Latin America.

Petchesky, R. (1986) *Abortion and Women's Choice: the state, sexuality and reproductive freedom* (Verso). A historical and theoretical introduction to the debate about reproductive rights. This detailed analysis of contraception and abortion politics concentrates on experiences in developed countries and offers invaluable insights into the relationship between reproduction and wider feminist issues.

The best sources of women-centred and up-to-date information in this rapidly changing area are *Reproductive Health Matters* published twice yearly and available from 1 London Bridge Street, London SE1 9SG, England, and *Newsletter of the Women's Global Network on Reproductive Rights*, published quarterly and available from NZ Voorburgwal 32, 1012 RZ Amsterdam, Netherlands.

5

A Labour of Love

Introduction

In developed countries the maternal mortality rate has fallen dramatically over the past century. In most it now stands at about ten deaths per 100 000 live births. Thus for some women at least, childbirth is now easier and safer than it has ever been in human history. However for others it remains extremely dangerous. More than half a million still die from pregnancy-related causes each year, almost all of them in the third world, where 86 per cent of all births take place. A woman living in one of the developed countries has a lifetime risk of between one in 4000 and one in 10 000 of dying as a result of pregnancy, while the risk in some third world countries can be as high as one in 15. Indeed there are more maternal deaths in India in one day than in all the developed countries in a month (Royston and Armstrong, 1989, pp. 30–1). Significantly, the maternal mortality rate has risen in the past few years in many post-communist states. Maternal mortality in the newly independent states of the former Soviet Union is now twice as high as in Central and Eastern Europe and four times higher than in Western Europe (World Health Organisation, 1994).

The huge reduction in maternal mortality observed in developed countries was not simply the result of better access to obstetric care. Women's enhanced capacity for safe motherhood was achieved primarily through better nutrition, improvements in housing and working conditions, and the wider availability of more effective birth control. The opening up of access to basic maternity care also played an important part in ensuring safer births. However there is considerable controversy about the value of more recent developments in obstetric technology (Oakley, 1987, pp. 55–6; Rooney, 1992). We will examine these questions in more depth by looking first at the consequences of too little care during pregnancy and birth, and then at the risks engendered by what may sometimes be a surfeit of the wrong kind of treatment.

Dying for a Baby

Childbirth is a universally celebrated event and an occasion for dancing, fireworks, flowers or gifts. Yet for many thousands of women each day, childbirth is experienced not as the joyful event it should be but as a private hell that may end in death (Royston and Armstrong, 1989, p. 9).

The official figure of half a million women dying from pregnancy-related causes each year is certainly an underestimate. Even in developed countries, where registration systems are sophisticated and maternal deaths rare, studies have shown that some are missed (Cates *et al.*, 1982; Graham and Airey, 1987). In most third world countries figures are rudimentary, with the majority of deaths occurring in rural areas away from medical surveillance. In Egypt for instance the true level of maternal deaths is said to be at least twice the official figure (WHO, 1986b).

These problems are further compounded by the official definition of maternal mortality:

the death of a woman while pregnant or within 42 days of pregnancy irrespective of the duration and site of the pregnancy, from any cause related to or aggravated by the pregnancy or its management but not from accidental or incidental causes (International Classification of Diseases, 9th revision).

There is considerable evidence that maternity-related deaths may occur more than 42 days after birth, especially when medical services are available to temporarily prolong life (Fauveau *et al.*, 1988, p. 647). It is also clear that some apparently accidental deaths may have a social if not a biological relationship to the victim's pregnancy.

Evidence from a number of countries suggests that pregnant women are more likely than others to be battered, and that battering may end in death. A study in the United States found that only about 14 per cent of deaths of pregnant women from homicide and suicide were detected for inclusion in maternal mortality data, yet the pregnancy itself was often a major factor in instigating the act (Rochat *et al.*, 1988, p. 96). More than a third of the physically abused women at one Ontario refuge had been battered during pregnancy (Sinclair, 1985, pp. 23, 164), while a study of maternal deaths in rural Bangladesh found that 9 per cent were due to accidents or violence (Fauveau *et al.*, 1988, p. 646).

Despite these limitations, extremely high mortality rates continue to be recorded in many parts of the world. Ghana, Bhutan and Burkina Faso top the league table with rates of 1000, 1700 and 1810 deaths per 100 000 live births respectively (UN, 1991, p. 58). A woman from one of the poorer countries of Africa or Asia is at least a hundred times more likely to die in a single pregnancy than a woman giving birth in one of the developed countries. High fertility rates mean that she also faces that risk many more times during her reproductive life.

> If women the world over had the same chance of survival when they become pregnant as do women in the developed world, 460,000 fewer women would die, 1.5 million children would not lose their mothers and millions more women would be spared lifelong handicaps (Royston and Armstrong, 1989, pp. 41–2).

Though the majority of maternal deaths happen to women in the third world, poor women in rich countries may also be damaged by childbearing. A recent study in Massachusetts reported a maternal mortality rate of 35 per 100 000 for black women compared with only 9.6 per 100 000 for their white compatriots (Sachs *et al.*, 1982). Even in the United Kingdom the existence of the National Health Service has not eliminated class inequalities in maternal mortality. Women married to unskilled workers are twice as likely to die of causes related to childbirth as the wives of professional men (Whitehead, 1988, p. 62).

The Social Roots of Maternal Mortality

> Maternal mortality should not be viewed as a chance event so much as a chronic disease developing over a long period, for the outcome of a pregnancy is profoundly influenced by the circumstances of a woman's life (Royston and Armstrong, 1989, p. 45).

A deadly combination of poverty and sexual discrimination leaves many women unfit for the physical demands of childbearing. As we have seen, inadequate access to nutrition and health care in childhood, illiteracy and heavy burdens of domestic work all have damaging effects on women's general health, and therefore on their potential for healthy childbearing. In many societies these lifelong disadvantages are compounded by cultural and economic pressures towards early marriage and pregnancy.

Women who bear children while still young themselves run a great risk of damaging their own health (WHO, 1989). One survey of childbearing in Bangladesh found that pregnant girls aged 15–19 were twice as likely to die as women aged 20–24, while those aged 10–14 had five times the risk (Chen *et al.*, 1974, p. 337). Adolescent pregnancies show a higher rate of direct obstetric complications, including obstructed labour and toxaemia, especially when the mother is under 16. When the pregnancy is unwanted, illicit abortion is also common.

Despite these risks teenage marriage and early childbearing continue to be expected of many young women, especially in parts of Africa and Asia. Nearly all Bangladeshi women are already married by the age of 18, half have children by the age of 17, and a third have at least two by the time they are 19 (Royston and Armstrong, 1989, p. 38). In South Asia as a whole, 54 per cent of girls aged 15–19 are married. In the United States too, as in some other developed countries, an increasing number of teenage girls are becoming pregnant.

The reasons for the high rate of teenage pregnancies are complex. In many Asian countries early marriage has a long history. It has considerable economic importance as well as reflecting a desire to prevent young women becoming pregnant outside the bounds of marriage. In other countries a complex of social and cultural factors encourage unmarried adolescent girls to become sexually active at an early age. For some this leads directly to pregnancy. Paradoxically motherhood may hold out similar hope for social status and recognition to young women in very different circumstances. But what little they gain will often be at the cost of their health. In many parts of the world early sexual activity launches women on a lifetime of childbearing, which continues until they are no longer able to conceive.

As many commentators have pointed out, the social context of childbirth in third world countries is often – but by no means always – a supportive one (Jordan, 1983; Kitzinger, 1989). The presence of loved ones, the care of a midwife and the reassurance of familiar surroundings can be of great value at what may be a time of anxiety and pain. Indeed, as we shall see in later sections, it is precisely this intimacy and solidarity that many women in developed countries feel they have lost as a result of the institutionalisation of childbirth. However moral support is not enough when things go wrong, and some traditional practices can be dangerous. Thus all women need access to safe and effective medical care.

The Perils of Pregnancy

As we saw in the previous chapter, between one third and a half of all maternal deaths come early in pregnancy as a result of clandestine abortions. Most others occur during or immediately after labour. Some of these are the result of diseases from which the mother already suffers. Hepatitis for instance is still a major cause of maternal death in Ethiopia, India, Nigeria, Somalia and Sudan. However most result directly from complications of the birth process, often compounded by anaemia.

An astonishing 50 per cent of all women of reproductive age in third world countries outside China are thought to be anaemic (DeMaeyer and Adiels-Tegman, 1985, p. 303). This makes them exhausted, listless and highly susceptible to infection. At least 60 per cent of pregnant women in the third world are anaemic (compared with only 14 per cent in developed countries) and this considerably increases their risk of dying in childbirth (UN, 1991, p. 58). Maternal anaemia usually results from an inadequate diet, which may begin in childhood and continue into adult life.

Hypertensive disease, obstructed labour, haemorrhage and infection are the major causes of maternal death and impose a heavy burden of chronic disease on many who survive the immediate crisis. They are frequently the result of a woman's adverse social and economic circumstances, and their severity will be strongly influenced by her access to effective medical care. Though we will examine each in turn, they are of course often found in combination, especially in women already debilitated by hard work and frequent childbearing.

The hypertensive disease pre-eclampsia causes high blood pressure, protein in the urine and swelling of tissues. For some women the condition may remain mild, but for others it can deteriorate rapidly, causing headaches, vomiting, pain and impaired vision. If no treatment is given, convulsions begin, followed by coma and death within a very short time. The average survival time from onset of eclampsia to death is about two days (Royston and Armstrong, 1989, p. 77).

Negisti was 18, unmarried and a 12th grade student. She lived with her parents about 20km outside the city. Negisti had become pregnant unintentionally and, afraid of her parents, had left home to hide her pregnancy. She came back at the end of nine months and confided in her mother, who hid the fact from Negisti's father. Negisti had had no antenatal care. She had headaches and frequently vomited.

At 5am one morning, Negisti complained of lower abdominal pain. Her contractions increased in regularity and intensity. At 1pm Negisti started convulsions. At this point her mother hid her in a little outhouse in the field. However, Negisti's convulsions worsened and late that afternoon her frightened mother told her husband everything. They arranged for transport and arrived at the city hospital at 9pm.

On admission, Negisti was unconscious. Her breathing was loud and her tongue was bleeding from small wounds due to the seizures. Negisti was sedated and her full bladder was catheterised. Internal examination revealed that she was ready to deliver, but the baby was dead. Vacuum extraction was used. It now became clear that this was a twin pregnancy and the second child, also dead, was delivered.

Negisti went into an irreversible coma, probably due to a cerebral haemorrhage caused by the severe convulsions and died at 3am the next morning (Kwast, 1987).

Obstructed labour is most common among young mothers, and usually occurs when the mother's pelvis is too small to allow the baby's skull to pass through. At the onset of menstruation a young woman's pelvic bones can be expected to grow a further 12–18 per cent yet many are already embarking on their first pregnancy (Howard, 1987, p. 4). Women who are short in stature (often as a result of nutritional deficiency in childhood) are also at high risk. If specialist care is not available, obstructed labour may result in the death of the mother through exhaustion and infection.

Those who survive obstructed labour may well face chronic health problems. One of the most devastating is the creation of a passage between the bladder and the vagina (vesico-vaginal fistula or VVF), or between the rectum and the vagina (recto-vaginal fistula or RVF), (Cottingham and Royston, 1991). Fistulae cause urine and/or faeces to leak constantly from the vagina. They are commonest in Africa and frequently afflict women who start childbearing early. One study in Northern Nigeria found that 45 per cent of new fistula patients were aged between 14–16. Most were also poor and illiterate (Murphy, 1981).

The social consequences of fistulae are usually devastating. Women may be stigmatised or may isolate themselves because of shame at the condition in general and the smell in particular. According to a Professor of Obstetrics in Pakistan,

Obstetric fistulae are a serious social problem in the Indian subcontinent. To live with it, or even to think of it is dreadful and awesome. Women who suffer from this disease are confined to their homes and are rendered unsocial. They are highly prone to psychosocial ailments (Shah, 1989, p. 5).

In Northern Nigeria only 11 per cent of long-term fistula patients were found to be living with their husbands and three quarters had been living apart for two years or more. Many were expected to live alone, were not allowed to pray and had lost the support of their families (Murphy, 1981, p. 145). Most women with fistulae remain childless following the death of their first child. The few who go on to become pregnant again only do so at great risk to their health.

Lete was married at thirteen years of age. Her first child was born dead in hospital following a labour which lasted for four days. Lete survived the ordeal, but the obstructed labour resulted in a fistula between bladder and vagina, so she had reconstructive surgery in a specialist hospital.

Lete became pregnant three years after fistula surgery and wanted the child very much. However her home was too far from a health centre and she had no antenatal care. When she was seven months pregnant, she started to bleed suddenly from the genital tract after fetching water from the river. Labour started on that day and the membranes also ruptured. She was admitted to hospital at 8pm after she had been in labour at home for three days.

She was in distress and had a high temperature and rapid pulse. Although the baby was small, birth could not progress because the vagina was severely scarred from the early surgery. The baby was dead. . . . By the third day after delivery Lete was very ill. . . . The fistula repair had broken down and she was again incontinent. . . .

Lete had a hysterectomy because of extensive septic necrosis of the ruptured uterus. Her outlook was poor . . . Lete talked little. She tried to eat but she was tired by vomiting. . . . She was very frightened of dying. She vomited blood intermittently until her death 27 days after the birth of her premature infant (Kwast, 1987).

Women who already have several children run the highest risk of dying from haemorrhage or internal bleeding. Most will live for only two to twelve hours if treatment is not available, yet many are miles from appropriate help. Infection too requires rapid treatment. During labour and immediately afterwards, mothers are especially susceptible to infection in the genital area. Reduced resistance can be caused by anaemia, shock and exhaustion or haemorrhage, while external bacteria may be introduced by those trying to help the woman to give birth. Leaves, mud, cow-dung, milk fat and oil, mustard and coconut oil are all commonly used to try to ease an obstructed labour (Howard, 1987, pp. 13–14). Treatment with antibiotics can help with straightforward cases but careful monitoring is needed to prevent the onset of septicaemia, which can cause death within a few days.

Crying Out for Care

Despite these severe hazards, effective maternity care is still only a dream for millions of women. A WHO study in the early 1980s found that in many countries less than 40 per cent of women had seen a qualified health worker during their pregnancy. This was true in countries as far apart as Madagascar, Honduras, Zimbabwe, Ecuador and Iran (Royston and Armstrong, 1989, p. 164). In developed countries too some groups of women may be disadvantaged in their access to services. Between 25 per cent and 30 per cent of women in the inner cities of the United States receive little or no pre-natal care (Gerber Fried, 1990, p. 158).

Even during birth itself, women are often without appropriate support. About 12 per cent of births in Latin America and the Caribbean, over half in South-East Asia, about two thirds in Africa and three quarters in Southern Asia still take place in the absence of a trained midwife or doctor (UN, 1991). While this will not pose a problem for women whose deliveries are uncomplicated, it can be a sentence of death for others.

The experience of a woman doctor in the Philippines provides a poignant reminder that lack of care is common even in major cities, where most facilities are concentrated:

On the way to work everyone sidestepped the woman and the child asleep at her breast. They were lying on pieces of cardboard. The child was completely naked, the mother was naked from the waist up. Across the street was the country's biggest tertiary care hospital (Estrada-Claudio, 1988).

However the majority of those without care live in rural areas. Many cannot reach their nearest medical centre because they have no access to transport, while others are denied help because of the inability or unwillingness of their husbands or families to pay the costs (Thaddeus and Maine, 1991).

If a woman does reach hospital the care is often inadequate, with few qualified staff and insufficient blood and other supplies. Clinical mismanagement is common. A study in a Zambian hospital in 1983 found that between 50 per cent and 85 per cent of maternal deaths were due to avoidable hospital factors (ibid.) Many women have also reported harsh and unfeeling treatment when they are at their most vulnerable. This is illustrated by the experience of Rabjallah, a woman living in North India:

> Inside the labour room the auxiliary nurse-midwife (ANM) began chiding Rajballah's in-laws for not heeding her advice. 'If you had stopped her eating so much rice and brought her for treatment, this would never have happened'. Then as Rajballah began moaning she turned to her sharply, and said 'Be quiet. Keep your mouth closed. . . . They'll hit you here if you make a noise'. 'Yes' agreed a nurse, 'Is she a goat or a buffalo that she cannot suffer even light pains?' (Jeffery *et al.*, 1989, p. 116).

We are left then with a disturbing picture of the paradox facing women in many parts of the world. Motherhood is not only a woman's duty but also the only path to social status and personal achievement. Yet it is a hazardous route to take. Though most survive childbearing, hundreds of thousands each year do not, and millions more can only experience their maternity as physical and psychological distress.

The New Obstetrics: Science or Social Control?

For pregnant women living in the rich countries, risks of this kind are now a thing of the past. Very few die in childbirth or suffer long-term problems as a result of pregnancy. The importance of these developments for women's health and well-being cannot be overestimated. However they do not mean that all maternity services are now as effective as they might be. Nor are all mothers satisfied with the care they receive. Indeed many have argued that recent developments in 'high-tech' obstetrics may be meeting doctors' needs more effectively than they meet those of their patients.

New Technologies for Old Skills

Over the past hundred years or so the place of birth, the participants and the techniques employed have all changed in ways that have profoundly affected women (Arney, 1985; Garcia *et al.*, 1990; Oakley, 1984). In most of the developed countries births have now been removed from the home. Ninety-eight per cent of British women currently deliver their babies in hospital, despite the lack of compelling evidence that this is safer than a home birth (Campbell and Macfarlane, 1990). The only exception to this pattern is the Netherlands, where about a third of deliveries still take place at home. As births have been institutionalised, the hospitals themselves have also grown larger, sometimes creating an inflexible and depersonalised environment for women in labour.

Most women now give birth in the presence of people whom they do not know. One study found that women in labour in a Canadian hospital faced an average of 6.4 unfamiliar professionals (Keirse *et al.*, 1989, p. 807). Another noted that a low-risk mother in a British teaching hospital saw sixteen people in six hours, yet was often alone at crucial moments (Chard and Richards, 1977).

Assessing women's response to such situations is difficult, since they will have very different experiences and expectations. Many feel relieved to have their babies safely delivered, are grateful for whatever care they have received and are reluctant to complain. However others report feeling uncared for, and research in a number of countries has shown that they often lack both the emotional support and the factual information they would like (Kitzinger, 1978; Oakley, 1979; Reid and Garcia, 1989). In one British study the average time women spent with a doctor on ante-natal visits was 3.9 minutes (Oakley, 1984, p. 229). Similar experiences have been reported by women in Australia:

The medical care which I received at the clinic was adequate. However waiting times of up to three hours, a different doctor each time and being invariably told 'not to worry' in reply to many of my questions, and a three-minute consultation did little to make me feel I was being 'cared for' in any way (Health Department, Victoria, 1990, p. 28).

There is a wealth of evidence to show the importance of social and psychological support in enhancing the well-being of mothers and babies, yet these are often given very low priority (Elbourne *et al.*, 1989).

Childbirth is increasingly defined as 'doctors' business' and as a result most pregnancies are treated as pathological unless proved otherwise. Most women begin their labour in a healthy condition and want medical care on hand in case it might be needed. Most doctors, on the other hand, have been trained to see labouring mothers as 'at risk' patients, whose 'normality' can only be proved after the event. This leads many to intervene in straightforward labours when it may be unnecessary and possibly even damaging. While some women will be prepared to accept whatever treatment is offered, others will be reluctant and it is this unwillingness to accede to medical control that lies at the heart of many women's dissatisfaction with their experience of contemporary childbirth. Again, an Australian mother expressed the feeling reported by many others:

> The doctor seemed to be working to an unspoken timetable. If I hadn't delivered in a certain time, he was going in there to bring the baby out, whether it was necessary or not. I thought, 'what the heck, I may as well give up, let him do the lot' (Health Department, Victoria, 1990, p. 35).

Mothers in many countries have voiced their disquiet about the inflexibility of hospital routines as well as the demeaning nature of much medicalised childbirth. The rituals of shaving of pubic hair for instance, or giving an enema at the onset of labour, can cause considerable discomfort, yet there is no evidence that they are effective in achieving a more successful outcome. Indeed enemas can actually be hazardous as documented cases of rectal irritation, colitis, gangrene and anaphylactic shock have demonstrated (Garforth and Garcia, 1989, pp. 823–4).

Similarly, there are no data to show that routine episiotomies do anything to improve either delivery or post-partum recovery (Chalmers *et al.*, 1989). Sheila Kitzinger has described such procedures as 'genital mutilation' and they are certainly the commonest cause of perineal damage (Kitzinger, 1989, p. 107). An episiotomy can be painful, leaves a wound that requires suturing and forms a scar. It remains the most frequently performed surgical operation in the United States and in several European countries, yet many women do not even realise it is being done to them and certainly do not give their active consent (Banta and Thacker, 1982; World Health Organisation, 1986a).

These concerns about modern obstetrics have intensified with the growth of what has been called 'active management of labour'. During the 1960s and 1970s the science of pregnancy developed dramatically (Schwartz, 1990). Obstetricians were no longer reliant on rudimentary empirical techniques and a 'wait and see' approach. Instead they were able to utilise a whole array of new technologies that facilitated the electronic surveillance of women in labour and encouraged early intervention at any sign of apparent abnormality. For obstetricians these developments have meant an enhancement of their professional status and a bolstering of their scientific respectability. They have also been able to lay claim to a new patient – the foetus – who had hitherto been hidden from view and largely untouchable. However the implications for women and their babies remain a matter for debate.

The new reproductive technologies have attracted a great deal of attention and a large amount of resources. However we still know very little about their effectiveness since few clinical trials preceded their introduction (Chalmers, 1989). Their impact on women's psychological experiences of childbearing and on the emotional relationship between mother and baby have received even less attention. As a result many of those on whom they are used have been made into unwitting 'pioneers' on the road to medicalised birth (Rapp, 1987). As the routine use of these new technologies increases, there is growing concern that women are not consenting to them in any active way – or sometimes in any way at all (Faden, 1991; Whitbeck, 1991).

Managing Labour

The new interventionism in obstetrics began with the development of a range of technologies for monitoring the foetus in utero. These include biochemical tests such as amniocentesis to identify genetic abnormalities, ultrasound imaging to give a visual impression, and electronic monitoring to assess various aspects of physiological functioning. In most countries the growing use of these surveillance techniques has been accompanied by an increased rate of other interventions in labour – more induced births and caesarean sections in particular. They have also led to a growing desire on the part of many doctors to 'manage' the unborn baby, sometimes at the expense of the mother. Thus it is doctors who are increasingly active in labour while women take it lying down, too often becoming the passive recipients of medical ministrations.

Significantly, doctors often initiate labour itself through inducing contractions by artificial means. Most commonly a hormonal drip is used either to start the uterus contracting or to speed it up if the process is judged to be too slow. While there are clearly circumstances in which such techniques can be valuable, their use cannot always be justified in terms of immediate clinical need. In the United Kingdom inductions rose rapidly in the late 1960s and early 1970s, reaching a high of 40 per cent of all births. Numbers levelled off in the mid 1970s, but by 1978 about a third of all labours were still being started by artificial means (Macfarlane and Mugford, 1984, p. 162). The World Health Organisation recently recommended that the induction of labour should be reserved for specific medical indications and that no geographical region should have rates of induced labour over 10 per cent (World Health Organisation, 1985).

These techniques are no longer confined to sophisticated hospitals. There have recently been alarming reports of a growth in their use on women giving birth at home without medical back-up. Fifteen per cent of mothers interviewed in a North Indian village had been given an injection of synthetic oxytocin if labour did not proceed as expected. As the authors of the study comment,

> The popularity of these injections could hardly be more ironic. Male practitioners display no inhibition about administering them, relying simply on the dai's assessment of cervical dilatation and the baby's presentation. The injection of a standard dose of oxytocin (rather than a steadily monitored intravenous drip) results in acute discomfort from the almost instantly amplified pains. Moreover there are risks of rupturing the uterus, damaging the cervix or causing severe foetal distress or after-pains (Jeffery *et al.*, 1989, p. 112).

In developed countries most induced labours also involve continuous electronic foetal monitoring (EFM) of the baby through electrodes attached either inside or outside the mother's body. In the United States EFM is now used in at least 50 per cent of all births, though randomised controlled trials have failed to demonstrate that it benefits either mother or child (Grant, 1989; Simkin, 1986). On the contrary, a 'managed' labour of this kind may involve a significant loss of autonomy for the mother, causing both physical and psychological distress: 'I felt my labour had been taken over by strangers and machines . . . any fragile confidence I may have had in my body's ability to handle birth had vanished. I was frightened and despairing' (Health Department, Victoria, 1990, p. 100).

While some women will find the presence of technology reassuring, others resent the inevitable restrictions on their freedom. Many find that medical attention is focused not on their own judgements or feelings but on the messages coming from the machines. Thus the new technologies have frequently led to a deterioration in personal care, with women left to labour under the less than tender gaze of a bank of machines.

> I was put on a drip which was switched off at frequent intervals to 'get some action here'. After four or five hours I was told that my baby was distressed and I was only two centimetres dilated. I believe this was because I was induced when my cervix wasn't ready.
>
> They were helpful and sympathetic but they could not allay my feeling that the baby's distress and the Caesarean section could have been avoided if I'd been left alone (Phillips and Rakusen, 1989, p. 391).

As well as the experiential problems associated with induction there is also a clinical literature connecting it with increased rates of premature labour, foetal distress, jaundice and maternal infections (Chard and Richards, 1977). Both induction and EFM appear to have contributed to the recent increase in other forms of active intervention, particularly caesarean section. Between 1968 and 1983 the proportion of babies born by caesarean section rose by 250 per cent in England and Wales, by 300 per cent in the Netherlands, and by 380 per cent in the United States (Grant, 1989, p. 1185). Increases have also been noted in some third world countries, especially in Latin America (Janowitz *et al.*, 1982). Attempts to reduce the rate of operative deliveries have met with considerable resistance from doctors (Ruzek, 1991; Stafford, 1990). By 1986 about a quarter of all North American babies were being delivered by surgical means, and some commentators have suggested that this figure could reach 40 per cent by the year 2000 (Placek *et al.*, 1988, p. 562).

Clinical Freedom or Medical Domination?

Neither the overall increase nor the marked variations between countries can be explained in terms of objective differences in medical need. Instead the professional interests of the 'new obstetricians' appear to be having a major effect on clinical decision making. In the United States at least 80 per cent of caesareans are directly associated with the use of EFM, so that the new technologies themselves seem to be generating a greater need for surgical intervention (Banta and Thacker, 1979).

Financial factors also play a part. In 1986 19 per cent of US women paying their own medical bills were delivered by caesarean section compared with 21 per cent paid for by the government and 27 per cent with Blue Cross insurance (Placek *et al.*, 1988, p. 562). Brazil now has one of the highest rates of caesareans in the world and here too richer women are more likely to be the recipients (Janowitz *et al.*, 1982). One study of women in nine hospitals in southern Brazil showed that an astonishing 75 per cent of deliveries to private patients were by caesarean section compared with 40 per cent of public or privately insured patients, and less than 25 per cent of those without resources (Ruzek, 1991, pp. 75–6). Paradoxically however, treatment of this kind may not be of advantage to the recipient.

Caesarean section is a major surgical procedure with a mortality rate some four times higher than a vaginal delivery, as well as a substantially greater morbidity rate. There is a relatively high risk of infection and most patients report considerable abdominal and intestinal pain, weakness and difficulty in holding their infants. Few studies have been designed to assess women's emotional and psychological reactions to this or any other obstetric intervention. However there is evidence that 'high tech' births in general and caesarean sections in particular may exacerbate the problems most women face during the early weeks of motherhood (Oakley and Richards, 1990).

While most mothers are delighted with the safe delivery of a healthy baby, disappointment, guilt, anger and low self-esteem are also common reactions and many feel sorrow that they were not able to give birth 'naturally' (ibid.) This distress reflects the invasive experience of abdominal surgery combined with the heavy demands put on all new mothers. It is essential therefore that such potentially damaging procedures be used only in response to clearly identified clinical need, with the mother participating as fully as possible in the decision. However this is by no means always achieved.

The growing problems surrounding informed consent in obstetric practice were highlighted by a rash of court-ordered caesarean sections in the United States (Gallagher, 1987). In 1981 the Georgia Supreme Court ordered a caesarean section to be carried out on a woman with placenta praevia who had refused to give her consent to the operation. Immediately after the order was granted, ultrasound showed that the placenta had shifted and the woman was able to deliver vaginally (Daniels, 1990; Gallagher, 1987; Kolder *et al.*, 1987). Since that time a number of other attempts have been made to use the courts to enforce obstetric interventions on women whose legal competence has not been questioned. This has led to growing concern about the potential conflict between maternal and foetal rights.

A survey carried out in 1986 revealed a total of 21 such court orders sought by US hospitals in the previous five years. Fifteen involved caesarean sections; three, hospital detention for medical treatment, and three, intrauterine blood transfusions. 86 per cent were granted. Nearly all of the women who were the subject of requests for court orders were black, Asian or Hispanic and 24 per cent did not speak English as their first language; 44 per cent were unmarried and all were being treated at a clinic in a teaching hospital or were receiving public assistance (Kolder *et al.*, 1987, pp. 1192–3).

Most doctors seeking court orders do so in the belief that they are acting in the best interests of the foetus – their newly discovered second patient. However such cases obviously raise a number of serious concerns. In the first place it is difficult for doctors to achieve certainty in obstetric decisions (Banta and Thacker, 1979), yet judges may have to decide in a matter of hours or even minutes on an issue about which they know very little.

This problem of uncertainty is compounded by the fact that the woman concerned is unlikely to have effective legal representation, though a judgment against her constitutes a major threat to her civil liberties. It places the perceived interests of the foetus firmly against the common law right of the mother to maintain her bodily integrity and to refuse medical treatment. Indeed it requires her to undergo a painful and potentially risky medical procedure to which she does not consent, for the sake of another 'person' – a situation for which it is difficult to find an easy parallel.

As several commentators have pointed out, arguments of this kind can be extended indefinitely to control all aspects of a woman's life during pregnancy and even before conception. This is no longer a hypothetical fear, since a Californian woman was arrested in 1986 and held in jail for six days on charges of medical neglect of her foetus (Gallagher, 1987, p. 45). While such interventions are unlikely to happen on a mass scale they do illustrate the potential risk of new technologies being used to advance both the professional power of doctors and the cause of the 'right to life' movement. Significantly, only 24 per cent of obstetricians interviewed in a US study were unequivocal in their belief that pregnant women have a right to refuse medical treatment (Kolder *et al.*, 1987, p. 1194).

At the heart of feminist concerns about obstetric technologies is a fear that the medicalisation of birth has too often been against the interests of mothers, turning actively labouring women into the passive object of medical ministration. Similar anxieties about medical power have been raised in relation to the new techniques designed to diagnose genetic abnormalities in utero.

A Doctor's Right to Choose

The past decade has seen major advances in prenatal diagnosis but relatively little progress in treatment. Serious birth defects occur in about twenty-three per thousand live births, but very few are amenable to medical intervention (Birke *et al.*, 1990, p. 159). Hence the main rationale for detecting genetic disease is still to enable the parents to make an informed choice about whether or not to abort a damaged foetus (ibid., Ch. 7). However it is ultimately doctors who control access to the technology, to the interpretation and presentation of the findings and to any medical strategies that may be devised as a result. Under these circumstances the woman's freedom of choice may again be compromised and the liberatory potential of the technologies constrained.

The earliest of these 'new wave' diagnostic devices was ultrasound, first used in a clinical context in Glasgow in 1957 (Oakley, 1984). It is widely employed both for routine screening of foetal development and also as a diagnostic tool for identifying major congenital defects such as anencephaly or spina bifida. However more precise and reliable diagnosis is now available either from amniocentesis or from the new technique of chorionic villus sampling (CVS). Both procedures are usually carried out under the guidance of ultrasound imaging, often following a blood test for alpha foetoprotein (AFP).

Amniocentesis is done between the sixteenth and twentieth weeks of pregnancy through inserting a needle into the uterus to draw out a small amount of amniotic fluid. This is then grown in a culture and the results are known at nineteen or twenty weeks. The test can pick up chromosomal abnormalities such as Downs Syndrome as well as neural tube defects, but it has the major disadvantage that results are generated so late in pregnancy that an abortion becomes extremely traumatic. CVS on the other hand can be carried out at eight to twelve weeks. It involves the removal of a small sample of tissue from the chorionic villi, the tissue developing around the placenta, and the result is known in a few days. The test can show chromosomal abnormalities and inherited disorders such as Tay-Sachs disease but not neural tube defects (Birke *et al.*, 1990, p. 177).

These diagnostic and screening techniques can be of considerable value to parents. They can provide relief from anxiety and many women have expressed particular pleasure in seeing their child on a routine ultrasound. They can also help parents of an impaired foetus to make an informed choice about abortion and to prepare themselves for the child if they decide to continue with the pregnancy. Although the information generated is not always definitive, these techniques do represent an important source of data to facilitate reproductive choices. However there is serious concern about how far their potential is being realised by those they are designed to help.

Women who are at increased risk of having an impaired foetus do not always have access to the technology. Evidence from the United States suggests that poor women may face practical and financial barriers in attempting to use it (Adler *et al.*, 1991). In most third world countries screening is virtually unavailable to all but very wealthy women living in urban areas.

Those women who do gain access to genetic screening are not always adequately informed about the risks and benefits. Indeed some are not even given the chance to decide whether or not to participate. In one study carried out in London, a quarter of consultant physicians reported that they routinely carried out AFP screening without informing the women involved – a practice in direct conflict with British government guidelines (Farrant, 1985, p. 110). The same study found that immediately *after* amniocentesis 24 per cent of women were apparently unaware that it carried a significant risk of miscarriage (ibid., p. 111).

Thus far we know very little about the effects of diagnostic screening on women's emotional and psychological responses to pregnancy. However preliminary research indicates that they may well be profound. Most women report a positive response to developmental ultrasound if the images on the screen are sensitively communicated. A scan makes the pregnancy seem 'real' and promotes closer identification with the child within. However it can also cause unnecessary anxiety: 'A scan showed that the baby did not have enough body fat and that there was a low level of fluid in the womb. Or did it? When the baby was born, before the date set for induction, neither "fact" was correct' (Health Department Victoria, 1990, p. 101).

Amniocentesis and CVS are inevitably more disturbing. The insertion of a needle into the uterus can be invasive and unpleasant and many are afraid it will damage the baby. The risk of miscarriage is estimated to be between 0.5 per cent and 1.7 per cent with amniocentesis and about 2.0 per cent with CVS – a chance some women will not wish to take. Studies have shown that participating in amniocentesis causes high levels of anxiety for women, especially when previous screening has indicated that an impaired pregnancy is a real possibility (Evers-Kiebooms *et al.*, 1988; Farrant, 1985; Hibbard, 1987). These fears represent a realistic response to the genuine dilemma women may have to face if the tests reveal impairment (Adler *et al.*, 1991; Robinson *et al.*, 1984; Rothman, 1988). However they can be exacerbated by inadequate counselling and poor social support. As one American woman told Barbara Rothman:

> I alternated between being convinced that since statistically the odds were in my favour, everything would be fine, and dreading the possibility that everything wouldn't be fine and I'd have to go through an abortion at my stage of pregnancy. I wanted to know, and yet I dreaded the doctor's phone call (Rothman, 1988, p. 102).

One consequence of amniocentesis seems to be a state of suspended animation in which the pregnancy can only be 'tentative' until the results are known. This is especially difficult if the baby is beginning to move. Indeed many of Rothman's respondents reported that they did not feel movement until after the pregnancy had been 'confirmed' by a normal test result (ibid., pp. 100–7). Whatever the results eventually show, many women report continuing anxiety. A negative result obviously offers relief but the testing procedure itself may have raised fundamental questions that might otherwise have been avoided. Women will have a heightened awareness of what can go wrong, and lingering doubts will often remain.

If the news is bad – if the test is positive for Downs Syndrome for instance – then a very difficult decision will have to be made by the mother and her partner. It is at this point that the techniques of prenatal diagnosis can potentially maximise a woman's capacity to determine her own future and that of her family. However the evidence points to a number of obstacles that can impede such choices. In the first place a diagnosis is often limited in what it can predict about the child's potential quality of life. While certain conditions are inevitably fatal – Tay-Sachs Disease for instance – the degree of impairment in a child with Downs Syndrome cannot be predicted. Ambiguous diagnoses of this kind often make the decision about abortion much harder (ibid., Ch. 6).

More fundamentally, experience of the use of these technologies indicates that as the opportunity to abort opens up, so the option not to do so appears to be increasingly unavailable. While some women receive non-directive counselling, others have found that their doctors strongly encourage the termination of impaired foetuses. Research carried out in London in the mid 1980s indicated that the majority of doctors were unwilling to perform amniocentesis if the woman was not willing to agree *in advance* to a termination should the results prove positive (Farrant, 1985). The unreasonable demands imposed by such a requirement are illustrated by the feelings of another American woman in Barbara Rothman's study:

> It was easy to say at the beginning of the pregnancy that I would have an abortion. However, as part of the procedure, an ultrasound is done. We could see the baby and she became real to us. After that it was extremely difficult to think of abortion. . . . The procedure is performed so late and the pregnancy is advanced enough that abortion is not a simple matter. It seems more like murder (Rothman, 1988, pp. 58–9).

Most subtle pressures can also be involved. A woman who decides to continue with an impaired foetus may well be held responsible for her own fate and therefore undeserving of sympathy or social support. As one London woman described it, 'The decision was made by the doctors. They said 'it's no use, the tests show it's abnormal. It's up to you what you do, but if you keep it you will live with the problem' (Farrant, 1985, pp. 116–17).

The power conferred on doctors by these new technologies is highlighted by the distressing experience of another London woman in the same study, who had to undergo an abortion for foetal abnormality at five months. She had previously been refused an early termination of the same pregnancy, which she had not wished to continue. Only after amniocentesis did the doctor accept that she had a 'good' reason for termination.

> [The gynaecologist] didn't really want to do it [abortion for medico-social reasons]. . . . He kept saying you're young and healthy, you

can cope. . . . He said you'll be risking your life and everything having it at four months, so I had to accept it. . . . They shouldn't try to talk you out of something you really want in the beginning. . . . They try to push you into getting rid of it when there's something wrong with it – they keep saying it's best for you and that (Farrant, 1985, p. 117).

Looking at the broader context of reproductive choice, increased diagnostic screening may well lead to reductions in provision for the smaller number of children who are born with disabilities. Since these are most likely to be the children whose mothers cannot afford access to diagnostic technology, there is a danger that disability may increasingly become a problem of the poor, with diminished resources reducing parental choice. Comparable developments are evident in India, where the abortion of female foetuses continues to be seen by some parents as an appropriate response to gender inequalities in the wider society.

Infertility: A Life Sentence?

So far we have been concerned only with fertile women and their strategies for managing their reproductive lives. We have ignored the experiences of millions of infertile women, many of whom are drawn by their desire for a child into the epicentre of high technology gynaecology and obstetrics. New technologies such as in vitro fertilisation (IVF) or gamete intrafallopian tube transfer (GIFT) have recently been hailed as the miracle solution for all those who cannot conceive within their own bodies. However they are suitable for only a small percentage of infertile women and only a few of these can afford them. As a result the majority remain childless. This includes millions of women in third world countries for whom infertility may be a cause not just of sorrow but of social exclusion.

Worldwide, between 8 per cent and 12 per cent of couples experience some period of infertility during their reproductive lives (WHO, 1991). In the United Kingdom more than 50 000 men and women bring infertility problems to the NHS each year and between one and two million are being treated at any one time (Pfeffer and Woollett, 1983, pp. 2, 27). In the United States a 1982 study estimated that just over 8 per cent of married women were infertile, with the rate being one and a half times greater among black women than among white women

(Mosher and Pratt, 1985). In many parts of the third world the incidence is much higher, reaching an astonishing 50 per cent of the female population in some countries in Sub-Saharan Africa (WHO, 1991). For infertile women or the partners of infertile men, the inability to create a child can be a major life crisis, yet their plight has frequently been ignored.

Men and women with reproductive impairments are disabled because they are unable to participate in the basic human activity of procreation (Rothman, 1989, pp. 143–51). Of course the degree of their handicap will vary according to individual and social circumstances. For individuals not wishing to have their own biological children, reproductive impairment will impose no constraints at all. However for others the consequences of infertility may be very great indeed.

Both members of an infertile couple will be concerned, but recent research suggests that it is usually the woman who experiences the greatest distress and is also the most disabled by her failure to conceive (Greil *et al.*, 1988). Despite major changes in the nature of women's lives, the status of 'mother' continues in most cultures to be a central element in the definition of a 'normal' adult female. Under these circumstances an inability to become a biological parent may have a profound effect on women's sense of themselves and their well-being. One American woman described the impact of infertility on all areas of her life:

> It affects your ego. It has an immense effect on self concept in all kinds of crazy ways. You ask 'how can I be a real woman?' By affecting the self-concept it affects sexuality and it affected work for me for a while. How can I be good at this: I'm not a normal person (Greil *et al.*, 1988, p. 181).

While many men may feel disappointed and sometimes even stigmatised by their inability to father a child, few report feeling the same degree of loss.

> I think she reacted a lot stronger in terms of her body not working and it being her responsibility and not being a mother. I reacted and got angry more at the inconvenience and the unfairness of it. She took it more to heart and personally. I feel like I probably dealt more with her response. I probably got more frustrated by her response than by the whole thing just as myself (Greil *et al.*, 1988, p. 183).

The handicap imposed by reproductive impairment will be at its most severe for an uneducated woman living in a small community where few options other than motherhood are culturally sanctioned. When her 'barrenness' becomes apparent she is likely to suffer extreme pressure not just from her husband but also from his family. If the problem is not resolved she may be abused, divorced or abandoned. She will have no daughters to comfort her and no sons to support her in old age. Under such circumstances infertility is clearly an individual tragedy of major proportions that may even threaten a woman's chance of survival, as this report from North India demonstrates:

> A childbearing career is an essential part of adult women's lives. Not to want children is unthinkable, to fail to conceive or to have no living children is usually calamitous . . . failure is just cause for a man to return his wife to her parents and several women in Dharmanagri and Thakvi (who ultimately bore children) recall worrying times when their husbands were pestered to replace them (Jeffery *et al.*, 1989, p. 87).

Thus infertility can be a major disability and its treatment should be seen as a basic element in reproductive self-determination, along with abortion, contraception and maternity care. Yet many infertile men and women get little or no help from medicine. In most third world countries the cost and inaccessibility of services are compounded by the low priority of conception on a medical agenda dominated by birth control. As a result only the very rich can expect to receive treatment. In developed countries, on the other hand, spending on infertility is growing each year. Yet there are considerable doubts about the benefits achieved from this expenditure (US Congress Office of Technology Assessment, 1988).

Techniques for treating women's infertility remained largely unchanged for over a century until the introduction of the new 'fertility drugs' in the 1960s. This was followed in the late 1970s by the dramatic advent of IVF and its associated techniques. Doctors can now engineer the fertilisation of an ovum outside a woman's body and replace it there to grow to maturity. This highly publicised innovation gave new hope to millions of infertile couples, but it is suitable only for very few. For the rest, medicine still has little to offer. Moreover the new conceptive techniques have been subjected to extensive criticism from a variety of perspectives.

The most vociferous critics have been concerned largely with the status of cellular life. As a result public debate in most countries has been centred on the need to safeguard human embryos (Warnock, 1985). In contrast there has been widespread neglect of ethical issues in the treatment of those who provide these embryos (Scritchfield, 1989; Stanworth, 1987; Whitbeck, 1991). There can be no doubt that the new conceptive technology does meet very real needs for some women. About 2000 healthy babies had been born through IVF in the United Kingdom by the end of 1988 (Stacey, 1992, p. 31). However closer scrutiny of current practices reveals very similar contradictions to those we have observed in other areas of reproductive medicine.

The most immediate problem with the new technologies is their exclusivity. Even in the richer countries access is strongly influenced by income. In the United Kingdom the National Health Service has given a low priority to infertility treatment. Most attempts at assisted reproduction take place in the private sector, so only those able to find considerable sums of money can consider the possibility of IVF (Doyal, 1987; Pfeffer, 1992). This inequality is reinforced in many countries by the exclusion of infertility treatment from medical insurance schemes.

However money is not the only thing needed to ensure that infertility is taken seriously. A woman also needs to be part of a 'suitable couple'. Despite an apparent belief in the universality of the 'maternal instinct', it is only heterosexual women in long-term relationships with men who are deemed appropriate for medical help to achieve motherhood. Single women and those in lesbian relationships have experienced great difficulty in having their infertility recognised and in many countries they are specifically excluded from IVF programmes (Doyal, 1994b; Warnock, 1985). Disability too is often used as a reason to deny women access to assisted motherhood. Thus whatever benefits IVF may have to offer are currently limited almost entirely to those able-bodied women who have both money and social respectability.

For those women who do manage to reach the operating theatre, the experience of infertility treatment may be extremely stressful, and they may have little appreciation of the real chance of a successful outcome. Not surprisingly, research suggests that most participants in IVF programmes greatly overestimate the likelihood of ending up with a baby (Adler *et al.*, 1991, p. 113). Accurate data on the success rates of individual clinics are difficult to obtain, not least because they are easily manipulated by those who have an interest in promoting the technologies. However national figures for the United Kingdom in 1991 suggested that a live birth – or a 'take home baby' – results for 13.8 per cent of those who have their ovulation cycle stimulated, for 17.9 per cent of those who also have an egg retrieved, and for 18.1 per cent of those who finally have an embryo transferred (Human Fertilisation and Embryology Authority, 1993). These figures vary dramatically between centres, but even in the best the procedure ends in success for less than a third of those who embark on it.

Against this have to be set the considerable distress, pain and anxiety reported by many participants in IVF programmes, as well as possible long-term risks from the drugs used to induce ovulation (Scritchfield, 1989). The techniques can be highly invasive. Not only do they subject women's bodies to continuous monitoring and manipulation but they can also distort some of the most intimate parts of their lives. Yet there is evidence that many of those involved are failing to take women's emotional health seriously.

Women who enter IVF programmes are already vulnerable. In the United States they have experienced an average of 6.4 years' infertility with associated anxiety and loss of self esteem (Adler *et al.*, 1991, p. 112). Most find IVF extremely stressful, referring to the 'emotional roller coaster' that characterises each reproductive cycle (Stewart and Glazer, 1986). Many talk about their feelings of loss of control and of depersonalisation. The procedures themselves may be inherently stressful, but it is significant that women frequently identify the insensitivity of health care workers as a contributory factor in their distress (Adler *et al.*, 1991, p. 115). No doubt the small minority who end up with a healthy baby will find these costs acceptable, but we know little about the majority who go away with empty arms.

Given their very high cost as well as their relatively low success rate, it seems unlikely that IVF, GIFT and other 'high tech' solutions will ever provide the solution to global infertility problems. Yet their very existence may be diverting resources away from broader strategies for responding to reproductive impairment. In particular they have contributed to a neglect of preventive strategies, which could greatly reduce the need for curative services.

There is probably a core of between 5 per cent and 7 per cent of female infertility that is anatomical or genetic in origin, and therefore difficult to prevent. However a significant proportion of the remainder has its origin in gynaecological infection. As we have seen, failure to treat reproductive tract infections such as gonorrhoea and chlamydia, the promotion of IUDs for contraception, and the continuation of unsafe practices during childbirth and abortion can all be a cause of pelvic inflammatory disease, which in turn can lead to infertility. A recent WHO study found that in developed countries about 20–25 per cent of infertility is caused by infectious organisms, while in Africa the proportion is as high as 50 per cent (WHO, 1991).

It is also clear that there are occupational and environmental factors promoting infertility. Women who smoke for instance are more susceptible to infections of the reproductive tract, and those who smoke more than twenty cigarettes a day are three times more likely than non-smokers to take over a year to conceive (Chollat-Traquet, 1992, p. 48). A number of chemical hazards in the workplace can affect the fertility of both men and women. There is also evidence from animal research that stress can significantly affect fertility, though as yet we know little about such effects in humans.

An effective strategy for preventing infertility would therefore extend the quality and availability of reproductive health services. These services would pay particular attention to the identification and treatment of reproductive tract infections, and the promotion of safe contraception. They would be accompanied by policies to minimise the impact of occupational and environmental factors on women's (and men's) reproductive potential. At the same time a wider range of more sensitive policies is needed to meet the varied needs of those unable to procreate. Some will be designed to alleviate the reproductive impairment itself but others will involve a variety of strategies for facilitating social rather than biological parenting.

Conclusion

In this chapter and in the one that preceded it we have identified the complex ways in which social, economic and cultural circumstances shape reproductive experiences. At the same time we have glimpsed the biological reality that lies behind women's continuing struggle to control their procreativity. Our exploration of their lives as lovers, mothers and would-be mothers showed the enormous diversity in women's material circumstances and in the way they make sense of them. However it also showed their common need for access to the means to regulate their reproductive potential. This will be explored in more detail in the final chapter, where we look at women's campaigns for reproductive rights.

Further Reading

Birke, L., Himmelweit, S. and Vines, G. (1990) *Tomorrow's Child: reproductive technologies in the nineties* (London: Virago). An extremely useful introduction to the science of the new reproductive technologies. As well as giving the facts, this book also outlines current policy debates and places them in a broader feminist context.

Chalmers, I., Enkin, M. and Keirse, M. (eds) (1989) *Effective Care in Pregnancy and Childbirth*, Vols. I and II. (Oxford: Clarendon Press). A classic compendium of articles investigating the effectiveness of medical care in pregnancy and childbirth. It covers a wide range of medical techniques and processes, summarising what we know and don't know about their impact on mothers and babies.

Jeffery, P., Jeffery, R. and Lyon, A. (1989) *Labour Pains and Labour Power: women and childbearing in India* (London: Zed Books). An anthropological account of the centrality of childbearing in the lives of women in two North Indian villages. This detailed investigation offers invaluable insights into the reality behind current policy debates about maternal health and well-being.

Rothman, B. (1988) *The Tentative Pregnancy: prenatal diagnosis and the future of motherhood* (London: Pandora). An American study that explores the experiences of women undergoing prenatal testing. It provides a unique account of the impact of these new technologies on women's reproductive consciousness, highlighting ethical and social dilemmas that are often ignored by doctors and policy makers.

Royston, E. and Armstrong, S. (1989) *Preventing Maternal Deaths* (Geneva: WHO). A monograph produced under the auspices of the World Health Organisation, as part of its campaign against maternal mortality. It provides a clear and comprehensive overview of the causes and consequences of morbidity and mortality during childbearing and discusses possible solutions.

6

Waged Work and Well-Being

Introduction

One of the most striking developments of the postwar period has been the increase in female work outside the home. Worldwide, women now make up over one third of the paid labour force. The proportion of women in employment and in the informal sector of the economy varies between regions, but in most there is an upward trend with a particularly rapid rise in many parts of the third world (Moore, 1988, Ch. 4; United Nations, 1991, pp. 88–96). For most women, staying at home is no longer an option, and many move in and out of employment as financial need, personal preference, domestic circumstances and job opportunities dictate (Bullock, 1994). Since their place in the labour force is now well established, we need to assess the implications this has for women's health.

Sexual Divisions in Waged Work

Nowhere in the world have women entered the labour force on equal terms with men. In most countries they are concentrated in particular sectors of the economy – in service jobs or in selected areas of manufacturing such as clothing and footwear, textiles, food processing and precision and electronic engineering. In most third world countries they make up a significant proportion of the labour force in agriculture. Within each area of work there is also a concentration of women in the jobs with lowest pay and least status (Moore, 1988, pp. 98–103; United Nations, 1991, pp. 87–8).

During the 1960s and 1970s legislation was passed in the United States, Canada, Australia and many European countries making it unlawful to pay women less than men for doing the same job or to discriminate against them in selection and promotion (Meehan, 1985).

However women have not achieved parity with men's earnings and many continue to be crowded into female 'employment ghettos', doing unskilled, monotonous jobs in shops, canteens, laundries, factories and hospitals. In most third world countries the lack of equal opportunities legislation means that women are entering employment under even less advantageous conditions. All over the world women are more likely than men to be homeworkers, to be self-employed or to work in small unregulated businesses, and are less likely to be members of trade unions.

It is also significant that much of the recent expansion of the female labour force has taken place among married women with children. Again this pattern varies between countries, but it is clear that mothers with dependent children form an increasingly large proportion of the world's labour force, fitting their hours around their children's needs and their domestic responsibilities, and often leaving little time for themselves. Though there is evidence from some countries that the degree of inequality in the division of household labour is beginning to decrease, employed women everywhere still retain primary responsibility for household work. When this is combined with employment it can have serious effects on their well-being (Berk, 1985; Morris, 1990, Ch. 5; UN, 1991, pp. 81–2).

Women Work and Health

For decades middle-class married women in developed countries were threatened with sterility, cancer, madness and all manner of other diseases if they left their homes for the world of work (Ehrenreich and English, 1979). However it was not until the 1970s that any systematic investigation was undertaken into the health effects of women's employment (Chavkin, 1984; Frankenhaueser *et al.*, 1991; Repetti *et al.*, 1989; Sorensen and Verbrugge, 1987; Waldron, 1991). Though evidence is now beginning to accumulate about both the positive and the negative effects of waged work on women's well-being, most research has concentrated on major industries in developed countries. As a result the impact of waged work on millions of women in both the formal and informal sectors of the global economy continues to go unrecorded and unregulated.

Most studies have been undertaken in the United States and involve large-scale comparisons of the physical and mental health of women in employment with that of non-employed women. The findings of some studies have been inconclusive, but most show that employed women as a group have better mental health than those outside the labour market (Repetti *et al.*, 1989; Waldron and Jacobs, 1989). Similarly, most suggest that women's physical health benefits from waged work (Rosenfeld, 1992). Some of these apparent improvements in well-being may simply reflect the prior exclusion of unhealthy women from employment. However the positive effects of paid work should not surprise us, in light of the health problems we have already identified in women who remain outside the labour market.

The first benefit for women entering the labour force is the financial reward it brings. Many give income as their prime motivation for employment and recent research in the United Kingdom suggests that at least four times more families than at present would be below the official poverty line if married women stopped going out to work (Glendinning and Millar, 1987, p. 6). In many third world countries the economic pressures are even greater, drawing women into agricultural labour and plantation work as well as industrial employment (Moore, 1988, Ch. 4).

For women living in poverty, income from waged work may offer significant health benefits to themselves and their families since it will allow them to purchase basic necessities such as housing and food. However the effects may be contradictory since the nutritional status of some women may deteriorate if long hours of labour keep them from tending family plots. Lack of food combined with overwork may therefore damage their health, though it may improve that of their dependants (Mebrahtu, 1991; Raikes, 1989, p. 454).

Income from work outside the home can also enhance women's autonomy and hence their mental well-being through reducing their economic and social dependence on a male partner. As one woman working in a Cairo factory expressed it, 'Work strengthens a woman's position. The woman who works doesn't have to beg her husband for every piastre she needs. She can command respect in her home and can raise her voice in any decision' (Ibrahim, 1985, quoted in Moore, 1988, p. 111). But again these potential benefits should not be overstated. Some women continue to be denied their right to autonomy and self-determination despite their economic contribution. In a recent study in a Punjab village, not one of the women interviewed said she alone could decide whether or not to work. Twenty-one out of twenty-nine said their husbands decided, three said their sons, and the rest mentioned other relatives. Only two said they and their partners would decide together. None were free to decide how their wages would be spent (Horowitz and Kishwar, 1984, p. 95).

Finally, employment outside the home can be a source of companionship and provide a network of relationships to alleviate the isolation and feelings of worthlessness commonly expressed by women at home (Brown and Harris, 1978; Warr and Parry, 1982). American research suggests that the social support many women receive from work is a central element in promoting both physical and mental health. Co-workers are often highly valued, offering help with both domestic and work problems, and support of this kind seems to be especially important to single mothers (Aneshensel, 1986; Repetti *et al.*, 1989, pp. 1398–9).

The potential benefits of waged work are therefore clear. But we have seen that they can be negated either by the domestic circumstances of the woman herself or by the nature of the job. Neither 'women' nor 'work' are homogenous categories. Factors such as a woman's marital status, whether or not she is a single parent, the domestic division of labour in her household, her age, the number of her dependants, her skills and her attitudes to employment will all affect the influence of work on her well-being, as will the nature of the job itself (Arber *et al.*, 1985). Hence large-scale studies comparing 'housewives' with those who are also employed can tell us very little either about the impact of work experiences on the health of different groups of women, or about the differences between the occupational health of men and women.

The importance of taking these various factors into account can be illustrated by recent research on the health of women workers in the United Kingdom (Arber *et al.*, 1985; Bartley *et al.*, 1992). In this particular social context, part-time work seems on balance to be beneficial to the health of women with young children while full-time work does not. This is especially true for women in the lowest socio-economic groups. The research also suggests that the psychological benefits are much greater than the physical ones, though of course this relationship may be reversed in situations of extreme poverty where waged work is essential to buy the necessities for health.

Thus the key question is not whether paid work in general is good for all women, but rather which types of work will be harmful or beneficial for which women and under what circumstances. In this chapter we examine some of the health effects of different types of work through exploring the potential hazards in a variety of jobs now done by large numbers of women.

Danger: Women at Work

A detailed examination of women's roles in the global economy suggests that many are now employed in jobs involving both physical and psychological risks. As we shall see, these hazards are not random but reflect gender divisions in waged work and in the wider society.

Hazards of Industrial Employment

Many more women are now working in industry, coming into contact with the sorts of hazard some men (and a few women) have been facing for decades (WHO Regional Office for Europe, 1983). Though men still suffer the majority of fatal accidents, women are increasingly exposed to hazardous chemicals, dusts, fumes and other toxic substances, as well as the physical strains of heavy labour. This is especially true in East and South-East Asia, where women now make up over a quarter of the manufacturing workforce (UN, 1991, p. 87). A brief account of the life of one Indian worker serves to challenge any stereotype of weak and passive third world women.

> Jayamma, a woman working for a brick kiln on the outskirts of Trivandrum, the capital of Kerala State, is almost fifty years old. . . . As part of her equipment a woman brick-worker carries her own wooden plank, two feet by eight inches, to be used as a base on which to place the bricks. . . . An adult woman carries twenty bricks, each weighing approximately one kilo, at a time. She must stack the bricks on her head by herself and carry them to the kiln, which may be ten or twenty minutes' walk. The main brunt of the weight falls on her neck. . . . And still these women virtually run (Gulati, 1982, p. 39).

During the nineteenth century many thousands of women in Europe, the United States and India laboured in the unhealthy factories of the industrial revolution. For many this carried on the traditional role of their mothers and grandmothers, who had dominated the weaving trades before mechanisation (Lown and Chenut, 1983). Today women workers still predominate in the industry, which has been forced into rapid restructuring to cope with recession. While the textile industry has shrunk in Europe, it still employs many thousands of women, often in depressed areas with a largely female and non-unionised labour force. In Asia women are entering textile factories in increasing numbers as multinational companies search the world for a cheap and 'docile' labour force (Chapkis and Enloe, 1983).

Yet work in the industry is still hazardous. Exposure to cotton dust can produce the debilitating respiratory disease byssinosis, or 'brown lung'. In the early stages this leads to tightness in the chest, coughing and shortness of breath, and in the long run to severe congestion of the lungs and varying degrees of disability. Textile workers are also at risk from chemicals used in processing and dyeing the cloth while garment workers are prone to accidents from needles. Formaldehyde, which is a suspected carcinogen, is widely used, as are other chemicals likely to produce allergies and industrial dermatitis.

In the electronics industry, too, jobs are opening up for women both in developed countries and in the third world. At first sight these factories appear to pose little risk to health. In practice however a great many hazards lie concealed from the needy and often unorganised women who flock to work in them. Around the world more than 50 per cent of workers on electronics production lines are women. In California's Silicon Valley, for instance, about 70 000 are involved in the lowest levels of production, and about 40 per cent of these are Asians and Hispanics (Baker and Woodrow, 1984, p. 22). In other developed countries electronics is expanding in areas of high unemployment, where traditional industries have declined.

In many third world countries the benefits for employers are very great, especially in export processing zones (EPZs), where governments offer tax exemption, free repatriation of profits, freedom from foreign exchange controls and loans at favourable rates of interest (Elson and Pearson, 1981; Lim, 1978; Lin, 1986; Mitter, 1986). In addition most have little in the way of environmental controls or occupational health and safety regulation. As a result, electronics, like textiles, is increasingly moving towards South and South-East Asia and Latin America, where the majority of workers in EPZs are now female (Mitter, 1986).

These developments do provide women with jobs in countries that traditionally offered them few opportunities for employment. However there is growing evidence that for many work may mean risking their health (McCurdy *et al.*, 1989). Despite its image of cleanliness the electronics industry relies on hundreds of potentially dangerous substances to make its products. Organic solvents such as xylene, trichloroethane, chlorofluorocarbons, trichloroethylene (TCE), freons and methyl ethyl ketone (MEK) are extensively used (Baker and Woodrow, 1984; Bowler *et al.*, 1991a, 1991b). Corrosive acids are also common, while gases such as arsine and phosphine pose additional threats. These highly potent chemicals are often used in new and untested combinations, putting workers at considerable risk. A 1977 report from the US Occupational Health and Safety Administration put the scientific instruments industry in the first place and electrical equipment manufacturers in third place among hazardous industries exposing their workers to carcinogens (Baker and Woodrow, 1984, p. 25).

Evidence from California shows the rate of occupational illness among microelectronics workers to be some three times that of workers in general manufacturing industry (LaDou, 1986, pp. 2–3). There have also been frequent reports of symptoms such as headaches, dizziness, nausea, blurred vision and numbness. Many women on the production lines suffer at some time from conjunctivitis and bad eyesight forces some to leave their jobs (Grossman, 1979; Lim, 1978; Lin, 1986). As well as the physical hazards, work in electronics plants can be psychologically distressing, particularly for young women who leave their rural extended families to work in the expanding towns of South-East Asia (Lin, 1986).

Factory discipline is strict, with frequent overtime and shift work producing distress and fatigue. These pressures have sometimes led to mass outbreaks of illness. While some stem from exposure to toxic chemicals, others are probably the expression of psychological tensions. The apparent outbreaks of mass possession by spirits that have occurred in several South-East Asian plants have been described by some observers as 'covert industrial conflict'. Among employers however, they have usually been rationalised away as hysteria or 'mass psychogenic illness', not requiring any changes in employment practices or working conditions.

Despite growing epidemiological and toxicological evidence of hazards there have been few studies of the health of workers in the electronics industry. Companies are secretive and the labour force has a high turnover rate, making it difficult to exert pressure for investigation and regulation. However formal evidence of neuropsychological damage to electronics workers is now beginning to emerge. In a comparison between a group of former electronics workers and a sample of matched controls, the former manifested inferior verbal ability, memory functions, visuospatial function, visuomotor speed, cognitive flexibility, psychomotor speed and reaction time and grip strength (Bowler *et al.*, 1991a). High rates of anxiety, depression and psychosis were also found among the sample of predominantly Hispanic workers (Bowler *et al.*, 1991b). The authors of the study attribute their findings to excessive solvent exposure and compare the effects to senile dementia. Women workers at the GTE Lenkurt plant in New Mexico experience them first hand every day.

One woman said, 'My kids laugh at me. I used to keep a perfect house, and now they'll find the sugar bowl in the freezer. I put it there'. Several women related getting lost on the freeway, which is difficult to do in Albuquerque because there are only two. Three had had the same experience – having to pull over and wait to remember where they had set out to go. Some of the stories come from husbands and children: mom is so out of it lately (Fox, 1991, 'p. 89).

Agricultural Labour: Growing Dangers

Like the electronics industry, the agricultural sector is often thought of as a safe workplace, providing labour in the open air and plenty of exercise. In reality however, it too can pose threats to women's health (Taattola and Susitaival, 1993). According to official estimates nearly 80 per cent of economically active women in Sub- Saharan Africa and at least half in Asia are in agriculture (UN, 1991, p. 89). Many work extremely hard and in very harsh conditions. In Saba Mebrahtu's study of women farmers in Nigeria, many were concerned about the impact of work on their health. In the women's own words, 'farming consumes a lot of energy . . . women age faster . . . they do not feel good . . . and their stomach turns upside down' (Mebrahtu, 1991, p. 100).

Similar experiences have been reported from all parts of the world where women do agricultural labour – whether paid or unpaid. For most, the exhaustion and physical depletion engendered by their work is reinforced by overexposure to heat, sun and other elements as well as the large burden of domestic labour that is inextricably interwoven with waged work in many rural environments.

Travelling on a road in a large-scale farming area in Zimbabwe, one commonly sees poorly dressed, thin women bending over huge plowed fields, weeding, planting or harvesting. Many work with babies on their backs, entering the fields at sunrise and leaving after sunset. These are the women whose labor contributes to Zimbabwe's rich export harvests and southern African food security, while their own children experience some of the highest rates of malnutrition in the country (Loewenson 1991, p. 35).

Most female agricultural workers have no employment rights and little money. As a result many work during pregnancy, which may damage the health of both mother and baby. A research project carried out in Maharashtra, India, found a high incidence of stillbirths, premature births and deaths at the peak of the rice cultivation season. The work involves squatting and bending for hours, leading to physical strain and pressure in the uterus (Asian and Pacific Women's Resource Collection Network, 1989, p. 105).

It was a hot and humid late morning when I met Parvathi, eight months pregnant with her ninth child. She was on the top of a five feet high ladder tapping her 500 plus rubber trees. Tired, sweat glistening on her dark skin, Parvathi was panting as she spoke. She works for a contractor and therefore is not entitled to paid maternity leave. She will be back in the plantation a week after her delivery for her income is vital for the family's survival (Asian and Pacific Women's Resource Collection Network, 1989, p. 106).

Millions of women working on the land are also at risk from exposure to agrochemicals, many wrongly used and inadequately labelled. Again, the dangers are especially great in poorer parts of the world. A recent WHO estimate suggested that some three million people are hospitalised each year as a result of acute pesticide poisoning and there are about 220 000 deaths. (Jeyeratnam, 1990, p. 140). These chemicals can also cause chronic and long-term health effects such as cancers, birth defects and sterility, while dust from rice husks can cause asthma, corneal scars and other eye problems (Asian and Pacific Women's Resource Collection Network, 1989, p. 105). We do not know how much of this damage is borne by women, but where they are substantially involved in agricultural production and/or live near the fields, they will inevitably figure prominently among the victims.

Since women are the lowest paid workers they often end up with the least popular jobs and this frequently includes chemical spraying. On Malaysian plantations about 80 per cent of those spreading herbicides are women (Ling, 1991, p. 23). They have little protective clothing or equipment when using highly toxic chemicals such as paraquat which can cause damage to the lungs, heart, kidney, liver and central nervous system.

Many agricultural hazards are at their most serious for women who work as migrant farmhands, moving around either alone or with their families to take on seasonal jobs. In the United States there are said to be around five million seasonal farmworkers and their dependants, many of them black or Hispanic. They do not have access to clean water or effective sanitation, and temporary living quarters are usually inadequate, increasing the incidence of infectious diseases. One Texan woman described her daily life to a tribunal investigating the need for toilet provision in the fields: 'Whenever there is a ditch or woods nearby, we go there. When this does not exist, we just have to wait. Or otherwise a group of us get together and stand around the person and cover him or her up' (Jasso and Mazorra, 1984, p. 90). Not surprisingly, prolonged retention of urine has been associated with the high rate of urinary tract infections among farmworking women.

Male Bias in Occupational Health Research

We have identified many of the potential hazards women face in both industrial and agricultural employment. However the degree of damage caused to their health is difficult to assess since most research has concentrated on men doing jobs traditionally reserved for males. Women's biology differs from that of men, they often do different jobs under different conditions and they have a heavier burden of domestic tasks. All these factors need to be taken into account when assessing the impact of waged work on their health (Messing *et al.*, 1993).

The bias in occupational health research is especially clear in chemical risk assessment Workers are presumed safe unless their exposure to a dangerou' ibstance exceeds what has been set as the 'safe level'. However bo. he development and the implementation of these measures have been widely criticised. Many chemicals remain untested, there is considerable doubt about the validity of some of the levels currently applied, and regulatory mechanisms are often rudimentary (Doyal *et al.*, 1983, Ch. 3). All occupational health and safety experts are therefore operating to a considerable extent in the dark, especially when the workers are women.

The United States is still the major centre in the world for toxicity testing and the chemicals in question are usually tested on 'average' white male workers. Hence safe exposure levels rarely take into account the physiology of the large, the small, the old, the ill, the young, or those who are just healthy women. Females may be affected differently by a particular substance because they have a different weight, metabolism and fat distribution. Their response may also be influenced by the functioning of their reproductive systems, but as yet we know very little about this relationship.

Researchers have been concerned for some time to determine whether or not menstruation interferes with women's capacity to work. They have been much less interested in how women's work affects their experiences of menstruation (Harlow, 1986). It is known that cold can cause menstrual problems, as can exposure to certain substances including carbon disulphide (used in spinning rayon), the hormones used in the manufacture of oral contraceptives, and lead styrene (used in the making of polystyrene) (Harlow, 1986; Mergler and Vézina, 1985). However we need much more information about the relationship between women's body chemistry – including menstruation and lactation – and their exposure to occupational hazards (Messing *et al.*, 1993).

This failure to take the occupational health of women seriously is reflected in the methods used to determine appropriate standards for physical working conditions such as temperature, as well as maximum weights to be lifted (ibid., p. 50). If these are to be appropriate they need to take into account both the physical stressors women experience at work and those they return to at home. It is also significant that few manufacturers produce protective clothing or devices suited to women's size and shape. As a result many are either denied jobs because they 'cannot be protected' or face additional hazards from ill-fitting protective clothing (Kaplan and Knutson, 1980).

Because women's employment is still not taken seriously, any hazards it may pose for their health are often ignored. Such complacency is reinforced by the increasing importance of women as a cheap and flexible source of labour. Despite their changing circumstances, women continue to be seen predominantly as mothers. Hence the potential threats posed by employment to their unborn children are often taken more seriously than those affecting women themselves.

Reproductive Risks: Counting the Future Cost

Concern that waged work would destroy women's capacity for successful motherhood was widespread during the nineteenth century in those countries where the industrial revolution brought women into factory work. Indeed it was concern for their children – both born and unborn – that provided the major impetus for the first phase of protective legislation enacted during the Victorian era. However it was not until the latter part of the century that physical evidence of these risks began to emerge. In 1897 a study of 77 English females in the lead industry found that they had produced only 61 living children between them (Rom, 1976, p. 543).

This early research led several countries to implement special regulations prohibiting women from working in the lead industry, and these were later extended to other areas of employment. However protective legislation has not solved the problem of exposure to reproductive hazards, either in the lead industry or elsewhere. It is clear that a wide range of agents still have a serious impact on reproductive health (Hatch, 1984; Lindbohm *et al.*, 1985; Rosenberg *et al.*, 1987; Stein and Hatch, 1986). Indeed it seems likely that the risks may be growing as women encounter new chemicals not just in the workplace but in the home, in food and other consumer products, and in the physical environment surrounding them (Lindbohm *et al.*, 1985).

Evidence is still limited but we know that reproductive damage can be caused before conception, during pregnancy and during lactation, and the effects may not show up until some time after birth. Both male and female reproductive systems can be affected. At the earliest phase of the reproductive cycle, toxic chemicals can lead to sexual dysfunction through loss of libido and impotence, and can also damage the sperm or the egg. They can lead to infertility in both men and women, making it difficult either for conception to occur or for a live baby to be produced.

We know for instance that parental exposure to vinyl chloride and anaesthetic gases is associated with an increased incidence of spontaneous abortions (Infante *et al.*, 1976). Similarly a series of Finnish studies have shown that women working with organic solvents in the metal industry, in laundries, in dry cleaning and in pharmaceutical factories have an increased risk of miscarriage (Hemminki *et al.*, 1980; Lindbohm *et al.*, 1993, pp. 67–8). In Finland a study among hospital staff involved in sterilising instruments found an increased risk of spontaneous abortion among those using ethylene oxide (Hemminki *et al.*, 1982).

The literature on the effects of maternal exposure to chemicals on subsequent child health is also extensive. Female industrial and construction workers in Finland have an increased risk of bearing children with central nervous system malformations (Hemminki *et al.*, 1981; Holmberg, 1978) while Swedish studies also found high rates among women in chemical laboratories (Meirik *et al.*, 1979; Strandberg *et al.*, 1978). Increased rates of spontaneous abortion, reduced birth-weight and malformations have been noted in women working in or living in close proximity to a Swedish lead-arsenic smelter (Nordstrom *et al.*, 1979a, 1979b).

In many countries this evidence has been ignored. Where action has been taken it has rarely involved changes in the workplace. Instead protective legislation has been enacted to prevent women from working in conditions where they might endanger their offspring. Individual employers too have begun actively to exclude pregnant or even fertile women from potentially hazardous circumstances.

In 1978 five women employed at the Willow Island plant of the American Cynamid Corporation submitted to sterilisation in order to keep their jobs. A year earlier the company had stated that all fertile women working in lead-exposed areas would have to be transferred to other tasks with lower earning potential or lose their job completely. This was to protect any unborn child from harm and to protect the company from possible law suits. As one of the women explained, 'They don't have to hold a hammer to your head – all they have to do is tell you that's the only way you can keep your job' (Scott, 1984, p. 180).

In many countries the introduction of equal rights laws has highlighted the contradictions inherent in protective legislation and led to concerns about both its effectiveness and its equity. Critics have pointed out that it has been used very selectively so that women are excluded from some jobs but allowed to continue in others that are equally dangerous but are considered the proper province of women (Bayer, 1982; Covell and Refshauge, 1986; Petchesky, 1979). Many jobs in the medical field, for instance, involve both reproductive hazards and shift work, yet there has been no suggestion that women should not be doing them. Moreover legislation that excludes women but leaves men exposed can provide only partial protection for the foetus. Current laws therefore protect the existing division of labour between men and women but are ineffective in preventing damage to potential mothers and fathers and their children.

Occupational Stress and Gender: Adding Insult to Injury

So far we have concentrated mainly on the physical hazards imposed by waged work. However it is widely recognised that employment can also impose psychological costs. The 1970s and 1980s saw a growth of interest in the measurement of occupational 'stress' and its implications for health, though few of these studies paid attention to the particular experiences of women (Haw, 1982). This gap is now beginning to be filled, as researchers examine the stressors women are likely to encounter in their working lives (Baruch *et al.*, 1987; Frankenhaueser *et al.*, 1991).

Pressures of Work

The conditions under which many women are employed have already been identified as stressful in studies of men. That is to say, they are poorly paid, low status jobs that make high demands but offer little opportunity for control. Most factory work fits into this category since it involves monotonous, uncreative, rigid tasks with a high level of supervision, sometimes carried out by machines. 'High strain' jobs of this kind have been shown to cause dissatisfaction and distress and to have a negative impact on men's health (Karasek, 1979; Karasek *et al.*, 1981, 1982). In the past few years a number of studies have suggested that they may have the same effect on women (Haynes, 1991; Haynes *et al.*, 1987).

A recent study of several thousand Swedish women found that those doing hectic, monotonous work with little control over their hours or conditions of employment were significantly more likely than their fellows to suffer from alcohol-related or gastro-intestinal illness or to be hospitalised as a result of a heart attack (Alfredsson *et al.*, 1985). Similar findings came from a Finnish study of metal fabrication workers, where cardiovascular disease doubled among both women and men with high levels of job strain (Haan, 1985). Even more striking results are now available from the Framingham Heart Study in the United States. Over a ten-year period women with 'high strain' jobs had nearly three times more chance of developing coronary heart disease than a comparable group employed in other jobs (Haynes *et al.*, 1987; LaCroix and Haynes, 1987).

Workers who have direct responsibility for the fate of others often report more distress than those dealing only with the manipulation of inanimate objects. Again, this affects women in particular since so many are either in 'caring' jobs or are expected to take on the mothering role in other workplaces. Recent research suggests that helping others – or being unable to do so – often has a greater impact on women's mental health than on men's (Barnett and Marshall, 1991). The ability to help people may counterbalance a number of negative factors in a job, and the inability to do so may be devastating: 'The hassles at work are all the more intolerable if I can't help someone' (Barnett and Marshall, 1991, p. 122).

In many of the service jobs done by women there are particular pressures generated by the requirement to be nice to people. Arlie Hochschild has documented these effects in her work on Delta airline stewardesses. Her analysis shows that these women are expected to sell their 'emotional labour' – to pretend to have positive feelings they are not experiencing and to deny their negative responses in order to make passengers feel they are being cared for in a safe and convivial place (Hochschild, 1983, p. 7). This often results in what she calls emotional dissonance: 'There are many sources of stress . . . but there is also a general source of stress,. . . a thread woven through the whole work experience: the task of managing an estrangement between self and feeling and between self and display' (ibid., p. 131).

For many this can lead to 'burn-out', and loss of self as feelings and emotions are dulled as a defence against an intolerable situation. One result of this can be loss of sexual desire as the stewardesses become estranged from the female role they play for the company. Hochschild suggests that this can be seen as a 'pre-political form of protest against the over-extension and over-use of their traditional femininity'. 'Burn-out' in various forms is also common among women in other female-dominated occupations such as social work and teaching (Otto, 1986).

It is clear that the types of jobs women do, the expectations that others have of them and that they have of themselves, can all make the workplace a stressful environment. This is often exacerbated by what has come to be called 'sexual harassment'. This term was first coined around 1975 to describe a range of behaviours that form part of the working conditions of most women. Abusive behaviour by men has always been a problem for working women, as historical evidence shows (Bularzik, 1978). However it was not until the second wave of feminism in the 1970s that it was identified as a public issue.

The scope of this distressing behaviour can be very broad, ranging from nude calendars on the wall through sexual jokes and propositions to unwanted touching and caressing and even rape. The vast majority of incidents involve women being harassed by men, very often those in a position of authority over them. As a result many victims have to choose between sexual harassment and lack of promotion, low pay or even loss of their jobs. Sexual politics were made very clear at one clothing factory or 'maquiladora' on the Mexican–American border:

During the first years of the maquiladora program, sexual harassment was especially blatant. There were ingenieros who insisted on
having only the prettiest women under their command. They
developed a sort of factory 'harem'. Sandra knew of a man –
'would you believe this?' – who wanted as much female diversity as
possible. All of the women on his crew, at his request had eyes and
hair of a different color. Another man boasted that every women on
his line had borne him a child (Fernandez Kelly, 1984, p. 241).

South African women interviewed after a strike in a textile factory in
1973 indicated that sexual harassment was high on their list of
complaints.

The women reported that the men workers in their factory have no
respect for them. On the factory floor they ill treat women, make
fools of them and become vulgar by 'touching the women in
embarrassing parts'. Others mentioned that the men assault the
women that they work with, one noting that if this is reported to the
authorities the latter take the part of the men (Berger, 1983, p. 228).

There has been little systematic research on the impact of these
experiences on women's well-being. However the Working Women's
Institute in the United States documented the health effects reported by
women who wrote to them for help in harassment cases (Crull, 1984, p.
107). Nearly half reported a deterioration in their work performance
with many doubting their own abilities and even their career choice.
Others reported that harassment exacerbated existing hazards either
because those involved were not concentrating properly, or because the
men in question were deliberately behaving in a dangerous way.
Virtually all the women reported at least one symptom of distress,
with anxiety, depression, anger, guilt and fear being common. For
many this resulted in physical symptoms such as sleeplessness, sexual
and eating problems, nausea, tiredness and headaches. One woman
said: 'I would vomit every day before going to work and I was so tired
that even the smallest job seemed like too much effort. I really knew
something was wrong when I had an accident driving to work for the
night shift (Crull, 1984, p. 109). Many reported using alcohol and
tranquillisers in an attempt to cope and about 25 per cent of the sample
had sought medical help. Other studies have reported very similar
findings (Gruber and Bjorn, 1982; US Merit Systems Protection Board,
1981).

None of this research has been tightly controlled to show a cause and effect relationship between sexual harassment añd health problems. However the woman who is harassed at work is in a classically stressful situation. She does not want this interference in her life but equally she may not want to risk her job. Thus her only choice is to remain in a constant state of vigilance, and research has shown that a chronic stress response of this kind can lead to long-term physical problems such as high blood pressure, ulcers or heart disease. In addition, mental health problems may well result from the need to deny fear, suppress anger and cope with the irrational guilt that so many harassed women feel.

Low Status, High Stress

We have identified a number of factors that may potentially cause distress to women in their working lives. There are no statistics indicating the extent of such distress but a survey by the National Association of Working Women in the United States suggests that it may be very high. More than 40 000 American women in a wide range of jobs returned a detailed questionnaire. Only 5 per cent of these respondents said that their job was not at all stressful. For 62 per cent work was 'somewhat stressful' and for 33 per cent 'very stressful' (Working Woman, 1984).

Although women in jobs with the greatest responsibility reported the most stress, it was those with the least say over their working lives who suffered the worst effects. Of those women doing pressurised jobs without authority or control, 59 per cent suffered frequently from severe fatigue (compared with 35 per cent of those not doing such jobs). Nearly half the women whose work was uninteresting or unchallenging regularly felt exhausted at the end of the day. Twenty-three per cent had recurrent digestive problems, 30 per cent felt depressed and more than a third had recently been treated by a physician for one or more related symptoms. In comparison women who felt positively challenged by their work reported much better health.

These findings cast doubt on the widespread belief that it is only male members of the elite who suffer from work-related distress. In fact it is lower status jobs of the kind that most women occupy that appear to be particularly stressful. We can explore this in more detail by looking at two jobs – nursing and clerical work. Despite their benign image both can expose women to physical as well as psychological stressors.

Jobs Fit for Women?

It is widely believed that 'female' jobs are neither physically hazardous nor particularly stressful. Recent research has illustrated the fallacy of both these assumptions. Though nursing and clerical work are often seen as 'soft options', they continue to put the health of millions of women at risk.

Do Nurses Need Nursing?

About 90 per cent of all nurses are women. Though the content of nursing work varies between societies, the universal element is care of those in need (Holden and Littlewood, 1991). Many women gain a great deal of satisfaction from this labour, but some damage their own health in the process of caring (Rogers and Salvage, 1988). As we shall see, nurses working in hospitals face hazards similar to those in industry, yet health and safety legislation has rarely been extended from the factory to the ward.

Accidents are common in health work, especially those caused by lifting heavy patients. There are controls over the weight women can lift in industrial settings, but no such regulations exist in health care and appropriate equipment is rarely available. In Britain this is estimated to cause the loss of at least 764 000 working days each year from back problems (Rogers and Salvage, 1988, p. 123). Many nurses report puncture wounds and cuts while wet floors and crowded spaces can cause injuries, not just among nurses but among other women working in hospital kitchens and laundries. There is no accurate recording of these accidents but according to the United States Department of Labor occupational injury and illness is 55 per cent higher among hospital workers than among those in other service industries (Coleman and Dickinson, 1984, p. 44).

Nurses are also at risk from toxic chemicals. Antibiotics, detergents, disinfectants and sterilising fluids can all be a threat to health. They can lead to skin irritation or dermatitis and in some cases to more long-term problems. Therapeutic drugs such as penicillin and streptomycin are potential sensitisers that can eventually produce severe allergic reactions. Even more seriously, the cytotoxic drugs used to treat cancer patients can not only cause local toxic or allergic reactions, but are themselves carcinogenic and teratogenic (Lindbohm *et al.*, 1993). Yet adequate precautions are not always taken to protect those nurses and doctors who administer them (Falk *et al.*, 1979). Anaesthetic gases can lead to headaches, irritability and depression and have also been implicated in the causation of spontaneous abortions and birth defects (Edling, 1980; Vessey and Nunn, 1980).

Finally, nurses may also be at risk from radiation. In many hospitals, records are kept of the exposure levels of radiologists and radiographers but not of nurses and other technicians. Much of this risk occurs outside the X-ray department: nurses can be exposed to scatter from portable X-ray machines when positioning patients and from patients with cobalt or radium implants. Thus nursing can be a hard and dangerous job, as traditional risks such as infection are combined with the new hazards accompanying high technology medicine.

It can also be psychologically stressful (Marshall, 1980; Smith, 1992). As we saw earlier, the task of caring for others can exert a powerful influence on women's mental health in both positive and negative ways. Different types of nursing vary in their psychological impact, with certain specialties involving more potentially stressful tasks than others. Different work settings will also have more or less supportive cultures. However all nurses take on a significant degree of responsibility for managing the emotional as well as the physical needs of others.

Pam Smith has transferred Arlie Hochschild's notion of emotional labour from air hostesses to nurses in an attempt to understand the nature of this work. She documents the way in which some nurses have to suppress very powerful feelings of their own in order to promote the well-being of those they are caring for.

> They think 'Oh yea, you're a nurse, you can manage'. But you can't really. . . . Outwardly you might be managing, but you know I used to go home and cry my eyes out sometimes. It was dreadful. But I've found that at work you've almost got to be, well people expect you to be happy and not cross. And you can't be cross even though you feel like wringing someone's neck (Smith, P., 1992, p. 14).

The inevitable pressures of caring for others can be handled positively with appropriate training and support. However they can also be extremely damaging as many nurses struggle with little help to maintain their own well-being. As one British psychiatric nurse expressed it:

> We have no way of escaping . . . and sometimes if I've put a lot of effort in and they demand more and more then it begins to feel like

'You're taking my blood' – and it's not good to get into that position where you feel you've given someone a pound of flesh (Handy, 1991, p. 827).

Nurses are expected to take a great deal of responsibility for patient care but few have ultimate control over their work. Too often they continue to be seen as the 'handmaidens' of doctors with their working lives heavily supervised by nursing superiors, managers and medical staff (Gamarnikow, 1991; Game and Pringle, 1984, Ch. 5; Salvage, 1985). Even where their skills and knowledge are greater they may have to 'defer' to those with higher status. A recent study of Canadian nurses found that the degree of control they had over their work was significantly associated with their job satisfaction and well-being (McLaney and Hurrell, 1988).

In many parts of the world, reductions in public expenditure have increased the pressure on nurses over the last decade. Both hospitals and community services are often understaffed so that the pace of work is speeded up for individual nurses, who feel unable to care adequately for their patients (Glazer, 1988). The continuing financial constraints on the British health service have meant a damaging degree of overload for many nurses.

Practical work conditions left me feeling pressured and stressed. . . . Ironically, it is because I wanted to remain 'caring' that I left nursing. Trying to care in the present system was a little like being flung in at the deep end with weights round my neck and told to swim. I think many nurses are in fact drowning, not waving, even if they have fixed smiles on their faces (*Medicine in Society*, 1983, p. 21).

Similar testimonies can be found from nurses in the United States:

My first nursing job was on a forty bed medical ward in one of New York City's municipal hospitals. I had a lot of responsibility for my patients . . . I quickly learned that unless my day was organised with clockwork routine and precise time allotments, I would soon fall behind. Then I would feel panic set in as things began to go wrong – an intravenous line that went dry, a medication error or omission, a forgotten promise to a patient . . . I'd begin to cut corners, hoping that there would be no serious repercussions, that no-one would die, that no-one would find out (Coleman and Dickinson, 1984, p. 37).

The stress of nursing is evidenced by the very high rates of turnover and drop-out found in many countries. In the United States it was formally demonstrated in a study by the National Institutes for Occupational Safety and Health (NIOSH), which ranked 130 occupations according to their incidence of mental health problems. Licensed practical nurses, nursing aides and registered nurses were ranked 3, 10 and 27 respectively (Colligan *et al.*, 1977).

'My Boss Gets on My Nerves': The Hidden Hazards of Office Work

In many parts of the world clerical work has been the fastest growing occupational category over the last decade. In the United States some 80 per cent of clerical workers are women and about one third of all women workers are in clerical jobs. Other industrialised countries show very similar trends, with more women now employed in offices than in any other single workplace. Again, recent research has shattered complacency about 'female' jobs with the identification of significant physical hazards in what had been assumed to be a safe environment (Craig, 1981; Fleishman, 1984; Stellman and Henifin, 1989).

Offices are often ill designed and badly constructed, with little attention paid to the health of occupants. Unsuitable lighting, inadequate temperature and ventilation control, excessive noise and poorly constructed seating can all have deleterious effects on health, especially in the long term. There is also growing evidence of chemical hazards in the office. Solvents and correcting and cleaning fluids can cause dermatitis, eye and skin irritation, dizziness, headaches and allergic reactions. Some of the major correcting fluids contain perchloroethylene or 1.1.1 trichloroethane, which are suspected of causing cancer, while carbonless copy forms emit formaldehyde – an irritant and possible carcinogen (Fleishman, 1984).

Office machinery can also be hazardous to health. The use of photocopying machines involves exposure to several chemicals used mainly as cleaners and toners. Many of these are known to carry a significant risk if recommended exposure levels are exceeded (Stellman, 1977). Some photocopying machines also emit ozone – a highly toxic gas that can cause nervous system, lung and genetic damage. Energy conservation policies have led to the tighter sealing of buildings, trapping chemical hazards inside. Although toxic exposure in offices usually occurs at levels traditionally considered safe, the effects over a working life are not yet understood.

In recent years millions of women have also begun to use video display units (VDUs), often for a very high percentage of their working time (Westlander and Magnusson, 1988). For some, these machines have caused significant health problems (Henifin, 1984; Marschall and Gregory, 1983). Seven studies in the United States all found greater health problems among VDU users than among those not using the machines (Haynes, 1991, p. 161). There have been frequent reports of sore and tired eyes, prickling and burning sensations, twitching of the eye muscles and conjunctivitis. Staring at a VDU for many hours without sufficient breaks can also lead to nausea, headaches and digestive problems (Haynes *et al.*, 1987; Henifin, 1984).

VDU operators are one of the groups most likely to suffer from a syndrome that has come to be called repetitive strain injury (RSI). This term was first used in Australia in the mid 1970s to describe the condition of workers suffering from pain and stiffness in particular muscles as a result of their repetitive use or the maintenance of constrained positions (London Hazards Centre, 1988; National Occupational Health and Safety Commission, 1986). Symptoms include fatigue, weakness, pain, muscle tightness, swelling and pins and needles. Feelings of frustration and depression also appear to be common, with RSI being found most often among those who have least control over their work.

Many women with symptoms of RSI have experienced serious difficulties in getting their problems understood and accepted by doctors, causing further frustration and distress (Ewan *et al.*, 1991). As a result the symptoms of RSI can affect all aspects of their life, sending them on a 'pilgrimage of pain' in search of relief (Reid *et al.*, 1991).

As well as concerns about health problems resulting from the use of VDUs, there have also been reports about the ill effects of working near the machines. Clusters of adverse reproductive outcomes have been reported in a number of different workplaces, including the *Toronto Star* newspaper, the Southern Bell Telephone Company in Atlanta and the public library in Aarhus, Denmark (De Matteo, 1985). Attempts to explore these further have come up with contradictory results. Two Swedish studies found no relationship between VDU use and risk of miscarriage, while a study of 60 000 Canadian women had similar negative results (Ericson and Källen, 1986a, 1986b; McDonald *et al.*, 1986). However research among 1500 pregnant women in the United States found a significantly higher risk of miscarriage among those who reported using VDUs for more than 20 hours a week during the first three months of pregnancy (Goldhaber *et al.*, 1988).

Although some women are beginning to move on from clerical and secretarial jobs to more senior positions, many are restricted to dead-end jobs with little chance of promotion. They are often expected to take on considerable responsibility but are not recognised or paid accordingly. Again this 'job strain' appears to be reflected in their health. US research has shown that women in clerical jobs have significantly higher rates of coronary heart disease than other women (Haynes and Feinleib, 1980). Those most at risk have an unsupportive boss, lack of job change over a ten-year period, and difficulty in expressing anger.

Conclusion

We have seen that there is a complex relationship between women's waged work and their health. On the one hand it can provide much needed material resources and the psychological benefits of improved status and greater independence, as well as important networks of social support. However many women may have to purchase these benefits at the price of exposure to serious hazards, potential threats to their reproductive capacities, and considerable mental and physical distress. Any attempt to evaluate the health effects of waged work on particular groups of women will need to take these complex processes into account.

It is also clear that waged work cannot be separated from the rest of women's lives. The boundaries of work and home are more permeable for women than for men and their mental and physical health will be moulded by their experiences as waged workers, parents and partners. Each area of life will have its own positive or negative effects, but they also interact together. In some circumstances the combination will be health promoting as resources and support from one part of a woman's life compensate for difficulties in another. However in other circumstances it will create conflict and contradictions that are not conducive to well-being. As more women enter the labour force it becomes increasingly urgent for further research to clarify these issues through an exploration of the relationships between working women's health and their experiences of daily life.

Further Reading

Bullock, S. (1994) *Women and Work* (London: Zed Books). A general introduction to global trends in women's work. Within the broad framework of women and development, it provides an overview of female labour and of women's initiatives to improve their circumstances.

Chavkin, W. (ed.) (1984) *Double Exposure: women's health hazards on the job and at home* (New York: Monthly Review Press). An American collection surveying the health hazards facing women working inside and outside the home. It includes case studies of a number of different occupations as well as lucid debates on policy issues.

Frankenhaueser, M., Lundberg, U. and Chesney, M. (eds) (1991) *Women, Work and Health: stress and opportunities* (New York: Plenum Press). An international compendium of articles exploring the relationship between women's paid employment and their health. Three of the articles are particularly useful since they provide overviews of current research in important areas: Barnett, R. and Marshall, N., 'The relationship between women's work and family roles and their subjective well-being and psychological distress'; Haynes, S., 'The effect of job demands, job control and new technologies on the health of employed women: a review'; and Waldron, I., 'Effects of labor force participation on sex differences in mortality and morbidity'.

Stellman, J. and Henifin, M. (1989) *Office Work can be Dangerous to your Health* (New York: Pantheon). A review and updated version of an earlier publication. This provides a useful summary of current information on the hazards of office work.

7

Abusing Women

Introduction

Millions of women consume legal but potentially hazardous substances every day in an attempt to ensure their own well-being and that of their families. In this chapter we explore some of the reasons behind this paradox. In particular we look at women's use of food, alcohol, cigarettes and tranquillisers, linking this with patterns of inequality and discrimination that have already emerged in earlier chapters.

Blowing Her Mind

All societies have devised a variety of artificial means for reducing stress and promoting feelings of well-being. These usually include the ingestion of mood-altering substances that may or may not be damaging to health. Traditionally it is men who have had easiest access to these resources, because of their superior purchasing power. In addition there is usually a gender bias in the social codes regulating the use of intoxicating substances. In the case of alcohol for instance, some societies condemn drunken women much more heavily than their male counterparts (Heath, 1991). This 'double standard' reflects the fact that women are often regarded not only as the caretakers of dependent children but also as the guardians of public morality (Lisansky Gomberg, 1982; Morgan, 1987). Any loss of control is perceived as either a symbolic or a real threat to the social order, and is punished accordingly.

During the postwar period many of these traditional constraints on female behaviour have begun to break down, while many women have had more income to spend on themselves. The effect of these trends on their health has been contradictory. On the one hand some women are now able to indulge in harmless pleasures that were previously monopolised by men. Moderate drinking, for example, can be pleasurable and possibly health promoting. On the other hand there is evidence that growing numbers of women are using or abusing substances in ways that pose a serious threat to their health (Ettore, 1992). The reality of their lives as workers and carers has put many women under increasing strain. In the absence of other socially accepted mechanisms for resolving tension and conflict, many are turning to addictive substances in an attempt to sustain themselves in an otherwise unsupportable environment.

Detailed evidence of these changing patterns of consumption is difficult to obtain. However it is clear that the pattern is a complex one. While women's intake of some potentially addictive substances is certainly increasing, their consumption of others remains stable, or is even declining. There is little sign of a significant increase in social problems caused by women's use of addictive substances, but there is considerable evidence of a growing health risk to women themselves.

Women's rates of alcohol abuse are not approaching those of men in any of the countries for which data are available (Wilsnack and Wilsnack, 1991). But research does show that younger women in many parts of the world are now drinking more than was the case in the past, and in Scandinavia this pattern is evident among older women too (Hammer and Vaglum, 1989). This does appear to have led to a slight increase in alcohol-related health problems in some of the developed countries and many commentators have expressed concern about the effects as this cohort of younger women get older. However men are still three or four times more likely than women to experience physical or psychological problems from drinking. They are also, of course, much more likely to hurt others as a result of their own alcohol consumption (Christensen, 1989).

Female patterns of tobacco use are very different. In many of the developed countries the gap between male and female smoking rates is rapidly diminishing as more girls than boys take up the habit (Chollat-Traquet, 1992). Current estimates suggest that by the end of the century women will outnumber men in the population of smokers in many of the developed countries, and women in the third world are also taking up the habit in increasing numbers. Unlike alcohol, there is no safe level for tobacco consumption, and it is clear that smoking will constitute a major threat to women's health over the coming decades.

Tranquillisers differ from both alcohol and cigarettes in that they have always been taken in greater quantities by women than by men. The introduction of the benzodiazepines in the early 1960s offered for the first time a socially acceptable means for millions of women to alter their consciousness – often on a daily basis over long periods. Though access was controlled by doctors, the medical profession responded enthusiastically, prescribing drugs such as valium and librium in huge quantities – twice as often for women as for men. These drugs do appear to cause less physical damage than cigarettes or heavy alcohol consumption but by the 1980s there was growing concern about dependency in long-term users. As a result there has been a decline in their consumption but women continue to be the major recipients (Ashton, 1991).

Thus the pattern of women's use of legal mood-altering substances is a complex one. In order to make it clearer, we will disentangle the potential effects of each in turn, assessing their meaning and significance in the lives of different groups of women. However it is important to begin by acknowledging that women can also damage their health through the use of a wide range of substances not normally recognised as addictive. Many appear to be dependent on coffee or over-the-counter analgesics for instance, while food can be a source of both psychological and physical problems.

Easting Her Heart Out

Food is clearly very different from the psychoactive substances usually associated with dependence. For both men and women it can be a source of intense pleasure as well as an essential element in maintaining their health. It is a basic necessity for survival and is not addictive in the orthodox medical sense. However many women have a problematic relationship with food throughout their lives. For some this can amount to an 'abuse' of food, causing significant damage to both physical and mental health.

As we have seen in earlier chapters, millions of women in third world countries and some in the developed world struggle to remain healthy without adequate nutrition. Viewed on a global scale this is certainly the most serious aspect of the problematic relationship between women and food. However we also need to consider the plight of those relatively affluent women who are obsessed with food, caught in a never-ending cycle of dieting and over-eating which makes them feel humiliated and self-destructive (Lawrence, 1987). For some this can become a significant threat to health, with clinically diagnosed eating disorders being ten times more common among women than among men (Krahn, 1991).

The factors influencing women's relationship with food are complex (Chernin, 1983; Lawrence, 1987; Orbach, 1978, 1986). Social pressures to conform to an idealised body-image mean that many are doomed to feel like constant failures. Paradoxically only the rich can afford to be healthy and thin while poor women are often both overweight and badly nourished. If women cannot control their weight, many believe that they cannot control the rest of their lives, and their sense of their own powerlessness is reinforced. Women also report using food as a way of controlling their emotions, of eating to suppress anger or hostility (Epstein, 1987).

For many, these contradictory pressures lead not just to unhappiness and low self-esteem, but to the more extreme symptoms associated with anorexia, bulimia and compulsive eating. These are especially common among girls and young women facing what is sometimes a painful process of adolescence. One US study estimated that anything between 8 and 20 per cent of female high school and college students in the United States are now bulimic (Pope *et al.*, 1983). A 1984 national poll of American women found that only 25 per cent were 'overweight' by orthodox standards but more than 40 per cent were unhappy with their bodies and 80 per cent felt that they needed to be thin to attract men. Many had started to feel this way when they were very young. They often expressed a desperate desire to control their weight with more than 50 per cent having tried diet pills, 27 per cent liquid formula diets and 18 per cent diuretics (Anderson, 1988, p. 197).

Not surprisingly there is growing evidence of a link between these eating disorders and more traditional forms of substance use. Female patients seeking medical help with bulimia and anorexia have high rates of alcohol and other drug abuse (Krahn, 1991, p. 241). Just over a third of one group of bulimic women in the United States reported that they had a history of problems with alcohol or other drugs (Mitchell *et al.*, 1985), while half of another bulimic group had significant alcohol abuse problems (Beary *et al.*, 1986). Conversely there is a high prevalence of eating disorders among women presenting with other forms of substance abuse (Beary *et al.*, 1986; Krahn, 1991). Often these overlapping problems are related to a history of violence in women's lives.

It would appear then that many women use food along with or instead of more traditional 'drugs' to deal with complex feelings for which they have few alternative means of expression. In the following sections we explore this theme in more detail by looking at the 'big three' – alcohol, tranquillisers and cigarettes. As we shall see, all are promoted by multinational corporations with a vested interest in maintaining women's dependence. Yet many women would find it difficult to manage without them. Far from being a sign of their liberation, substance abuse is, for many, a symptom of the inequality and disadvantage that continues to characterise their daily lives.

Fallen Angels: Alcohol

Until the early 1980s the predominance of men in the population of problem drinkers meant that both research and treatment were heavily male-oriented. Most studies either excluded women from their sample or failed to use gender as a variable in the analysis (Vannicelli and Nash, 1984). Where gender issues were raised, women were simply compared with men rather than being studied in their own right. As a result the specificity of female alcohol abuse remained unexplored and those women having the courage to seek treatment were offered therapies geared to male needs (Ettore, 1992).

Over the past decade or so this pattern has begun to change, as women with drinking problems have become increasingly visible (Wilsnack and Wilsnack, 1991). Male stereotypes have been challenged both by problem drinkers themselves and by some researchers, and preliminary studies have identified a number of factors frequently associated with female alcohol abuse. It appears that many women drink heavily to relieve feelings of helplessness, powerlessness, ineffectiveness and lack of self-esteem in the face of stressful life events (Beckman, 1980; Reed, 1985; Snell *et al.*, 1987). More research is needed to relate these characteristics to the concrete reality of women's lives, but certain important clues are beginning to emerge.

First we know that in most societies women are more likely than men to abuse alcohol at home (Corrigan and Butler, 1991). This may indicate a continuation of the double standard whereby women drinkers are more severely stigmatised than their male counterparts as well as reflecting women's lack of transport and other factors necessary for access to the public domain. We also know that their responsibilities continue to confine many women within a stressful domestic environment which may in itself contribute to their alcohol abuse. True, an American woman attributed her problem drinking to her home circumstances:

> I took to buying a bottle of wine at the 7-Eleven every day, then drinking the whole thing all by myself in the evening. It made me feel

less empty and less lonely. The loneliness was really beginning to get to me. I had gotten married to escape from loneliness and here I was lonelier than ever (Sandmaier, 1992, p. 116).

Many women have their drinking reinforced by a male partner who is himself an alcohol abuser (Hammer and Vaglum, 1989; Jacob and Bremer, 1986; Wilsnack and Wilsnack, 1991, pp. 149–50). Drinking then becomes an important and sometimes immutable part of the central relationship in their lives. It is also increasingly clear that a significant proportion of women with drinking problems have experienced incest or sexual abuse at some point in their lives (Rohsenow *et al.*, 1988; Swett *et al.*, 1991). One survey in the United States found that twice as many problem drinkers (23 per cent) as non-problem drinkers (10 per cent) reported having been sexually abused before the age of 18 (Wilsnack and Wilsnack, 1991, p. 149).

A number of different factors in women's domestic lives may therefore contribute to their unhealthy drinking. For many, these problems will be relieved by the companionship and greater independence offered by waged work (Wilsnack and Cheloha, 1987). However employment may increase the likelihood of alcohol-related problems for others (Wilsnack *et al.*, 1984). Those who work in male-dominated occupations are especially likely to drink heavily (Hammer and Vaglum, 1989; La Rosa, 1990).

The need to understand the specificity of the female route to alcohol abuse is made more urgent by the recognition that women are more susceptible than men to psychological and physical damage from drinking (Dunne, 1988). Since women's bodies are, on average, smaller than men's and have a higher proportion of fat to water, alcohol becomes more concentrated in their bodily fluids. They are more prone than men to liver disease, digestive and nutritional problems, and brain damage, and appear to develop alcohol-related disease earlier than men with the same levels of intake. Hence women who are dependent on alcohol may be putting their health at greater risk than their male counterparts, especially if they combine drinking with the use of tranquillisers. Though the risk is sometimes over-emphasised, women also have to face the possibility that drinking during pregnancy may damage their unborn child. Each year in the United States at least 300000 infants are born with alcohol-related defects of some degree of severity (Little and Wendt, 1991, p. 187).

Despite these obvious problems women often find it difficult to get help with alcohol abuse. They are less likely than men to receive encouragement from their families to seek counselling. This may be due in part to the stigma still attached to female drinkers and by extension to their families. However it may also reflect the relatively low level of disruption female drinkers cause. Many women with drinking problems remain largely invisible and hence are unlikely to be offered help.

The structure of the services themselves may also contribute to women's reluctance to use them (Beckman, 1984; Duckert, 1989). For those with dependants, residential programmes may be inappropriate and some will not have the money to pay. Many will not feel confident in a male-dominated environment and they are often pressed into traditional female roles with their treatment needs subordinated to those of men (Duckert, 1989). Research in the United States has identified particular problems faced by black women seeking help in predominantly white environments (Amaro *et al.*, 1987). Similarly, many Native American and Australian Aboriginal women have been damaged by alcohol but there are very few services designed to meet their needs (Asetoyer, 1993).

This brief exploration of female patterns of alcohol abuse has shown that women may drink in different ways and for different reasons than men, and the effects on their health may be different. Hence their treatment needs may also be gender-specific. It has also indicated that female drinkers are themselves a heterogeneous group and more research is needed to identify the complex reality of their use and abuse of alcohol. As we shall see, detailed information on women's consumption of tranquillisers also remains to be collected but similar themes can already be observed.

A Pill for Every Ill

Chlordiazepoxide (or librium), the first of the new breed of minor tranquillisers, was introduced in 1960, followed by diazepam (or valium) in 1963. Since they were more effective and less dangerous than their predecessors, the barbiturates, both were soon prescribed on a huge scale. Throughout the 1970s librium and valium were the most widely prescribed drugs in the world (Ray, 1991, p. 140).

During this 'benzodiazepine era' one in every ten US adults was using valium or librium at any given moment, with the volume of tranquilliser prescriptions rising by 78 per cent between 1964 and 1970 (Silverman and Lee, 1974, p. 293). A similar increase occurred in the United Kingdom. By 1975 one in five of all National Health Service prescriptions were for minor tranquillisers, of which 70 per cent were for librium or valium (Ray, 1991, p. 140). Though consumption fell markedly during the 1980s, the number of people taking tranquillisers remains high. Long-term users form a 'hard core' and many are now dependent on a regular supply of drugs from their doctor.

Throughout this period it is women who have been the major consumers of benzodiazepines. In Europe and North America women are about twice as likely as men to be prescribed tranquillisers (Ashton, 1991). One cross-national study carried out in 1980 found the highest rate of psychotropic drug use in Belgium, where about 13 per cent of men and 21 per cent of women used them regularly to sleep or to control anxiety (Balter *et al.*, 1984). Use is especially high among older women (Glantz and Backenheimer, 1988; Harding, 1986). In the United Kingdom 60 per cent of benzodiazepine prescriptions are written for women over 40, and 40 per cent go to those over 65 (Glantz and Backenheimer, 1988; Taylor, 1987).

Why are women so consistently overrepresented among the recipients of minor tranquillisers? We can begin to answer this question by looking at the gender issues inherent in those medical consultations where tranquillisers are prescribed. First we examine the basis upon which doctors appear to make their treatment decisions and then we explore women's own accounts of their use of tranquillisers.

The Politics of Prescribing

Most critics of the 'tranquilliser epidemic' have focused on the actions of individual doctors as the cause of the problem. They emphasise the role of medical practice in the control of women, arguing that doctors prescribe tranquillisers for women they see as 'neurotic' rather than attempting to resolve the underlying cause of any distress (Edwards, 1988, Ch. 6; Illich, 1977; Zola, 1975). As a result doctors are able to demonstrate their competence, docile women continue to perform their daily tasks and the profits of the pharmaceutical industry are maintained.

There is certainly some evidence to confirm the belief that doctors operate with stereotypes of appropriate 'male' and 'female' behaviour. In this, they are of course no different from most of their fellow citizens, but their beliefs are particularly important since their actions can help to maintain a woman in a situation that is ultimately damaging to her health. We know from a classic study carried out in the late 1960s that many clinicians in the United States have very different conceptions of a 'normal healthy woman' and a 'normal healthy man'. The 'male' characteristics approximate to the social stereotype of a healthy person and the 'female' ones reflect sickness and instability (Broverman *et al.*, 1970). Other research has shown that when doctors are confronted with similar 'cases', they are more likely to attribute symptoms in women to psychological causes and those in men to physical problems (Bernstein and Kane, 1981; Miles, 1991, pp. 151–61; Verbrugge and Steiner, 1981; Verbrugge, 1984).

There is also evidence that despite doctors' inclination to attribute more psychosomatic problems to female patients, women who consult a general physician tend to receive more tests and treatment than their male counterparts (Verbrugge and Steiner, 1981). Women may represent their problems as more serious, doctors may feel less able to deny treatment to the 'weaker sex', or they may simply want to get rid of them. Whatever the factors involved, both participants will feel pressured to find a cure, and if mental distress is the presenting problem, a pill may seem to be the only solution.

Such decisions will often be reinforced by the techniques used to sell tranquillisers. During the late 1960s and early 1970s women featured in the majority of advertisements and were consistently represented as the most suitable recipients of psychotropic drugs (Prather and Fidell, 1986). They were presented as less serious than men, they were sometimes pictured in alluring poses and were often defined as irritating in their distress – as a problem for doctor and family alike. While the style of these advertisements has changed over the past decade, women are still used more often than men to sell tranquillisers (Prather, 1991, pp. 121–2).

The precise effect of this advertising on doctors' prescribing habits is difficult to assess. However it appears to play a significant part in alerting some physicians to new products on the market while at the same time suggesting women as the most appropriate recipients. In one recent study of the marketing of a new tranquilliser, 68 per cent of doctors who prescribed the drug said that they had first heard about it from commercial sources, and 59 per cent said promotional materials were the most important influence on their decision (Peay and Peay, 1988, p. 1185). The impact of drug advertising appears to be especially great in third world countries, where there are few alternative sources of information.

The growing criticism of tranquillisers does appear to have influenced a number of doctors. A recent study in the United

Kingdom showed that younger doctors in particular were increasingly reluctant to prescribe them, preferring other approaches such as counselling when they were available (Gabe and Lipshitz-Phillips, 1986, p. 280). However doctors around the world continue to be exposed to huge quantities of promotional material, and often have few alternative treatments to offer.

Clinical decisions are therefore shaped by a variety of factors, including broad gender stereotypes, the curative and technological orientation of the biomedical model, and the specific promotional activities of the pharmaceutical industry. However these factors alone cannot explain prescribing patterns. We also need to look at what women themselves bring to the medical encounter.

Women living in developed countries make more visits to their doctors than their male counterparts (Miles, 1991, p. 63). In part this reflects their greater longevity, since tranquillisers and anti-depressants are often prescribed to help with the anxiety associated with the chronic illnesses of old age. However it is women's higher consultation rates for psychological problems that are most often associated with gender differences in psychotropic drug prescribing.

In most of the developed countries the ratio of female to male consultations for what doctors would class as neurotic or psychosocial problems varies between 2:1 and 4:1 (Weissman and Klerman, 1977). This may not of course mean that more women than men actually experience mental distress. It may also reflect an apparently greater willingness among women than among men to admit their difficulties and seek medical help. They may be encouraged to go to their doctor by the general perception of women as more 'sickly' or be driven to do so by the lack of alternative sources of support. These different factors are extremely difficult to disentangle, making it impossible to obtain any precise comparison of the 'real' levels of psychological distress experienced by men and women. However the end result is that women are more likely than men to receive a tranquilliser prescription.

Pharmacology and Social Control

According to some commentators, many of these women are given psychotropic drugs to help them continue with an otherwise intolerable life, while their labour continues to benefit those around them. In Cecil Helman's study in North London, he described the feelings of 'Mrs B', a 'housewife' aged 70 and a long-term Mogadon user:

Without the drug she gets 'bad-tempered' with her husband – very 'snappy' with him and 'all groans and moans'. With the drug she is 'nice and calm' in relation to him. Both he and her daughter know of her taking the drug: he very much approves, though her daughter is against it (Helman, 1986, p. 219).

Ruth Cooperstock and Henry Lennard heard similar stories from the Canadian women they interviewed in the late 1970s. One mother with four teenagers reported:

> I take it to protect the family from my irritability because the kids are kids. I don't think it's fair for me to start yelling at them because their normal activity is bothering me. My husband says I over-react . . . I'm an emotional person, more so than my husband, who's an engineer and very calm and logical – he thinks (Cooperstock and Lennard, 1986, p. 232).

Quotes such as these suggest that tranquillisers can be a means of keeping women in their place. As Cooperstock and Lennard point out, the few men in their study tended to use tranquillisers to cope with employment problems while the women emphasised domestic concerns, thus reinforcing a gendered division of labour. However we cannot simply write off these drugs as a 'top down' method used by doctors to control helpless patients.

Tranquillisers as a Coping Strategy

Qualitative research in this area is rare, but it does appear that not all women are passive victims. Though many are extremely ambivalent about tranquillisers they choose to go on using them as an active strategy to sustain themselves in a situation they know to be damaging, but which they also believe they cannot change. In an attempt to explore these issues further, Jonathan Gabe and Nicki Thorogood interviewed a racially mixed group of working-class women in East London (Gabe and Thorogood, 1986). Their aim was to understand the use of tranquillisers within the context of the other 'resources' available to these women in the management of their everyday tasks and problems.

The women themselves identified the major resources at their disposal as paid work, housing, social supports, leisure activities, cigarettes, alcohol and religion. Each woman's access to these resources depended on her circumstances, and in this context at least the black women tended to have more at their disposal. More had full-time jobs that they enjoyed, more had children still living at home, especially daughters whom they found particularly supportive, and more were regular churchgoers. As a group the white women had fewer of these resources. They were also significantly more likely to be users of benzodiazepines (ibid., pp. 260–1).

Among the white women, those most likely to be long-term users were divorced and did not have children living at home. Few had any opportunity for leisure, few were regular churchgoers, and those who had jobs found them unrewarding. Thus the more 'positive' resources were rarely available to long-term users. Instead many used cigarettes as well as tranquillisers to manage the stresses in their lives.

In a linked study, a group of white women using tranquillisers were asked about their attitude to the drugs. Some saw them as a lifeline without which they would be unable to carry on: 'Well the valium I've got to take haven't I really because there's no doubt I do need something. I think even you would recognise. . .' (ibid., p. 252). Others saw them as a 'standby' to be used only intermittently when problems were acute:

> Valium does help if you're that desperate but I tend if I can to do without it – I do without it as long as I can and I only take it if it's absolutely necessary. I can go three or four weeks without and then I suddenly feel this need. That's why I keep some in my bag just in case I need it (ibid., p. 252).

Few users were uncritical of tranquillisers. Most of those who saw them as a standby, and some of those who saw them as a lifeline, were ambivalent about using them. However the benefits were seen to outweigh the risks, at least at that point in their lives.

Assessing Risks and Benefits of Drug Use

In the initial euphoria after their introduction, the benzodiazepines were hailed as risk-free and non-addictive, but problems have now emerged, mostly among long-term users. Small-scale studies indicate that about 5–10 per cent of users experience significant withdrawal symptoms after six months' continuous use, 25–45 per cent after 2–4 years, and 75 per cent after 6–8 years (Williams and Bellantuono, 1991, p. 79). These effects include sleep disturbance and anxiety, irritability, muscle pain, headaches, tremors, nausea and intolerance of sound and light. Some women have reported appalling experiences in their attempts to get off large doses of tranquillisers.

> The first two weeks I stuck to the programme, so I cut down quite drastically: from 20mg down to 15mg and then from 15mg down to 10mg, and that two weeks was awful, physically and mentally – it was frightening. Some of the worst things were the changes in perception that happened, I'd be in a room and it felt like the walls were coming in and out; I couldn't see straight and everything looked distorted . . . I was shaking and sweating and had terrible muscle tension and lots of pains in different parts of my body (Wolfson and Murray, 1986).

Others have had little or no physical problems in kicking the habit, though psychological dependence can be severe.

Women's use of tranquillisers therefore remains a complex and contradictory phenomenon. On the one hand there are conditions of acute anxiety and distress in which few would argue that the short-term use of benzodiazepines would be inappropriate (Clare, 1991, p. 184). However long-term use is clearly more complicated. Some women choose to continue using the drugs as a resource for dealing with very real distress and appear to obtain some benefit. But others find that the drugs themselves become a problem, causing physical and/or psychological dependence, sometimes greater than the distress they were originally designed to alleviate. Many of the women using tranquillisers do so in response to emotional problems directly caused by their social circumstances. While the drugs may help to alleviate some of the pain, they may also perpetuate the damaging situation itself. But without them the distress may be intolerable and the situation still unchangeable. As we shall see in the next section, very similar contradictions arise in understanding women's consumption of cigarettes.

A Smoking Epidemic

Cigarettes are the single most important cause of premature death in the world today. In most of the developed countries a growing recognition of this danger has contributed to a marked decline in consumption among both sexes. However men have been quicker to abandon the habit than women, and in some countries teenage girls are taking up the habit in greater numbers than their male counterparts. In 1991 27 per cent of 15 year old girls in the United Kingdom were smokers compared with only 18 per cent of boys (Chollat-Traquet, 1992, p. 16). Recent estimates from the United States suggest that if current trends continue, the majority of US smokers will be women by the year 2000. In most third world countries the gap between male and female smoking rates remains wide. However there are certain notable exceptions, including Nepal, Papua New Guinea, Uruguay and Brazil, where women's rates are catching up with those of men (Crofton, 1990, p. 165).

As women make up a growing proportion of the smoking popula-tion, cigarettes are increasingly linked with poverty and social disadvantage. In most of the developed countries female smokers are much more likely than non-smokers to have received little education and to have a low income. In the United States this association between smoking and social disadvantage is also reflected in racial differences in smoking patterns, with black women having very high rates of tobacco consumption. In Canada too, racial differences are marked, with an astonishing 78 per cent of Inuit women being smokers (Greaves, 1987, p. 28).

In most third world countries, the proportion of women who smoke is still less than 10 per cent. However in some this figure is rising rapidly, especially among women in towns who start smoking as part of their transition to a 'modern' way of life (Chollat-Traquet, 1992). It is this group who are the major targets of the tobacco industry. In 1988 cigarette consumption fell by 1 per cent in the developed countries, but rose by 2.3 per cent in the third world, largely as a result of these promotional efforts (Crofton, 1990, p. 164). Their impact can be seen with particular clarity in urban areas of Brazil, where the rate of female smoking is rapidly overtaking that in the United States.

Thus the effects of cigarette smoking seem set to cause further damage to some of the world's unhealthiest women. In developed countries the overall decline in smoking has led to its concentration among women whose rates of morbidity and mortality are already higher than those of their compatriots. In the third world rising cigarette consumption means that many more women will be burdened with the 'diseases of affluence' while the diseases of poverty remain unresolved.

Smoking and the Diseases of Equal Opportunity

In the developed countries, smoking now kills about 300 000 women every year (Chollat-Traquet, 1992, p. 34). Millions more suffer from tobacco-related illness and disability including impairment of their reproductive potential. More and more women are succumbing to what have traditionally been regarded as 'male' problems – heart disease and lung cancer in particular. Over the next thirty years tobacco-related deaths among women will more than double, and by the year 2020 well over a million women across the world will die each year from smoking-related illness (Chollat-Traquet, 1992, p. 3). Thus women smokers are achieving an equality in death that they never attained in life (Jacobson, 1981, p. vi).

Lung cancer has traditionally been ràre among women, but many of the developed countries are now witnessing a sharp rise. Most of the victims are women who took up smoking some thirty or forty years ago in the aftermath of the Second World War. In most of the EU countries, deaths of women from cancer of the lung rose by at least 15 per cent in every five-year period between 1955 and 1988. In Japan, Scotland and the United States lung cancer now kills more women than breast cancer, and a similar pattern is emerging in England and Wales, Australia and Denmark (Chollat-Traquet, 1992, p. 42).

This represents a major increase in the cancer toll among women and it is concentrated among the underprivileged. Data from the United Kingdom confirm that class differentials in female lung cancer deaths have widened markedly since the 1970s, with the least prosperous being more than twice as likely to be affected as their more affluent counterparts (Pugh *et al.*, 1991, p. 1106). While lung cancer remains an uncommon cause of death for women in most of the third world, Brazil again provides an important exception. Brazilian women already rank fourteenth in the world in the league table of female lung cancer deaths and they are moving up rapidly.

India is the third largest producer of tobacco in the world. Consumption is increasing by about 2 per cent per year and it is estimated that about 20 per cent of all cancer morbidity in women is related to tobacco (Stanley *et al.*, 1987, p. 276). While few can afford cigarettes, many smoke water pipes, bidis or chuttas, while others chew betel quid. In some regions women practise 'reverse smoking', where the lit end of a chutta or cheroot is turned around and kept burning inside the mouth (Jacobson, 1986, p. 33; Stanley *et al.*, 1987). This is considered more 'feminine' but it is extremely dangerous. The riskiest habit of all is pan chewing combined with smoking which gives a risk of mouth cancer thirty-six times greater than that of someone who does not use tobacco at all (International Agency for Research on Cancer, 1985; Jacobson, 1986, p. 34). In the Indian cities of Madras and

Bangalore the rate of oral cancer among women is the highest in the world (Stanley *et al.*, 1987, p. 276).

The health hazards faced by smokers are also evident in their high levels of respiratory disease. These effects are often exacerbated by occupational hazards and in parts of the third world by smoke from domestic fires, which affects women in particular. About 60 per cent of women in Nepal smoke, usually cupping their hands around bidis to prevent the smoke escaping (Jacobson, 1986, p. 35). Most live in tiny houses filled with smoke and as a result more than half of Nepalese men and women are afflicted with 'cigarette lung'. Thus female smokers face the same hazards as their male counterparts, and global mortality and morbidity rates are beginning to reflect this symmetry.

However women also face additional risks associated with reproduction. As we saw in Chapter 4, smokers who use the contraceptive pill significantly increase their chance of developing cardiovascular disease. There is also an association between smoking and reduced fertility (US Department of Health and Human Services, 1989). Those who do conceive have an increased risk of spontaneous abortion, of producing low-birth-weight babies, of stillbirth, premature rupture of the membranes and preterm delivery (Berman and Gritz, 1991; Chollat-Traquet, 1992, pp. 48–9). Maternal smoking may also be linked with sudden infant death syndrome (Berman and Gritz, 1991). When their childbearing years are over, women smokers are more likely than non-smokers to have an early menopause and health problems associated with osteoporosis (Chollat-Traquet, 1992, p. 49).

Seduced into Smoking

Any attempt to understand these trends in female smoking must look at two different processes – women's initiation into the habit, and its reinforcement and maintenance. In some countries female smoking has a long history embedded in particular cultural traditions. In others recent developments may have contributed to an increase in the number of women smokers. However it is evident that whatever their circumstances women smokers have a great deal in common, and it is this shared experience that we explore here.

Most immediately, they are all targets of a very powerful industry concerned to maintain or expand the world population of smokers. Over the past 60 years or so the style and content of the industry's appeal has varied but women have frequently been in their sights (Davis, 1987; Ernster, 1985). As existing smokers give up or die off, new recruits have always been sought and women's lower levels of smoking have made them natural targets for cigarette advertisers.

During the Victorian period women's temperance movements campaigned against cigarettes as well as alcohol, and women smokers were looked on with considerable disapproval. By the early 1920s this pattern was changing as advertisements were first directed specifically at women, presenting cigarettes as a symbol of female emancipation (Greaves, 1990, p. 5). Smoking rates continued to rise during the 1930s as advertisements portrayed cigarettes as glamorous and sophisticated, and the Second World War gave a further boost as women took on male jobs as well as some traditionally male habits. This was temporarily reflected in androgynous and egalitarian advertising images, but the postwar period saw a shift back to the themes of glamour and sexual attractiveness as women were pushed back into their homes.

As the health evidence against cigarettes began to pile up in the 1960s, women were again entering the labour force in large numbers. In this changing environment, advertisements represented smoking as a source of relaxation in a stressful world as well as a sign of independence and freedom from male dominance. Yet at the same time they also continued to associate them with 'thinness' and conformity to cultural stereotypes of female beauty. In the United States the 'targeting' of women of colour has caused particular concern. Thus tobacco companies have attempted to mould their advertisements to reflect the changing aspirations and circumstances of women, but always with the ultimate aim of turning them into smokers.

Until recently women in third world countries had largely escaped the attentions of the industry. However this is beginning to change as the number of smokers declines in developed countries and some third world women have increased their disposable income. While the first wave of advertising was directed at men, women are now being drawn in behind them (Stebbins, 1991). In 1973 less than 2 per cent of Nigerian female university students smoked, but by 1982 this figure had reached 21 per cent, with much of the increase resulting from specially targeted advertising (Jacobson, 1986, p. 36). Virginia Slims Light – the first specifically 'female' brand directed at women in the third world – was launched in Hong Kong in 1984 (Jacobson, 1986).

The companies themselves claim that these advertisements are designed only to ensure brand loyalty or to attract existing smokers to their particular product. However research suggests that they have a major influence on the behaviour of young people, who form the majority of new smokers. Teenage girls in particular are encouraged by enticing images of smoking to experiment with cigarettes, and many continue the habit into adulthood (ASH Women and Smoking Group, 1990a). Many read youth publications or women's magazines that contain glossy smoking advertisements and give little information on the health risks of cigarettes. Thus potential young smokers receive mainly positive messages (ASH Women and Smoking Group, 1990b).

Why are so many young women enticed by these commercial blandishments into becoming smokers? The reasons are complex, but we can identify a number of key factors. Social acceptability makes it much more likely that a girl will take up smoking, and both family and peers can be important role models. An adolescent girl is much more likely to start smoking if one or both parents is a smoker or if older siblings smoke (ASH Women and Smoking Group, 1990a).

Psychological factors too are important. Girls with low self-esteem are more likely to start smoking than their more confident peers, using cigarettes to generate a feeling of greater maturity and a stronger sense of identity (Piepe *et al.*, 1988). Rebellion, excitement, curiosity and a desire to be 'one of the gang' are also mentioned frequently by girls explaining their initiation into the smoking culture. In more affluent parts of the world a desire to be slim also appears to be a central feature in many girls' induction into smoking (Charlton, 1989).

Smoking for Life

Once the smoking habit has been established a complex mixture of psychological, pharmacological, physical and social factors combine to maintain it. Nicotine dependence plays a major part in preventing the majority of women who would like to quit from doing so. For some the appetite suppressant effect of cigarettes also continues to be important as they strive to be thin. However it is increasingly clear that for many the major benefit of smoking is an enhanced capacity to manage the difficulties they face in their daily lives. This appears to be especially true for those disadvantaged women who now make up the majority of female smokers.

A number of studies have shown that women are more likely than men to use cigarettes to cope with negative feelings (Greaves, 1987; Wells and Batten, 1990). Instead of focusing on the pleasures of smoking they frequently describe cigarettes as a means of keeping loneliness, sadness, anger and frustration under control. As one British woman explained:

> I think smoking stops me getting so irritable. I can cope with things better. If I was economising, I'd cut down on cigarettes but I wouldn't give up. I'd stop eating . . . food just isn't that important to me but having a cigarette is the only thing I do just for myself (Graham, 1987, p. 55).

Poor women have to face more stressful life events than their affluent counterparts and often have fewer resources to deal with them. As a result many who have to manage multiple responsibilities on a low income become dependent on cigarettes as a source of support. Hilary Graham's research in the United Kingdom showed that full-time child care on a low income is especially conducive to smoking. Stopping for a cigarette seems to offer a space and a reward in a life otherwise devoted mainly to the needs and demands of others (Graham, 1987). As one young mother put it:

> A cigarette is the only pleasure you can indulge in without the kids pestering you for their share – especially if you've had no break from them for hours or days and couldn't afford to go out even if you did have a babysitter. You're tired, they're whiny, bored and awful. Ten fags may be the only pleasure you can (just) afford. They are your substitute for leisure, pleasure and ordinary adult activities (Jacobson, 1986, p. 95).

Lorraine Greaves identified similar feelings in a sample of Canadian women (Greaves, 1990). Very few of the women 'liked' smoking and most used it to organise social relationships. Some smoke to create a self-image and a sense of identity as well as a feeling of bonding with others. However the most common experience was the use of cigarettes to cope with a variety of oppressions or intrusions into their bodies or lives (Greaves, 1990, p. 906).

Many of Greaves' respondents used smoking as a distancing strategy, designed to repel interaction with others and also to defuse situations of tension or disagreement. Some stated quite clearly that they would rather blunt their feelings than experience the effects of releasing their emotions (Greaves, 1990, p. 906). Some described 'smoking back their anger' for example. Very often this internalisation of emotions reflected the powerlessness these women felt in their most intimate relationships. Cigarettes were controllable, reliable and 'always there'. Significantly, these feelings were especially important for women with abusive partners, whose lives were often insecure and unpredictable.

Not surprisingly women appear to have much less confidence than men in their ability to give up smoking. Most claim to be addicted, reflecting the lack of control they experience in so many areas of their lives. Fewer women than men get support in their efforts to give up. Indeed some report encouragement from their families to carry on smoking.

More research is needed in a variety of cultures to explore the way smoking is closely integrated into so many women's lives. But it is already evident that cigarettes represent a paradox for all women smokers. They undoubtedly pose a serious threat to their physical health yet they are a central plank in the strategy that many have devised to maintain themselves in their roles as carers and workers. Like tranquillisers, they offer women the illusion of power over their emotions. But too often they end up controlling them – or even killing them.

Conclusion

This chapter has presented a preliminary exploration of women's use of 'drugs of solace'. It has not offered a unitary explanation of all women's use of all drugs, or even all women's use of a particular drug. However it has demonstrated that a gendered understanding of women's substance use and misuse is essential if their health is to be protected.

The last few decades have seen the convergence of a number of trends. The greater purchasing power of some women and their increased access to medication has given them more opportunity to acquire a wider range of legal but potentially hazardous substances. At the same time many find themselves in circumstances that are increasingly difficult to manage without traditional networks and sources of social support. These developments have led large numbers of women to abuse one or more substances in an attempt to manage in the here-and-now – a tactic encouraged by those industries who stand to make a massive profit from women's distress.

The need to interrupt this process is urgent, as more third world women are drawn into the trap. Short-term strategies would include more culturally aware and gender-sensitive education strategies and support and treatment services, as well as tougher regulation of advertising and promotion policies. However the long-term solution will clearly involve more fundamental change in the social and economic position of women. It is these political issues that we explore in more detail in the final chapter.

Further Reading

Ashton, H. (1991) 'Psychotropic drug prescribing for women', *British Journal of Psychiatry*, vol. 158, supplement 10, pp. 30–5. A summary of current trends in the prescribing of psychotropic drugs for women in Europe and North America. It includes a useful discussion of the reasons why women are prescribed these drugs so much more often than men, and highlights the problems that follow from this.

Chollat-Traquet, C. (1992) *Women and Tobacco* (Geneva: WHO). A global overview of current trends in female smoking. Produced with the support of WHO, this book highlights the growing number of women smokers around the world and documents the likely health effects.

Gabe, J. and Thorogood, N. (1986) 'Tranquillisers as a resource', in J. Gabe and P. Williams (eds), *Tranquillisers: social, psychological and clinical perspectives* (London: Tavistock). An important study challenging the notion that all women taking psychotropic drugs are passive victims. Through interviews with a group of working-class women in London, it illustrates their use of tranquillisers as a resource for coping with the contradictions of everyday life.

Jacobson, B. (1986) *Beating the Ladykillers: women and smoking* (London: Pluto Press). A campaigning book designed to reduce the female death toll from tobacco. It explores in depth the reasons why girls and women are drawn into the smoking habit and offers a guide to women who want to quit smoking themselves or to help others to do so.

Journal of Substance Abuse, vol. 3 (1991) special issue on women and substance abuse: A wide-ranging collection describing women's use and misuse of a number of different substances. Two survey articles are especially useful: Berman, B. and Gritz, E., 'Women and smoking: current trends and issues for the 1990s'; and Wilsnack, S. and Wilsnack, R., 'Epidemiology of women's drinking'.

8

Women's Movements for Health

Introduction

Preceding chapters have documented the economic, social and cultural constraints on women's capacity to realise their potential for health. However we caught only glimpses of the myriad of strategies they have adopted in response. In this concluding chapter the spotlight is firmly fixed on these struggles for health. Most women spend much of their lives involved in health promotion activities. But a few go further, taking collective action to promote health through social change. It is this complex mosaic of women's health politics that will be examined here.

The Global Politics of Women's Health

Health care was a major concern of second wave feminists in North America, Australia, New Zealand and Europe. However its political importance has now diminished in many of these countries, along with the decline of grassroots feminism itself. The centre of gravity of women's health politics has shifted to the third world, where campaigns have become increasingly vigorous in the face of recession, structural adjustment policies and widespread environmental deterioration. Latin America in particular has a very powerful and growing tradition of women's health advocacy and Asian organisations are also growing rapidly. Campaigners for women's health now represent a significant political reality in many parts of the world and their voices have grown stronger over the past decade.

As well as spreading to many different countries, the practice of women's health politics is also becoming increasingly international (Kisekka, 1992; Tudiver, 1986). This can be seen in part as a response to the multinational nature of many threats to women's well-being – dangerous reproductive technologies for instance, as well as the export of environmental and occupational hazards. However it also reflects the more general growth of international collaboration in women's politics that followed the 1975–85 UN Decade for the Advancement of Women. The first International Women and Health Meeting was held in Rome in 1977. This was followed by meetings in Hanover, Geneva and Amsterdam. In 1987 there was a shift away from Europe with a meeting in Costa Rica, followed by one in the Philippines in 1990 and in Uganda in 1993 (Keysers and Smyth, 1991).

Not surprisingly these have never been easy gatherings. They bring together women with varied interests, desires, commitments, styles of working and frameworks of meaning. In Manila these differences led to what were later described as 'little earthquakes of despair and distrust' (ibid., p. 30). Yet the meetings continue to attract large numbers of participants who share the common objective of improving women's health. It is significant that whatever their circumstances, these women have directed their energies towards broadly the same ends. As we shall see, reproductive self-determination, affordable, effective and humane medical care, satisfaction of basic needs, a safe workplace, and physical security continue to be high on all feminist health agendas.

Reproductive Rights and Wrongs

Reproductive rights issues are now central to women's health politics in most parts of the world (Garcia Moreno and Claro, 1994). Historically most initiatives have consisted of single-issue campaigns for birth control. However these are increasingly located within a broader framework that includes not just the right to prevent conception but also the right to sexual autonomy, to safe motherhood and to a healthy environment for child rearing (Correa and Petchesky, 1994; Dixon-Mueller, 1993; Gerber Fried, 1990a). At the end of the United Nations Conference on Women held in Nairobi in 1985, participants from forty three countries declared:

> Women in the third world demand access to all methods of family planning, including abortion as a back-up, and assert our right to choose for ourselves what's best for our situations. By protecting our lives we protect the lives of those children that we genuinely want

and can care for. This is our conception of being pro-life (German and Ordway, 1989, p. 7).

Campaigning for Change: Unity and Diversity

Most reproductive health campaigners work at community level empowering others through information, advice and care. However broader initiatives are also flourishing, as women identify and publicise the deficiencies of many family planning and abortion services, expose the hazards of some medical techniques and fight for greater participation in reproductive research and development.

In recent years many of these campaigning groups have begun to work together in regional and national alliances. The Latin American and Caribbean Women's Health Network coordinates many of the activities in that region, working in collaboration with Isis International. A similar network has recently been set up in South and South-East Asia. In Brazil the National Feminist Network for Health and Reproductive Rights now has nearly 50 member organisations and co-ordinating groups exist in Argentina, Chile and Colombia (Garcia Moreno and Claro, 1994). A variety of organisations are also working across north/south boundaries. International advocacy for women's health is especially strong in the area of reproductive rights and two organisations offer complementary models of political action.

The International Women's Health Coalition (IWHC) is a charity 'dedicated to promoting women's reproductive health and rights in Southern countries'. It is based in New York and works in alliance with women's organisations, health professionals and government officials in third world countries and with a variety of non-governmental organisations (NGOs) in the north. Its goal is to serve as a 'catalyst for change through research, consultancy and support for women-centred reproductive health services'. In furtherance of this aim the IWHC worked with WHO to set up one of the first meetings between women's health advocates and research scientists, held in Geneva in 1991 (WHO and IHWC, 1991).

The Women's Global Network for Reproductive Rights (WGNRR) operates on a more decentralised model. It is an autonomous network of groups and individuals from all parts of the world, has been in existence since 1978 and currently has members in over a hundred countries. A small office staff in Amsterdam coordinates the Network and major policy decisions are made at members' meetings held in conjunction with the International Women and Health meetings. The WGNRR acts as a resource centre, collecting, exchanging and responding to requests for information on reproductive health issues. It organises and participates in regional and international actions as well as responding to requests for solidarity from around the world. Every three months the network produces a substantial newsletter in English and Spanish, which is reproduced, translated and used in many different countries.

The volume of campaigning on reproductive issues and the growing links at both national and international levels testify to the vitality of this area of women's health politics. However this should not be allowed to obscure the very varied interests of the many groups of women involved. As we shall see, some are primarily concerned with increasing access to birth control. In much of Latin America, for instance, women have been drawn into political action by their inability to obtain safe and effective contraception and by the denial of abortion rights. In many Asian countries, on the other hand, women have been politicised by their experiences of coercive policies that gave them little right to refuse contraception or sterilisation.

Significant differences are also evident in debates about strategy. Some women believe that working with government agencies – with 'the state' – or with international family planning organisations can never be an appropriate means to achieve reproductive rights. They argue that only marginal gains will be made, and that these may be at the cost of legitimating existing population policies (Garcia Moreno and Claro, 1994, p. 53). Others believe that fundamental change is impossible without entering the corridors of power, either as workers or campaigners (Broom, 1993, Ch. 3; Watson, 1990).

There is also disagreement among feminist health activists about the acceptability or otherwise of certain medical practices. Some argue that the new reproductive technologies such as in vitro fertilisation (IVF) are inevitably damaging to women and that their use should be opposed under all circumstances. This is the position taken by the Feminist International Network of Resistance to Reproductive and Genetic Engineering (FINRRAGE). Others do not reject these technologies in principle but call for greater control by women over their development and use (Stanworth, 1987).

Disagreements are especially likely to emerge in sensitive areas of work that cross cultural boundaries, as the fight against genital mutilation illustrates. In recent years many women in Africa have campaigned against the public health hazards associated with female circumcision and its negative effects on women's well-being (Toubia, 1993). The Foundation for Women's Health Research and Development (FORWARD) is an independent non-governmental organisation founded by a woman from Ghana. It promotes the health of African women and children, placing special emphasis on education against genital mutilation (Dorkenoo and Elworthy, 1994).

White feminists have also spoken out against the practice, but this has sometimes led to criticism from African and Asian women who share their beliefs. This is because campaigns of this kind raise complex questions about the relationship between cultural imperialism and solidarity and about the 'ownership' of particular issues. While it is clear that genital mutilation can be extremely damaging to women's health, particular care is needed in the development of appropriate and effective strategies for its elimination.

Thus many groups of women are now working under the broad banner of reproductive rights. They share common goals but come from very different places, have followed a variety of routes and have very different levels of resources at their disposal. We can look in more detail at this 'unity in diversity' by exploring the various strands that make up the global movement for reproductive rights.

Seeking Sexual Self-Determination

A major feature separating 'new wave' reproductive rights campaigns from their predecessors has been an emerging demand for women's right to greater sexual autonomy. In developed countries campaigns for sexual freedom have a long history, especially within the lesbian and gay movements. However they have rarely been linked directly to health, and are sometimes divorced from wider social and economic issues (Gilliam, 1991). These important connections are now being made by many women in the context of a broader campaign for reproductive rights.

In Latin America, in particular, female sexuality has been a central concern for many women's health groups (ISIS International, 1985). They have emphasised the links between birth control and sexual pleasure, and campaigned for women's right to determine the nature of their own sexual lives. This reflects popular feeling. At a number of public meetings held for women in São Paulo and Rio de Janeiro in 1983, one of the main demands was the formation of male and female discussion groups on sexuality and reproduction in all health centres (ibid., p. 28).

The politics of women's sexuality was also taken up by a group of feminist researchers at the Chagas Foundation in São Paulo (Barroso and Bruschini, 1991). Using an action research approach they worked with the Mothers Club of Diadema, whose members are mostly low-income housewives. While these women wanted basic information about bodily functioning they also wanted to explore ideas about sexual pleasure. This led to extensive debate about the reality of sex where the family shares a single room, where safe contraception is difficult to obtain and where many men put their own pleasure before that of their partner. These were exciting but challenging discussions for all participants.

For the researchers, participatory ways of working sometimes presented difficult dilemmas. Should they keep silent for instance in the face of comments that 'homosexuality is sickness' or 'abortion is a crime'? For many of the members, too much disclosure of intimate secrets was threatening and strongly held beliefs were critically scrutinised. Though these issues were not easy to resolve, both groups were eventually able to develop a collective understanding of women's sexuality and its relationship to wider social issues. As a result of their discussions they worked together to produce a series of easily accessible pamphlets entitled *Esse Sexo que Nosso* (This Sex of Ours). After some pressure the Brazilian Ministry of Health agreed to publish 20 000 copies, which have been used for similar projects around the country.

In other parts of the world female sexuality has been less prominent in reproductive rights campaigns (Nowrojee, 1993). Indeed in some cultural contexts any reference to sexual autonomy may simply ensure continued denial of access to birth control. However this refusal to confront issues relating to women's sexuality is becoming increasingly untenable as the AIDS epidemic spreads. Without a clearer understanding of their own bodies and their own desires, women will be unable to achieve the sexual autonomy that will ultimately be their only means of protection against the HIV virus. It is recognition of this reality that has led women in many countries to set up groups to share their sexual knowledge and concerns (Berer and Ray, 1993, Ch. 14). One of the most active of these is the Society for Women and AIDS in Africa, which undertakes educational activities in many parts of the continent.

The Battle for Birth Control

Similar issues of autonomy and decision making lie at the heart of continuing campaigns for safe and effective contraception. The first large-scale efforts to achieve this goal began in Europe and the United States in the late nineteenth and early twentieth centuries. Women from many different backgrounds were involved in campaigns for the wider availability of birth control techniques (Gordon, 1976; Petchesky, 1986). Significantly however, divisions between middle-class and working-class women and black and white women were already evident as the eugenic implications of some policies became clear (Davis, 1990).

Today millions of women are still without effective means of contraception and the fight to achieve this continues. However it is now clear that access alone is not enough. As we have seen, women's health advocates have been highly critical both of the safety and the acceptability of many of the most commonly used methods and of the social inequalities embedded in many family planning services. Hence the emphasis in campaigning has now expanded to include not just availability but also safety and quality of care.

The hazards of the 'new' contraceptives first became apparent in developed countries during the 1970s, with the Dalkon Shield providing one of the most dramatic examples. Women in North America, Australia, New Zealand and many European countries were actively involved both in exposing its dangers and in campaigning for its removal from the market. The device was eventually withdrawn and many women who had been harmed by its use joined together to sue for compensation.

However 'double standards' in the regulation of this and other hazardous contraceptives soon became apparent (Ehrenreich *et al.*, 1979). Though dangerous drugs and devices might eventually be removed from the market in the rich countries, they continued to be exported in their millions to those areas where women had less knowledge and very little choice. In response to this unequal treatment, campaigns were mobilised both by international groups and by women in some third world countries.

In India the potential hazards of contraceptive use are now carefully documented and widely disseminated by a variety of women's organisations. Knowing the hazards of Depo Provera, several groups recently combined together to challenge the introduction of another injectable (Net-en) into the national family planning programme (Balasubrahmanyan, 1986; Daswani, 1987; Ghandi and Shah, 1992, pp. 120–5). Another focus of concern has been the dangers of high-dose oestrogen/progesterone formulations (HDEP) which many women use to try to induce abortions (Gandhi and Shah, 1992, pp. 125–8; Marcelis and Shiva, 1986).

International groups such as the WGNRR, the IWHC and the International Organisation of Consumer Unions (IOCU) have also played a major part in the global dissemination of knowledge about birth control techniques, garnered from women in a variety of social contexts. However judgements about the value of different methods can be difficult to make, since the circumstances of individual women will affect their contraceptive preferences. For some safety may be the most important criterion, for some efficacy in preventing conception, and for others invisibility.

The work of the Women and Pharmaceuticals Project, based in Holland, has played an important part in beginning to resolve some of these difficulties (Mintzes, 1992). Using both social and biological criteria they have evaluated a range of contraceptive methods in a way that is both scientific and women-centred (Hardon, 1992). Their publications have been widely used in many parts of the world, not just because of the information they provide, but also because of their sophisticated analysis of the methodological issues involved in assessing medical technology from a feminist perspective (Hansen and Launso, 1989; Morgall, 1993).

A Woman's Right to Choose?

But whatever the availability and effectiveness of contraception, women will always need access to safe termination of pregnancy, both as a back-up and sometimes as a preferred method of birth control. Recognition of this reality is manifest in continuing campaigns for the legalisation of abortion. In Ireland the struggle is still hard, despite pressure to harmonise with the rest of Europe (Murphy-Lawless, 1993). In Brazil women's groups managed to prevent the insertion of a foetal protection clause in the 1988 constitution, but the fight for decriminalisation continues (Garcia Moreno and Claro, 1994). In Hungary, Romania and Poland women have fought to retain abortion rights, which have come under threat as a result of the revitalisation of the power of the Catholic Church (Fuszara, 1993; Jankowska, 1993), while in East Germany campaigners have tried to maintain rights threatened by unification with the West (Funk, 1993). However it is in the United States that one of the most vigorous and certainly the best documented campaigns has been fought – first to legalise abortion and then to maintain that gain.

In 1973 the US Supreme Court legalised abortion in the historic Roe v. Wade case. However, this decision has been under attack for much of the intervening period (Gerber Fried, 1990b). As early as 1976 the Hyde Amendment removed Medicaid funding for abortions, except in the case of rape or severe illness. As a result many poor women were effectively denied access to their constitutional right. This was followed by attempts in many other states to stop public funding of abortion. In 1989 the Webster decision prohibited terminations both in public facilities and in private hospitals receiving public funds. Many states have also passed laws requiring parental consent for termination in minors. Thus the anti-choice movement has been successful in denying or limiting access to legal abortion for some of the most politically powerless women – those who are young, poor or living in rural areas. The battle to resist these moves has been a fierce one.

Before 1973 women had to search for abortions wherever they could find them. In response to this dilemma a group of women in Chicago set up a counselling and referral service called Jane (Bart, 1981; 'Jane', 1990). Within two years they had all learned the skills necessary to perform safe, supportive, low-cost terminations during the first six weeks of pregnancy. The service was illegal and operated underground, but by the time it ended in 1973 it had carried out over 11 000 abortions. About 250 women a week used the service and over a hundred were members at one time or another. As one of them later described it:

> We were ordinary women living in extraordinary times who seized an opportunity to act and despite all our failings accomplished something extraordinary. The need for our service, which grew rapidly as word of the service spread, pushed us to be as competent as possible. A woman came to us with a problem – she was pregnant and didn't want to be – and when she left the problem was solved. That daily experience of success gave us a feeling of incredible power and satisfaction. And the work itself was life-affirming ('Jane', 1990, p. 100).

'Jane' was able to help many women, but hundreds of thousands more were left to fend for themselves, often in fear and sometimes in poverty. It is a recognition of that still very recent reality that has made so many women (and men) determined to resist those anti-abortion activists who would wish to return to it. This commitment was evident in the March for Abortion Rights held in Washington DC in 1992 and attended by about three quarters of a million supporters.

Much of this campaigning has focused on legislative and policy issues – ensuring that terminations remain both legal and affordable. As a result abortion is now a major electoral issue in the United States. But increasingly pro-choice activists have been forced into civil disobedience and other forms of direct action. This has developed in response to organisations such as Operation Rescue, whose members have been picketing abortion clinics throughout the United States. The ferocity of these attacks offers an important warning about the contingency of all legal rights to abortion.

The US experience also highlights the political complexity of such campaigns. Abortion is a difficult moral issue and many women would not choose it for themselves – whatever the circumstances (Luker, 1984). Even among those who support a pregnant woman's right to choose, there are often disagreements about strategies and priorities. Women with disabilities for instance have questioned the validity of foetal abnormality as a criterion for termination, arguing that their interests have not been adequately represented in the abortion debate (Asch and Fine, 1990).

Black women too have been critical of the politics of some white campaigners. Though they have always been active in the movement, they have often felt marginalised (Ross, 1993). They point out that all too often black women who have abortions have not 'chosen' them in any real sense. For some, social and economic circumstances have meant that they cannot continue a pregnancy while others have been coerced by health care providers into abortion or sterilisation (Joseph and Lewis, 1981, p. 50; Ross, 1993; Shapiro, 1985). Angela Davis has painted a stark picture of the historical origins of this continuing reality:

> Black women have been aborting themselves since the earliest days of slavery. Many slave women refused to bring children into a world of interminable forced labour, where chains and flogging and sexual abuse for women were everyday conditions of life (Davis, 1990, p. 17).

Thus the politics of abortion needs to be placed in a wider context if the differing interests of all those involved are to be adequately recognised. As we shall see, similar complexities are apparent in the politics of maternity. Some women are fighting for access to the skills and technology necessary to ensure a safe delivery, while others are resisting what they see as the 'over medicalisation' of a major event in their lives.

Controlling Birth

Maternity continues to be a primary cause of morbidity and mortality for women in many parts of the world. Not surprisingly, those most at risk are least likely to have the resources to fight for change, and for generations these deaths were largely invisible. However a number of international organisations campaigned during the 1980s to put maternal mortality on the agenda and hundreds of women's groups have now taken up the cause.

In 1987 a 'Safe Motherhood Conference' was organised in Nairobi by WHO, the United Nations Fund for Population Activities (UNFPA) and the World Bank. The aim was 'to mobilise immediate and concerted action at the national and international levels to prevent the continued tragedies' (Starrs, 1987). In 1988 these same concerns were taken up by delegates at the Fifth International Women and Health Meeting in Costa Rica, who launched the Campaign against Maternal Mortality and Morbidity. This international initiative is coordinated by the WGNRR and the Latin American and Caribbean Women's Health Network.

As part of the Campaign, 28 May was designated International Day of Action for Women's Health. This has now become an annual focus of activity for many women's health groups, especially those working outside the developed countries. Significantly it has also been adopted by WHO, marking an important link between women's health advocates working in very different environments. The theme of the campaign varies from year to year and annual reports from the WGNRR reveal a kaleidoscope of events around the world.

In 1992 the scale of events was immense, with events occurring in dozens of different countries. In Nicaragua, for instance, activities were held in twenty-one towns and included video presentations, debates, theatre performances, meetings, training sessions, radio programmes and workshops. The Women's Health Network then presented the government with a petition calling among other things for the state to comply with the agreements laid down in the Constitution, the Universal Declaration of Human Rights, the Convention against Discrimination against Women and the commitments undertaken at the 1992 Safe Motherhood Conference (WGNRR, 1992). In the Philippines the GABRIELA Commission on Women's Health and Reproductive Rights put up posters in different communities in metropolitan Manila, emphasising the dangers of unwanted pregnancies. In Kampala the Safe Motherhood Project organised a workshop for market men and women to sensitise them to women's health issues, while in Equatorial Guinea the Association of Protestant Women distributed the Campaign's Call for Action in schools and hospitals (ibid.)

Women in many third world countries have used the campaign to call for access to effective and appropriate obstetric care tailored to meet the circumstances of their lives. For most this means a close link between maternity services and primary health care as well as the use of traditional methods where appropriate. By this means they hope to obtain the benefits of modern obstetric techniques without losing what is valuable about culturally specific 'low technology' care (Jordan, 1986). In developed countries too maternity campaigners have called for appropriate care, but not surprisingly the detail of their demands has been very different. Most are concerned not to increase levels of obstetric intervention, but to reduce them.

Some women living in rich countries do lack medical support. This is particularly evident in the United States where lack of funding often leaves poor mothers deprived of necessary services (Barbee and Little, 1993; Ruzek, 1978). However the major protagonists in the politics of pregnancy have been white middle-class women who can rely on a baseline of effective care for safe delivery but wish to prevent medical intervention exceeding what they regard as reasonable for the health of mother and child.

In Europe, North America and Australia the consumer movement in maternity care reached its height during the late 1970s and early 1980s (Kitzinger, 1990; Shearer, 1989). Its major themes were increased choice for women and greater control over their own labour. Specific demands included a less clinical birthing environment, the limiting of high technology intervention to genuine emergencies, and enhanced opportunities for the active participation of fathers. Campaigners pointed out that many of the new obstetric techniques were untested and that others had been shown to be harmful. They also emphasised the inadvisability of care policies that alienated mothers from the birth process and sometimes from the baby itself.

Despite their apparent unanimity the women (and men) involved in the movement do have widely divergent beliefs about the significance of birthing. Some have sought 'natural' childbirth as an end in itself. This is often part of a more general 'anti-technology' stance that emphasises the spiritual dimension of women's relationship with their own bodies and/or the centrality of the birth process in family life. Others reject such beliefs, arguing that they simply impose a different requirement on women – to give birth 'naturally' to prove their true femininity (Coward, 1989). Instead they emphasise women's right to determine their own labour – whether or not they opt for technological intervention.

Despite these differing philosophies, consumer campaigns do appear to have had a noticeable effect on medical practice in some countries. More mothers can now choose to give birth in 'home-like' surroundings. They are subjected to less intrusive procedures, are more likely to be cared for by a midwife and are not separated from their babies for lengthy periods. However these gains should not be overestimated. In many hospitals the incidence of procedures such as caesarean sections remain high and home births are rarely available. Even where care has been humanised, birth usually remains firmly under medical control. Indeed it is significant that some of the most visible innovations have occurred in the United States, where pregnant women with resources can command considerable market power. These changes have sometimes been apparent rather than real, reflecting not changes in medical philosophy but an economic imperative to keep patient numbers high as the birth rate declines (Ruzek, 1980; Worcester and Whatley, 1988).

We have seen that the global campaign for reproductive rights is a complex and multi-faceted political reality. It takes many different forms but has the common thread of a belief in women's right to determine what happens to their own bodies. This potential for collective action was amply demonstrated in the 'Women's Declaration on Population Policies', put together by over a hundred women's organisations across the globe for the International Conference on Population and Development held in Cairo in 1994.

It is evident that reproductive rights activists have often come into conflict with doctors and other health workers who continue to exert considerable control over an important part of women's lives. Yet women need some of what health workers have to offer. In the next section we explore this contradiction further by outlining the broader feminist critique of medicine.

Challenging Medicine

Whatever their social and economic circumstances, all women need high quality health care. For some this remains a remote and expensive dream. Others do have access to the benefits of good medicine but rarely on their own terms. Many share the experience of having little control over what should be a valued resource in their lives. Not surprisingly then, affordable, effective and humane medical care has always been high on their list of priorities.

The ease with which women can obtain health care varies dramatically. It is determined by their individual wealth or poverty and by the scope and cost of services in their local community. A few women are wealthy enough to ensure control over their own health care, but millions continue to experience the effects of professional domination and a denial of their right to participate in important decisions about their own lives (and deaths). As a result they have begun to challenge both the quantity and quality of the care available to them, and to question the basis upon which medicine itself is currently organised.

Women Help Themselves

In the late 1960s and early 1970s women's health politics in developed countries focused mainly on self help and on women's capacity to take care of themselves and each other. A starting point for many of these activities was the formation of small groups based on the feminist practice of sharing knowledge and experience. A core activity for many was self-examination of the vagina and cervix with the aid of a plastic speculum, a lamp and a mirror. By looking at this previously hidden part of their bodies women were able to learn about the normal and abnormal changes taking place, and sometimes to monitor them more effectively than a doctor. This helped them acquire knowledge and confidence to participate more effectively in their own health care.

As part of this process many women began to challenge the belief that all medical knowledge was always superior to their own, whatever the circumstances. Self-help groups were a form of consumer action that involved a redefinition of the role of the 'expert' and an attempt to change the accepted view that only a doctor can define medical need. Their potential was vividly described by the authors of *Our Bodies Ourselves*:

> Self help is women sharing experiences, knowledge, feelings – women supporting each other and learning together. Self help begins by working from a practical base, starting with learning from physical self examination, finding out what we *do* know, what we do *not* know, what we *want* to know and exploring from there. . . .
>
> Self help is women relating to ourselves in order to demystify health care, the professionals and our own bodies: it involves being

able to make personal choices based on our own very valid experiences and knowledge (Boston Women's Health Book Collective, 1971).

In developed countries most of these local groups have now disappeared, along with the broader 'consciousness raising' groups characteristic of second wave feminism. However many women continue to be involved in more specialised health groups, some of which operate at a national level. The majority of these are mutual support and aid groups organised around the needs of people facing particular challenges. Some are mixed but many are women-only with a focus on gender-specific problems (Foley, 1985; Hatch and Kickbusch, 1983).

The range of interests of these groups is diverse, but in most countries they include support for women with chronic problems such as depression, HIV infection, ME, cystitis, eating disorders, alcoholism and drug abuse as well as those recovering from the effects of medical interventions such as hysterectomy, mastectomy and inappropriate tranquilliser prescribing. In a number of countries there are also organisations catering for the health needs of particular groups of women. In the United States for instance there are many self-help groups for black women.

As well as providing mutual support and information, many of these groups are also involved in campaigns to ensure that the needs of their members are met more effectively. In the United States the National Women's Health Network now has some 17 000 members, both individuals and organisations. They have worked hard for changes in the US health care system and the combination of mutual aid and consumerist politics has often been a powerful one. In the United States in particular, many more women are now paid to work in health care politics and their impact has often been significant. While some of these groups may have moved a long way from the feminism of the 1970s, they continue to represent an important part of women's involvement in movements for change in health care.

Though they have declined in many of the developed countries, local health groups continue to be a vital source of support for women in many parts of the third world, especially when formal services are expensive and sparse. Most concentrate on education, confidence building and the sharing of experiences, and health often provides a lens through which to explore wider social and political issues. When a group of Guatemalan refugee women came together to share the problems of their new lives in Mexico City, it was health that provided the key to breaking down barriers of communication between them (Ball, 1991).

The women agreed that the greatest difficulty they faced was what they called 'tristeza de corazon' – literally 'broken heartedness' – resulting from their loss of home and loved ones (ibid., p. 265). Once the women understood that their distress was not a sign of 'madness' but a rational and shared response to their situation, they were able to think more positively about how to promote their own mental and physical health and that of others.

For some women's groups a major focus is the preservation of traditional healing practices. Members of the Irula Tribal Women's Welfare Society in Tamil Nadu have built a seed bank and a herbarium to safeguard their specialised knowledge. They cultivate medicinal herbs and plants and sell them in the neighbouring areas. This gives them a steady income but also helps to maintain their sense of self-worth and their traditional skills at a time when economic and environmental changes have turned them into landless labourers (*Womankind Newsletter*, 1994).

Creating Feminist Alternatives

Many women have used their own experiences to help others develop greater knowledge and understanding of health issues. The most famous of these feminist health education initiatives began in 1971 with the publication by the Boston Women's Health Book Collective of the first edition of *Our Bodies Ourselves* (Beckwith, 1985; Bell, 1994). This was not just a political success but also a commercial one. It has sold millions of copies and has now been translated into more than a dozen languages. The Boston initiative provided the inspiration for *Women's Lives and Health in Egypt*, published in Arabic in 1990 (Cairo Women's Health Book Collective, 1991; El-Mouelhy, 1993). According to one fourteen-year-old reader: 'I am recommending the book to all my friends in school and we plan to read it together with other friends and . . . to the women in our families who cannot read it on their own' (El-Mouelhy, 1993, p. 116). An older woman went even further: 'For the first time in my life I am feeling the depth of my deprivation as a non-literate woman. I am going to literacy classes so I can read the book on my own' (ibid.)

A wide range of feminist publications on women's health is now available. Some are very broad in their approach but others focus on the situation of women in specific communities. A group of women based in Malaysia produced a guide appropriate to women in their region (Asian and Pacific Women's Resource Collection Network, 1989). The National Black Women's Health Project in the United States offers a range of publications on problems such as hypertension and systemic lupus, which affect African American women in particular (Avery, 1990). Lesbian women too have been active in some countries, identifying the ignorance and homophobia that often dominate their experiences of health and health care (Browne *et al.*, 1985; Pies, 1985; Hepburn and Gutierrez, 1988). A number of resource centres have been set up to generate research and give women easier access to health-related knowledge. In the United States for instance, the Native American Women's Health Education Resource Center provides important information for an otherwise neglected group.

In some countries women have moved beyond these educational activities to set up their own health centres. However the viability of these initiatives has varied markedly, according to the social and economic context in which they have been developed. In Britain, for instance, very few services have been created outside the mainstream. This reflects in part the limited market for private care when it is available from the National Health Service without direct cost. But there is also a political reluctance to offer services that many women could not afford to buy. Only in the areas of mental health and substance abuse have alternative services been provided on any scale (Doyal, 1985a).

In the United States, on the other hand, the 1970s and early 1980s saw a proliferation of women's health centres offering reproductive care and a range of other services, on both a commercial and a charity basis (Ruzek, 1978; Zimmerman, 1987). Alternative birthing centres were especially common as women chose to remove themselves from the medical gaze during normal labour and delivery. These women's health centres were based on feminist principles, minimising status differences between health workers and maximising women's participation in their own care. Their number has markedly declined in recent years, but about a hundred are still operational; most make conscious efforts to cater for the diverse needs of different groups of women, offering sliding scales of fees as well as cultural variety in their personnel and resources.

It is probably in Australia that women's health centres have been most successful (Broom, 1993; Hunt, 1991, p. 25). Historically this reflects the priority they have been given within the Australian women's health movement and their subsequent incorporation into the National Women's Health Policy (Commonwealth Department of Community Services and Health, 1989, p. 89). The women involved continue to grapple with the contradictions inherent in any attempt to use state funding for radical initiatives (Broom, 1993, Chs. 3 and 5). However women's health centres in Australia offer important examples of gender-sensitive practice for other health care providers.

In most of the developed countries women's health centres are an alternative to the formal system. However in some parts of the world they are the only option available. This has drawn many women into voluntary organisations designed to fill this vacuum in basic medical care. They have used a variety of strategies to create a network of services, utilising both modern and traditional methods of healing.

The Bangladesh Women's Health Coalition now runs ten projects providing both reproductive and general health services for women and children (Kabir, 1992). They began by offering menstrual regulation as a way of helping women with unwanted pregnancies, but soon expanded to include not just abortion, contraception and maternity care, but also diagnosis and treatment of basic diseases. No distinction is made between medical care and wider community development, with the coalition offering literacy classes for women as well as workshops on family law. Workers and clients have also campaigned together for better national health services and more equitable development policies.

In Lima, Centro Flora Tristan and Vaso de Leche have worked together to create an integrated health service for women (SISMU). The project began with a process of *autodiagnostico*, during which women identified what they saw as their major problems. A variety of services, workshops and groups were then created in an attempt to help women meet their own health needs. Vaginal infections and cervical cancer were seen as key priorities and women have also been interested in learning more about herbal medicines. The project receives funding from Womankind Worldwide, a charity based in London.

All around the world examples can be found of clinics offering women-centred care to fill gaps in official provision. These are important initiatives offering much needed services as well as valuable examples of good practice. However individual projects can never meet the universal need for high quality health care. Hence women also continue to campaign for changes in the organisation, funding and content of mainstream health services. They are seeking improved access and affordability; greater effectiveness in curing diseases or relieving symptoms; and more humanity in caring relationships.

Reforming the System

In Brazil an alliance between the Ministry of Health and activists in the Women's Movement led to the creation of the Comprehensive Programme for Women's Health Care (PAISM). In Colombia women have been able to go a stage further with the implementation of a national women and health policy. Cooperation between the government, the Pan-American Health Organisation and feminist activists resulted in 'Health for Women, Women for Health'. This includes five programmes of care: health promotion and self help; reproductive health and sexuality; prevention and care for victims of violence; mental health; and occupational health (Garcia Moreno and Claro, 1994). Included in the policy is a written commitment to a comprehensive approach to women's health care:

> The woman has the right to treatment and care from the health services as a whole being with specific needs – according to her age, activity, social class, race and place of origin, and not to be treated exclusively as a biological reproducer (quoted in Garcia Moreno and Claro, 1994).

But even if women's access to comprehensive health services is increased, there are still major concerns about the effectiveness of much of the treatment available to them. Many are inappropriately diagnosed and treated by the doctors they consult. This is due in part to the lack of scientific evaluation of many medical procedures used on both sexes. But as we have seen it is exacerbated by gender bias in medical decision making. These distortions in the production and use of medical knowledge are now being challenged on a number of fronts (Rosser, 1992).

In the United States the massive death toll from breast cancer has been a major incentive for action. Taking their cue from both male and female AIDS activists, women have worked together to expose the relatively small sums spent on breast cancer research. One woman in nine in the United States can now expect to die from the disease, which kills about 45 000 each year. The death rate increased by an overwhelming 24 per cent between 1979 and 1986, yet research on prevention continues to receive relatively little funding (Rennie, 1993; US National Institutes of Health, 1992, p. 11). In an effort to change this, thousands of women – many of them breast cancer survivors – have formed campaigning organisations, including the Cancer Patients

Action Alliance, Breast Cancer Action and the Women's Cancer Resource Center (Brady, 1991). As well as providing mutual support they are fighting for higher levels of research funding and optimal treatment for all women.

Recent research in the United Kingdom and the United States has shown that there is systematic bias in some areas of clinical decision making. A woman undergoing renal dialysis in the United States has only 70 per cent of the chance of a man of obtaining a kidney transplant (Held *et al.*, 1988). In the case of cardiac surgery, American men are six times more likely to be given cardiac catheterisation than women with the same symptoms (Tobin *et al.*, 1987). Similar patterns are evident in the United Kingdom, despite the existence of the National Health Service (Petticrew *et al.*, 1993). In the United States women have a higher operative mortality rate than men for coronary bypass surgery and a higher mortality rate at the time of initial myocardial infarction (Wenger, 1990; Fiebach *et al.*, 1990).

The National Women's Health Network has played a major part in putting many aspects of gender bias in medical practice onto the American agenda. One result was the creation in 1990 of a new Office of Research on Women's Health within the National Institutes of Health (NIH). A major part of its work is the coordination of a fourteen-year women's health initiative designed to fill important gaps in medical knowledge. The project is studying 15 000 women at 45 centres across the United States in an attempt to find ways of decreasing the prevalence of cardiovascular disease, cancer and osteoporosis. In particular it is designed to generate practical advice on prevention for women and their doctors.

This study includes a representative mix of women from different social classes and races, as the NIH is responding to demands for a more balanced baseline for medical research. Guidelines have now been issued to ensure gender equity in the samples used in all government funded projects. As part of these new procedures all applicants have to demonstrate that any gender (or other) bias in their methodology is necessitated by the research problem itself, and would not be discriminatory to any group of potential patients (US National Institutes of Health, 1992, p. 2).

Empowering Women

But even if access and effectiveness can be improved, many of women's concerns about medicine remain. At the heart of all feminist critiques of medicine is the recognition that women lack power in health care institutions. This limits their ability to determine medical priorities or influence the allocation of scarce resources. It also has a significant impact on their individual experiences as users of health services. It affects their capacity to play an active part in their own treatment, and too often leaves them feeling uncared for.

As we have seen, when women use medical services, many have difficulty both in getting enough information and in being able to act on it (Faden, 1991; Holmes and Purdy, 1992; Whitbeck, 1991). This applies especially to those with few resources, whose problems often receive least time and attention (Doyal, 1985b; Whitehead, 1988). Many doctors appear to be reluctant to let women speak for themselves and many women find it difficult to assert their wishes (Fisher, 1986; Roberts, 1985). Lesbian women in particular report that their heterosexuality is usually taken for granted and attempts to correct this misconception may be denied or scorned (Robertson, 1992; Stevens, 1992). Women's own experience is devalued in comparison with that of doctors' expert 'knowledge' and many doctors are unwilling to admit ignorance or uncertainty (Graham and Oakley, 1981). As a result female patients frequently become the passive victims of doctors' ministrations, and for many this can be a distressing and demeaning experience (Healthsharing Women, 1990; O'Sullivan, 1987).

In some countries women's complaints about their treatment have led to changes in the education of doctors. However there are few controls on the quality of the encounter between individual patients and the physicians and surgeons whose skills they need. In order to empower women within this relationship, activists in some countries have attempted to guarantee them the right to 'informed consent' before any medical procedure is carried out.

Using the example of breast cancer again, there is evidence that more surgeons are now beginning to acknowledge the value of women's active involvement in decision making. For many years the standard treatment for breast cancer was a biopsy under anaesthetic followed by whatever the surgeon deemed appropriate. A variety of pressures, including those from women with cancer, have led to significant changes in this practice. In the United States about half of all states have now enacted informed consent legislation relating specifically to breast cancer (Montini and Ruzek, 1989). In Australia too there has been extensive public debate, leading to the introduction of national guidelines for all medical decision making and women have been at the forefront of that process. While this has not gone as far as many commentators would like, it has highlighted the need for informed consent for all medical procedures (Hancock, 1991).

Strategies of this kind go some way towards the humanisation of health services for women. However more fundamental changes are needed if 'women friendly' services are to become a reality. Health workers need to be both gender specific in their recognition of women's individual needs and also gender sensitive in devising appropriate strategies to meet them. This is unlikely to be achieved without better conditions and much greater power and authority for women working within the health care system itself. In many countries this aim is being pursued through the formation of groups of nurses, midwives and women doctors concerned both to enhance their own professional status and to use what influence they have to promote the well-being of the women they care for. Working in alliance with other feminist organisations, they are pushing for greater involvement of women as both users and workers in the management of health services (Doyal, 1994a).

We have seen that women are continuing to challenge medicine in an attempt to have their needs for both physical and mental health care met more effectively. Though some progress can be identified, much remains to be done. But even if it is radically transformed, medicine alone cannot guarantee the optimisation of women's health. They also need access to the basic resources necessary for promoting their own well-being and that of their families. As we shall see, lack of these essential components of health has brought an increasing number into the political arena.

Basic Needs and Sustainable Development

During the early nineteenth century women were major participants in the bread riots in Europe. If staple food was not available at a reasonable price they had little option but to take to the streets. With the gradual development of 'welfare states' this level of deprivation has largely disappeared in most of the developed countries. However deteriorating standards of living in many parts of the third world continue to draw women into similar struggles to meet basic needs.

Uncontrolled development and ecological degradation have also led many women into environmental politics (Braidotti *et al.*, 1994; Dankelman and Davidson, 1988; Rodda, 1991; Sontheimer, 1991). In developed countries their actions are usually fuelled by ethical concerns about the impact of current economic and social policies on the health of present and future generations. In third world countries many women share the same beliefs, but their commitment to change is heightened by the immediate impact of environmental degradation on their daily lives. For them, basic needs satisfaction is inextricably linked to the health or otherwise of their physical environment. Hence many are now campaigning for sustainable development policies. For some this builds on long-standing traditions of collective action, but for many it is the first step in a gradual process of self empowerment.

The Politics of Subsistence

Some of the most powerful campaigns can be found in Latin America, where a combination of recession and rapid industrialisation has led to a crisis in collective consumption. In Brazil the 1970s brought a serious decline in the standard of living of many people. This led thousands of women onto the streets for the first time, protesting against the high price of food and demanding nurseries as well as the return of missing relatives 'disappeared' by the police and military.

> Using the traditional values linked to the feminine figure – that of mother, wife and housewife – women have managed to make their presence felt where men are barred. They have faced up to dangers and undertaken actions to which this generation had not been accustomed . . . and this in turn gave them a new awareness of their social role (Blay, 1985, p. 300).

In Bolivia too women are fighting together to improve their own well-being and that of their families. The National Federation of Bolivian Peasant Women, Committees of Housewives of the Mines and Housewives of Popular Neighbourhoods have all been involved in campaigns against government austerity measures and military repression (Barrios de Chungara and Viezzer, 1978; Bronstein, 1982; Jelin, 1990; Léon, 1990).

For many millions of women, politics begins at home through local projects designed to improve their domestic environment. These involve a variety of strategies to increase women's access to food, fuel and housing, giving them a greater opportunity to meet their practical needs. However some go further, offering women the chance to challenge existing gender divisions and to effect real change in their economic and social circumstances (Moser, 1989).

Producing Food and Fuel

In 1981 a group of peasant women in the Chiapas region of Mexico formed the Pinatabel Women's Organisation to challenge continuing discrimination against them in the allocation of agricultural loans (Dankelman and Davidson, 1988, p. 24). After several years they accumulated enough money to buy their own land. The women worked collectively on a number of projects, including the cultivation of vegetables and the raising of sheep for wool and natural fertiliser. With support from Oxfam they also set up study groups and evaluation and planning sessions. The success of the project was demonstrated not only by improved food supply and income generation but also by the women's growing confidence and skills.

Like food, fuel is very difficult for some women to obtain in sufficient quantities. As deforestation spreads, many face significant threats to their health from the increasingly hard work of collection, or from chemical pollution if they are forced to use more hazardous fuels. For those women whose survival strategy includes the collection and sale of firewood, deforestation may seem to be a necessary evil. However the majority are concerned with conservation and it is these women who have been at the forefront of campaigns to save trees.

Chipko, the Hindi word for 'hugging' was adopted as the name of one of the most celebrated of these movements (Jain, 1991; Shiva, 1989). Begun in North India in the early 1970s, it employed Ghandian methods of non-violent resistance to oppose the cutting down of forests. Women simply hugged the trees when loggers arrived, saying they would have to cut off their heads to destroy the trees. Though they were often criticised for these public activities, many women gained strength through their participation and the movement grew rapidly. One notable success was the fifteen-year ban introduced by Indira Ghandi on green tree felling in the forests of Uttar Pradesh. *Chipko* now consists of hundreds of decentralised initiatives spread across the Himalayas. Though it continues to be a mixed movement, most local groups are organised by village women concerned to protect a basic component of their subsistence (Rodda, 1991, p. 111).

Similar experiences of empowerment have been reported by women in the Green Belt movement in Kenya. Begun by Professor Wangari Matthai, it was spread through the National Council of Women. The Council organises a programme of planting and distributes seedlings, but the daily management is done by a network of local women. As well as restoring an important part of Kenya's natural environment, the scheme has taught many women to be expert foresters and given them a cash income. According to one of the organisers: 'The successes have given women a positive image of themselves. They have gained economic power which has enabled them to raise standards of living for themselves and their families, and consequently that of the nation' (ibid.)

Ensuring Safe Water and Sanitation

Women's responsibilities for the supply, management and conservation of water have also led to their involvement in health-related initiatives (Dankelman and Davidson, 1988, Ch. 3; Sontheimer, 1991, Pt III). Bolivian women living around Lake Titicaca pressurised their men into petitioning the state for reliable water supplies. These have now been installed, with women trained as health promoters (Benton, 1993, p. 238). In urban areas too women have worked for improved water and sanitation services. One group living in a shanty town near La Paz were concerned about the effects on their children's health of rubbish tips containing human excrement (Rodda, 1991, p. 116). Women worked together to clear the tips while also building cheap latrines with local materials. One of the community leaders put the situation plainly: 'We're living on top of a load of trash. We're getting contaminated and our kids are getting sick. We have to deal with the problem ourselves until the authorities remember we exist' (quoted in Rodda, 1991, p. 116).

Recognition of women's central role in the conservation of water has led a number of organisations to involve them in innovative community projects. Funds have been provided for water and sanitation schemes in which women have important positions as managers and pump minders, and many also participate in the building of latrines and water closets. The SWACH Project in Rajasthan successfully trained several illiterate women to be mechanics, giving them greater economic independence as well as ensuring that the pumps remain in good order. Others have become 'animators', contacting women in the community to discuss health, hygiene and other water-related matters.

Homes Fit for Habitation

Housing problems are closely linked to water and sanitation issues, especially in rapidly growing urban areas, and here too women have used a variety of strategies in their campaigns for change (Moser and

Peake, 1987). In E Ward in the slums of Bombay, many have been active through the organisation Mahila Milan, which uses both direct action and community development techniques to increase self reliance among local women (Gahlot, 1993).

An initial survey of six thousand households identified the extensive social needs of pavement and slum dwellers. Women were then encouraged to work together to ensure that these needs were met. One outcome was a successful claim for compensation against Bombay Municipal Corporation after pavement dwellers' possessions were seized and destroyed. Members of the organisation have also worked with the National Slum Dwellers Federation to involve women in the design of their own houses. They have contested resettlement plans and set up cooperative savings schemes to build permanent, legal housing that women can afford. As evidence of their success, Mahila Milan branches have now been set up in a number of other areas in Bombay, and in Madras and Bangalore.

Similar action has been taken by women living in the tidal swamplands of Guayaquil in Ecuador (Moser, 1987). When families first arrived in the area of Indio Guayas, most had no house and no services – neither roads, electricity, water nor sewerage. All journeys required the negotiation of fragile catwalks over the water. These difficult circumstances threw many women together into self-help networks. A number then went on to become involved in barrio committees, campaigning for an improved infrastructure from the local municipality.

This was often exhausting and terrifying, generating opposition not just from political opponents but from local people who believed that women should stay at home with their families (Moser, 1987, pp. 180–90). However it is clear that these activities have been important not just in effecting social change but also in beginning to transform the women themselves. It is this potential for psychological and economic empowerment that makes campaigning for basic needs such an important element in the global politics of women's health. In the next section we explore similar processes in the context of waged work.

Working for Health

As we saw in Chapter 6, the impact of paid work on women's wellbeing is complex, reflecting not just the nature of the job itself but also their burden of domestic labour and their socio-economic circumstances. Not surprisingly this variety is reflected in the differing strategies women have devised to make their working environment a healthier one.

Organisational Strategies

Generally speaking, women's involvement in campaigns relating to occupational health and safety issues has been limited. Many are employed in small workplaces, in the 'informal' sector of the economy or in casualised work where there is little or no union organisation (Rowbotham and Mitter, 1994). Where unions do exist they have usually been male dominated, paying little attention to the specific concerns of women (War on Want, 1988). In recent years this pattern has begun to change, and some now recognise the importance of representing the needs of all their members equally. However for most unions health in general, and women's health in particular, have a low priority and this is likely to continue as the current economic climate continues to put jobs and wages at risk.

In response to this situation many women have developed new strategies, more appropriate to their circumstances than the traditional one of trade union bargaining. Most have been small-scale, local campaigns carried out in individual workplaces. However some have been more broadly based, involving extensive research to identify hitherto invisible hazards in predominantly female occupations. The results have then been disseminated to other women, sometimes culminating in campaigns for improved regulation. Much of this research has highlighted experiential aspects of the work environment, exploring psychological as well as physical hazards.

In India the Self Employed Women's Association (SEWA) has combined research into occupational health with organising, often involving women with no previous experience of political activity (Asian and Pacific Women's Resource Collection Network, 1989, p. 120). Surveys of living and working conditions are carried out with the active participation of the women themselves, and these form the basis of campaigns (Jhabvala, 1994). SEWA was instrumental in gaining recognition for women in national legislation and also in persuading the trade union movement and the International Labour Organisation to take up the cause of homeworkers. Similar action research methods have been reported from a number of countries including the Dominican Republic (Centro de Investigación Para la Acción Femenina, 1987).

Office Workers in Action

In developed countries new campaigning strategies can be found in the predominantly female arena of clerical and secretarial work. Most of the health hazards of office work were originally identified by clerical workers themselves, who conducted their own research and publicised their findings (Stellman and Henifin, 1989). The history of repetitive strain injury (RSI) offers a valuable case study.

First reported as a 'syndrome' among clerical and other workers in Australia in the early 1980s, its very existence was at first denied by employers and most doctors. A number of women then began a campaign to have the problem recognised, using existing medical research as well as first-hand testimonies collected from thousands of workers. The resulting reports described both the physical and the psychological effects of RSI as well as its devastating financial consequences for the many women who had been forced to give up their jobs. There have been notable successes in Australia and RSI has been recognised as a compensatable industrial disease. However much remains to be done in developing both preventive and curative services. Hence the campaign continues not just in Australia but in other countries where RSI has yet to be officially recognised.

Confronting Sexual Harassment

Women's experience of office work was also important in highlighting sexual harassment as a public health issue. Similar hazards are present in many other workplaces, but office workers played a major part in the campaign for their recognition. In those countries were sex discrimination legislation has already been enacted, some women have been able to take sexual harassment cases to court. In the United States in particular, legal action has been facilitated by the creation of advice and advocacy centres in various parts of the country. Many women have also been involved in their own workplaces in the drawing up of guidelines for the identification of harassment and the punishment of offenders.

In France this process has been aided by the creation of the European Association Against Violence Against Women (AVFT). Initially funded by the EEC, AVFT is now funded jointly by the French Secretary of State and the Ministry of Employment (Louis, 1994). Members of the organisation have organised conferences and workshops and publish a journal dedicated to the analysis and denunciation of violence against women. They have campaigned for changes in the laws relating to sexual harassment and also work in partnership with individual women who have been harassed in their workplace. Though the project is run by women, men are included in the membership as a recognition that changing gender roles are essential if abuse is to be prevented (ibid.)

Despite initiatives of this kind, women in most countries are still unable to seek formal redress if they are submitted to sexual pressure at work. Under these circumstances direct action may be the only solution. A group of young women working in one of the Free Trade Zones in Malaysia were regularly harassed on the road between the factory and their boarding house.

> The women workers went from house to house to get support for a campaign to change this situation. Finally a meeting was summoned of all village councils, youth groups, church groups and religious organisations to discuss this matter. The women themselves took the initiative and led the discussion. As a result a consensus was reached whereby the villagers pledged to see that such forms of harassment did not take place in the future. Churches, temples, public platforms were used to put this message across, and to a very large extent the menace has been lessened (Rosa, 1987, pp. 163–4).

Factory Workers Fight Back

This action reflects the growing levels of community organising by women in industries such as electronics and textiles (Asian and Pacific Women's Resource Collection Network, 1989, pp. 120–8). Though these campaigns have so far received little publicity, newspapers such as *Drops of Sweat* are beginning to spread the message more widely (Rosa, 1994, p. 73). In some factories women are working through unions, but in others their methods are more informal, generated out of living and working together. In the words of Rohini, a Sri Lankan zone worker:

> We have our own ways to organise ourselves. This is very important for us. After a period the workers have got used to those methods. They know how to act given a particular situation . . . for instance, if new production targets are introduced. It is at the beginning that this is difficult but after a while this changes and new and varied methods begin to develop (Rosa, 1994, p. 86).

Similar developments have been reported from Mexico City, where the Nineteenth of September Union was set up by female garment workers following the earthquake of 1985 (Tirado, 1994). Shocked by the callous response of employers when many of their colleagues were buried in the remains of sweatshops the women decided to improve their conditions. Both the goals of the union and its strategies have been broadly based. Their demands have included improved hygiene and safety in the workplace (including toilet paper in the lavatories, clean drinking water and adequate space), the elimination of sexual harassment, an end to the heavy work that makes some women miscarry and a halt to the practice of dismissing women when they become pregnant (Tirado, 1994, p. 111).

Health and Safety in Sex Work

In many countries a new group of workers have recently become involved in health and safety campaigns – those who work in the sex industry. Prostitution has always been a dangerous form of employment but this has intensified over the past decade with the spread of HIV and AIDS. Most official attempts to monitor the health of sex workers have been designed to protect clients and society at large from the risk of infection, and most have been punitive in their approach. In response prostitutes in many parts of the world have now become involved in organisations set up specifically to promote their own health.

One of the best known of these is the Empower project, which helps women working in Patpang, a sex centre in Thailand (Garcia Moreno and Claro, 1994). However similar schemes are now in operation in many parts of the world (Berer and Ray, 1993: Ch. 14). In San Francisco the California Prostitutes Education Project (CAL-PEP) develops initiatives to help women negotiate safer sex. Its services include education, information, referrals, safer sex workshops, support groups, HIV and STD testing and vocational rehabilitation for sex workers who choose to leave the industry.

Spreading the Word

International networks are now being formed to bring local occupational health campaigns together. Organisations such as Women Working Worldwide provide the means to share resources and information, facilitating direct contact between groups of workers in the same industries. Similar cooperation is encouraged on a regional basis by organisations such as the Asia Monitor Resource Centre in Hong Kong, and the Committee for Asian Women. The first international conference on sex workers, health and human rights was held in Yaounde, Cameroon, in December 1992. Further links will be developed through the Network of Sex Work-Related HIV/AIDS Projects set up in London to provide a network for those providing HIV/AIDS services to sex workers and their clients around the world.

We have seen that women are working on several fronts to change their conditions at home and in waged employment, as well as in the grey area between. Progress is being made as women are empowered by literacy, improved health care, greater control over their fertility and growing economic independence. However a major threat to their health and safety remains unresolved, and that is the continuing reality of male violence.

Putting Violence on the Political Agenda

Every day millions of women continue to be denied their right to physical security that is enshrined in the 1948 Declaration of Human Rights (Bunch and Carillo, 1990). When Match International carried out a survey among women's groups around the world, violence emerged as the number one priority. As the African American activist Byllie Avery has described it, 'When sisters take their shoes off and start talking about what's happening, the first thing we cry about is the violence in our lives' (Avery, 1990).

Because it is carried out in the sanctity of the home, domestic violence is too often ignored – treated only as a private 'squabble' and not a matter for public concern. Rape, too, remains largely a hidden problem.

Over the last two decades campaigns have been waged in a number of countries to make this huge burden of violence visible (Dobash and Dobash, 1992; United Nations, 1989). A recent survey by the feminist network ISIS documented nearly 400 separate groups fighting violence against women in Latin America (Heise, 1993). There have also been many international initiatives, reflecting the global nature of the problem. Largely as a result of pressure from Latin American and Caribbean women, 25 November has been designated International Day of Violence Against Women. Each year it provides an occasion for demonstrations and other actions in many countries. Violence has also been a central focus of the work of the United Nations Division for the Advancement of Women (United Nations, 1989b).

Significant gains have been made in many parts of the world, but much remains to be done, especially in those countries where violence is increasing. Growing landlessness and poverty, greater militarism and a shift towards fundamentalism in religious and social values have all been identified as factors in this intensification.

Supporting Survivors

One of the earliest strategies to deal with the consequences of male violence was the organisation of refuges for survivors. The first was set up in England in 1971 and the number there has now grown to over a hundred. Though the picture is constantly changing, recent estimates suggest that there are now more than 700 in the United States alone (United Nations, 1989b, p. 77). Rape crisis centres too have proliferated, offering support and advice to women who have suffered sexual attacks.

In third world countries both refuges and crisis centres spread rapidly during the 1980s. One of the most effective developments has been in Costa Rica, where the Centro Feminista de Información y Acción (CEFEMINA) provides a range of services for *mujeres violentadas* (Cox, 1994). The first women's aid shelter in Malaysia was set up in 1981 and a network of services for female survivors is now being created across Asia and Oceania and in some parts of Africa. In the former socialist states too, organisations for abused women are beginning to appear for the first time. The White Circle of Safety was set up in the Czech Republic in 1991. It offers counselling and sponsors seminars and workshops on legal rights and self-defence. Above all it attempts to break the taboo on discussing violence against women (Siklova and Hradlikova, 1994).

The immediate aim of refuges and crisis centres is to help women deal with the physical, emotional and practical consequences of violence. While their approaches to this task may vary, most emphasise the need for women to share their experiences with others in a similar situation and to learn positive lessons for the future. One volunteer described her work in a shelter in Kuala Lumpur:

The causes of violence are varied, and can differ slightly according to the ethnic group. For example, Indian women face poverty and alcoholism; Malay, love affairs; Chinese, money problems are common. However husbands who beat their wives can belong to any profession. . . . . Here women of different ethnic groups, mothers in similar circumstances encourage each other, heal their wounded feelings and recover confidence to start their lives again (Matsui, 1989, p. 154).

Women from different communities will not always be able to share their problems quite so easily, but this example from Malaysia provides an important illustration of the potential for support and learning across cultures.

Though the number of refuges is increasing, many are underfunded and dependent on volunteer labour. One example is a centre set up in Suva, Fiji, in 1983. In the first five years of its existence, workers looked after over a thousand women who had experienced violence (Ali, 1990, p. 167). Ten years later it was still dependent on donations, many of them from abroad. A grant application to the United Nations Fund for Population Activities (UNFPA) was twice turned down at government level, apparently because the very existence of the centre was seen to be bad for Fiji's image.

In contrast extensive lobbying has led some governments to take violence against women seriously. In Hong Kong, New Zealand, Japan, Brazil, Papua New Guinea and Malaysia women's refuges now receive state funding. In Australia in particular the strength of the women's movement led to significant state support as early as 1975. Sexual assault centres and refuges receive funds from the government but are operated independently by women's groups, often affiliated to other voluntary organisations. Police practices have also been a focus of attention. In Brazil nearly one hundred all-women police stations have been set up to help the victims of violence and in India 'crimes against women cells' have been created in several cities (Heise, 1993, p. 8).

Campaigning for Prevention

As well as providing services for survivors, women have also been involved in campaigns to change aspects of their social environment that continue to promote violence. Indian women for instance have attempted to change the legislation relating to sexual crimes (Gandhi and Shah, 1991: Ch. 3). The first demonstration against the existing rape laws was organised in Delhi on International Women's Day 1980.

It was attended by three thousand women, making it one of the first public affirmations of the need for an autonomous women's movement in India. Groups such as the Forum Against Oppression of Women have worked with other organisations to bring about changes in the laws relating to dowry death and *sati* (wife burning). Similar campaigns have been organised in Pakistan and in Bangladesh, where women's pressure played a major part in passing the Prohibition of Dowry Act in 1980 and the Cruelty to Women Ordinance in 1983 (Asian and Pacific Women's Resource Collection Network, 1989, p. 195; Matsui, 1989, p. 81).

In some countries therapy programmes have been developed for persistent batterers, but their effectiveness has yet to be demonstrated. Elsewhere community education strategies have attempted to reach a wider population of both actually and potentially violent men and those who could help to control them. These programmes have used a variety of strategies to alert the maximum number of people to the reality and unacceptability of violence against women. In Jamaica the theatre group Sistren produced a play to accompany their pamphlet 'No! to Sexual Violence' (Ford-Smith, 1994). This was the starting point for a series of educational and cultural initiatives designed to help women make sense of their own experiences and to generate greater concern about the rise in sexual violence.

In Australia a special domestic violence education initiative was implemented in 1989 as part of a wider prevention programme. In Papua New Guinea an impressive campaign has been developed, using leaflets, video and radio programmes. An accompanying action programme was worked out in collaboration with the National Council of Women. It included village meetings throughout the country as well as direct action by local groups to protect and support battered women. Some success has been reported, with the issue of violence being widely debated. However the threat to women remains very great.

It is clear that while some improvements can be achieved, a significant reduction in male violence is unlikely to be brought about without wider social change. Women will continue to be at risk as long as they remain socially and economically dependent on men within the context of unequal family relationships that remain stubbornly resistant to public scrutiny. The importance of these structural factors in perpetuating male attacks on women was highlighted in a recent speech by African National Congress member Frene Ginwala. She placed violence firmly in the context of wider gender inequalities and demanded that the constitution for the new South Africa should protect women from family practices that discriminate against them:

> We can no more accept even at a social level, a cultural practice that relegates the status of women than we would accept a claim by Afrikaaners that respect for their culture requires the separation or segregation of races. Just as commitment to racial equality is absolute, so too should we consider the commitment to the equality of women and the latter cannot be diminished on the grounds of sensitivity to cultural practices, or respect for the privacy of family relations (quoted in Hansson, 1991, p. 182).

Conclusion

This book began by identifying physical and psychological health as basic human needs for both women and men. It then explored the economic, social and cultural obstacles that prevent many women from meeting their needs. Some of these factors limit the potential of both sexes – global inequalities in income and wealth, for instance, as well as environmental degradation and the barriers of race and class that continue to divide both rich and poor countries. However others are gender specific – unequal burdens of domestic labour, discrimination in the allocation of household resources, constraints on women's capacity to determine their own sexuality and procreativity, inequalities in waged work and political power, and the continuing epidemic of male violence against women.

This final chapter explored women's responses to these constraints on their well-being. We saw that millions are now engaged both individually and collectively in the fight for better health. They have formulated goals, created strategies and devised methods appropriate for their own circumstances. Campaigns have been both 'bottom up' and 'top down' and interventions have been made at local, regional and international levels. Women have worked for change both inside and outside medical institutions and formal organisations, and have organised themselves in mixed as well as single sex groups. Some would define themselves as feminist while others would not. No single movement has emerged but all share a common belief in women's right to health.

Throughout, this book has documented the infinite variety of activities that constitute the fabric of women's lives. In particular it has highlighted their active participation in promoting the well-being of others. Unless women's health needs are met, their capacity to carry out these activities will be arbitrarily constrained and they will be unable to realise their own potential as human beings. Many more will die prematurely and even more will have the quality of their lives diminished. In order to prevent such damage, women's right to health and the formulation of appropriate strategies for its realisation must be a central concern not just in feminist politics but in wider campaigns for sustainable development, political freedom and economic and social justice.

Further Reading

Asian and Pacific Women's Resource Collection Network (1989) *Asian and Pacific Women's Resource and Action Series: health* (Kuala Lumpur: Asian and Pacific Development Centre). A text that provides resources and ideas for action for women in the Asian and Pacific Region. Covering sexuality, reproduction, domestic work, waged work and violence it provides a model that could be adopted by feminist health activists in other parts of the world.

Boston Women's Health Book Collective (1993) *The New Our Bodies Ourselves* (New York: Touchstone Publishing Co.). An old favourite that remains an essential resource for women wanting to take control of their bodies and their health.

Dankelman, I. and Davidson, J. (1988) *Women and Environment in the Third World: a blueprint for the future* (London: Earthscan). A stimulating account of the relationship between women and their physical environment in third world countries. It includes well documented case studies and interviews with women conservationists, examining the ways in which women can organise to meet environmental challenges.

Davis, M. (1994) *Women and Violence: realities and responses worldwide* (London: Zed Books). An impressive collection of articles on women's campaigns against violence. This contains extremely valuable case studies from around the world that raise key questions about the causes of sexual violence and the most effective ways of combating it.

Gerber Fried, M. (1990) *Abortion to Reproductive Freedom: transforming a movement* (Boston: South End Press). An anthology of articles from activists and academics involved in the fight for reproductive rights in the United States. It offers a history and critique of the abortion rights struggle from the 1960s to the present and argues for a more inclusive campaign for reproductive rights that recognises difference and diversity.

Sen, G., Germain, A. and Chen, C. (1994) *Population Policies Reconsidered: health, empowerment and human rights* (Cambridge Mass: Harvard University Press). A collection of articles from a diverse group of scholars, policy makers and women's health activists. It explores future directions for population politics and policies with an emphasis on health, empowerment and human rights.

Bibliography

Abdullah, T. and Zeidenstein, S. (1982) *Village Women of Bangladesh: prospects for change* (Oxford: Pergamon Press).

Adler, N., David. H., Major, B., Roth, S., Russo, N. and Wyatt, G. (1990) 'Psychological responses after abortion', *Science*, vol. 248, no. 6 (April), pp. 41–3.

Adler, N., Keyes, S., and Robertson, P. (1991) 'Psychological issues in new reproductive technologies: pregnancy-inducing technology and diagnostic screening', in J. Rodin and, A. Collins (eds) *Women and New Reproductive Technologies: Medical, Psychosocial, Legal and Ethical Dilemmas* (Hillsdale, NJ: Lawrence Erlbaum Associates).

Agarwal, B. (1986) *Cold Hearths and Barren Slopes: the woodfuel crisis in the third world* (London: Zed Press).

Alfredsson, L., Spetz, C. and Theorell, T. (1985) 'Type of occupation and near future hospitalization for myocardial infarction and some other diagnoses', *International Journal of Epidemiology*, vol. 14, no. 3, pp. 378–88.

Ali, S. (1990) 'It's been a long road: a women's crisis centre in Australia', in Health Sharing Women, *The Healthsharing Reader* (Sydney: Pandora).

Allen, S. and Wolkowitz, C. (1987) *Homeworking: myths and realities* (London: Macmillan).

Amaro, H., Beckman, L., and Mays, V. (1987) 'A comparison of black and white women entering alcoholism treatment', *Journal of Studies on Alcohol*, vol. 48, no. 3, pp. 220–8.

American Medical Association, Council on Ethical and Judicial Affairs (1991) 'Gender disparities in clinical decision making', *Journal of American Medical Association*, vol. 266, no. 4, pp. 559–62.

Amnesty International (1991) *Rape and Sexual Abuse: torture and ill-treatment of women in detention* (London: Amnesty International Secretariat).

Anastos, K. and Marte, C. (1991) 'Women – the missing persons in the AIDS epidemic', in N. McKenzie (ed.) *The AIDS Reader: social, political and ethical issues* (New York: Meridian).

Anastos, K. and Vermund, S. (1993) 'Epidemiology and natural history', in A. Kurth (ed.) *Until the Cure: caring for women with HIV* (London and New Haven: Yale University Press).

Anderson, M. (1988) *Thinking about Women: sociological perspectives on sex and gender* (London: Macmillan).

Andrews, B. and Brown, G. (1988) 'Violence in the community: a biographical approach', *British Journal of Psychiatry*, vol. 153, pp. 305–12.

Aneshensel, C. (1986) 'Marital and employment role-strain, social support and depression among adult women', in S. E. Hobfoll (ed.) *Stress, Social Support and Women* (New York: Hemisphere).

Aral, S. and Holmes, K. (1991) 'Sexually transmitted diseases in the AIDS era', *Scientific American*, vol. 264, no. 2, pp. 18–25.

Arber, S., Gilbert, N. and Dale, A. (1985) 'Paid employment and women's health: a benefit or a source of role strain?', *Sociology of Health and Illness*, vol. 7, no. 3, pp. 375–401.

Armstrong, S. (1994) 'Rape in South Africa: an invisible part of apartheid's legacy', *Focus on Gender*, vol. 2, no. 2, pp. 35–9.

Arney, W. R. (1985) *Power and the Profession of Obstetrics* (Chicago: University of Chicago Press).

Asch, A. and Fine, M. (1990) 'Shared dreams: a left perspective on disability rights and reproductive rights', in M. Gerber Fried (ed.) *Abortion to Reproductive Freedom: transforming a movement* (Boston: South End Press).

Asetoyer, C. (1993) 'Fetal alcohol syndrome: a nation in distress', in *Sojourner: the Women's Forum* (March).

ASH Women and Smoking Group (1990a) *Teenage Girls and Smoking: an expert report of the ASH Women and Smoking Group* (London: Action on Smoking and Health).

ASH Women and Smoking Group (1990b) *Smoke Still Gets in their Eyes: an expert report of the ASH Women and Smoking Group* (London: Action on Smoking and Health).

Ashton, H. (1991) 'Psychotropic drug prescribing for women', *British Journal of Psychiatry*, vol. 158, supplement 10, pp. 30–5.

Asian and Pacific Women's Resource Collection Network (1989) *Asian and Pacific Women's Resource and Action Series: health* (Kuala Lumpur: Asian and Pacific Development Centre).

Avery, B. (1990) 'Breathing life into ourselves: the evolution of the National Black Women's Health Project', in E. White (ed.) *The Black Women's Health Book: speaking for ourselves* (Seattle: Seal Press).

Baer, H. (ed.) (1987) *Encounters with Biomedicine: case studies in medical anthropology* (New York: Gordon and Breach).

Baker, R. and Woodrow, S. (1984) 'The clean, light image of the electronics industry: miracle or mirage?', in W. Chavkin (ed.) *Double Exposure: women's health hazards on the job and at home* (New York: Monthly Review Press).

Balasubrahmanyan, V. (1986) 'Finger in the dyke: the fight to keep injectables out of India', in K. McDonnell (ed.) *Adverse Effects: women and the pharmaceutical industry* (Penang, Malaysia: International Organisation of Consumer Unions).

Ball, C. (1991) 'When broken heartedness becomes a political issue', in T. Wallace with C. March (eds) *Changing Perceptions: writings on gender and development* (Oxford: Oxfam).

Balter, M., Manheimer, D., Mellinger, G. *et al* (1984) 'A cross-national comparison of anti-anxiety/sedative drug use', *Current Medical Research and Opinion*, vol. 8 (supplement 4), pp. 5–18.

Bang, A., Bang, M., Baitule, M., Choudhary, Y., Sarmukaddam, S. and Tale, O. (1989) 'High prevalence of gynaecological diseases in rural Indian women', *Lancet* vol. (i) pp. 85–8.

Bang, R. and Bang, A. (1992) 'Why women hide them: rural women's viewpoints on reproductive tract infections', *Manushi, A Journal About Women and Society*, vol. 69, pp. 27–30.

Banta, D. and Thacker, S. (1979) 'Assessing the costs and benefits of electronic fetal monitoring', *Obstetrical and Gynaecological Survey*, vol. 34, no. 8, pp. 627–42.

Banta, D. and Thacker, S. (1982) 'The risk and benefits of episiotomy: a review', *Birth*, vol. 9, no. 1, pp. 25–30.

Banzhaf, M. (1990) 'Race, women and AIDS: introduction', in ACT UP/NY Women and AIDS Book Group. *Women, AIDS and Activism* (Boston, Mass: South End Press).

Barbee, E. and Little, M. (1993) 'Health, social class and African-American women', in S. James and, A. Busia (eds) *Theorising Black Feminisms: the visionary pragmatism of black women*. Routledge.

Barnett, E. (1989) 'Notes on nervios: a disorder of menopause', *Health Care for Women International*, vol. 10, nos 2 and 3, pp. 159–69.

Barnett, R. and Marshall, N. (1991) 'The relationship between women's work and family roles and their subjective wellbeing and psychological distress', in M. Frankenhaeuser, U. Lundberg and, M. Chesney (eds) *Women, Work and Health: stress and opportunities* (New York: Plenum Press).

Barrett, M. and Phillips, A. (1992) *Destabilising Theory: contemporary feminist debates* (Cambridge: Polity Press).

Barrios de Chungara, D. with Viezzer, M. (1978) *Let Me Speak! Testimony of Domitila, a woman of the Bolivian mines* (London: Stage One Press).

Barroso, C. and Bruschini, C. (1991) 'Building politics from personal lives: discussions on sexuality among poor women in Brazil', in C. Mohanty, A. Russo and, L. Torres (eds) *Third World Women and the Politics of Feminism* (Bloomington and Indianapolis: Indiana University Press).

Barry, U. (1988) 'Abortion in the Republic of Ireland', *Feminist Review*, vol. 29, pp. 57–63.

Bart, P. (1981) 'Seizing the means of reproduction: an illegal feminist abortion collective and how it worked', in H. Roberts (ed.) *Women, Health and Reproduction* (London: Routledge and Kegan Paul).

Bartley, M. Popay, J. and Plewis, J. (1992) 'Domestic conditions, paid employment and women's experiences of ill health', *Sociology of Health and Illness*, vol. 14, no. 3, pp. 313–41.

Baruch, G. Biener, L. and Barnett, R. (1987) 'Women and gender in research on work and family stress', *American Psychologist*, vol. 42, no. 2, pp. 130–6.

Bassett, M. and Mhloyi, M. (1991) 'Women and AIDS in Zimbabwe: the making of an epidemic', *International Journal of Health Services*, vol. 21, no. 1, pp. 143–56.

Bayer, R. (1982) 'Reproductive hazards in the workplace: bearing the burden of fetal risk', *Millbank Memorial Fund Quarterly*, vol. 60, no. 4, pp. 633–56.

Beary, M., Lacey, J. and Merry, J. (1986) 'Alcoholism and eating disorders in women of fertile age', *British Journal of Addiction*, vol. 81, no. 5, pp. 685–9.

Becker, G. (1981) *Treatise on the Family* (Cambridge Mass: Harvard University Press).

Beckman, L. (1980) 'Perceived antecedents and effects of alcohol consumption in women', *Quarterly Journal of the Study of Alcohol*, vol. 41, no. 5, pp. 518–30.

Beckman, L. (1984) 'Treatment needs of women alcoholics', *Alcoholism Treatment Quarterly*, vol. 1, no. 2, pp. 101–14.

Beckwith, B. (1985) 'Boston Women's Health Book Collective: women empowering women', *Women and Health*, vol. 10, no. 1, pp. 1–7.

Bell, N. (1992) 'Women and AIDS: too little, too late?', in H. Bequaert Holmes and L. Purdy (eds) *Feminist Perspectives in Medical Ethics* (Bloomington: Indiana University Press).

Bell, S. (1994) 'Translating science to the people: updating the new *Our Bodies Ourselves*', *Women's Studies International Forum*, vol. 17, no. 1, pp. 9–18.

Belle, D. (1990) 'Poverty and women's mental health', *American Psychologist*, vol. 45, no. 3, pp. 385–9.

Benton, J. (1993) 'The role of women's organisations and groups in community development: a case study of Bolivia', in J. Momsen and V. Kinnaird (eds) *Different Places, Different Voices: gender and development in Africa, Asia and Latin America* (London: Routledge).

Berer, M. (1993) 'Population and family planning policies: women-centred perspectives', *Reproductive Health Matters*, no. 1, pp. 4–12.

Berer, M. and Ray, S. (1993) *Women and HIV/AIDS: an international resource book* (London: Pandora).

Berger, I. (1983) 'Sources of class consciousness: South African women in recent labor struggles', *International Journal of African Historical Studies*, vol. 16, no. 1, pp. 49–66.

Berk, S. (1985) *The Gender Factory: the apportionment of work in American households* (New York: Plenum).

Berman, B. and Gritz, E. (1991) 'Women and smoking: current trends and issues for the 1990s', *Journal of Substance Abuse*, vol. 3, pp. 221–38.

Bernard, J. (1972) *The Future of Marriage* (New York: World Publishing).

Bernstein, B. and Kane, R. (1981) 'Physicians' attitudes towards female patients', *Medical Care*, vol. 19, no. 6, pp. 600–8.

Binney, V., Harkell, G. and Nixon, J. (1981) *Leaving Violent Men: a study of refuges and housing for battered women* (Leeds: Women's Aid Federation).

Birke, L. (1986) *Women, Feminism and Biology* (Brighton: Wheatsheaf).

Birke, L., Himmelweit, S. and Vines, G. (1990) *Tomorrow's Child: reproductive technologies in the 90s* (London: Virago).

Blackburn, C. (1991) *Poverty and Health: working with families* (Milton Keynes: Open University Press).

Blaxter, M. (1990) *Health and Lifestyles* (London: Routledge).

Blay, E. (1985) 'Social movements and women's participation in Brazil', *International Political Science Review*, vol. 6, no. 3, pp. 297–305.

Boston Women's Health Book Collective (1971) *Our Bodies Ourselves* (New York: Simon and Schuster).

Boulton, M. (1983) *On Being a Mother* (London: Tavistock).

Bowler, R., Mergler, D., Huel, G., Harrison, R. and Cone, J. (1991a) 'Neuropsychological impairment among former microelectronics workers', *Neurotoxicology*, vol. 12, pp. 87–104.

Bowler, R., Mergler, D., Harrison, R., Rauch, S. and Cone, J. (1991b) 'Affective and personality disturbances among female former microelectronics workers', *Journal of Clinical Psychology*, vol. 47, no. 1, pp. 41–52.

Bradley, C. (1994) 'Why male violence against women is a development issue: reflections from Papua New Guinea', in M. Davis (ed.) *Women and Violence: responses and realities worldwide* (London: Zed Press).

Brady, J. (1991) *1 in 3: women with cancer confront an epidemic* (Pittsburg and San Francisco: Cleis Press).

Braidotti, R., Charkiewicz, E., Häusler, S. and Wieringa, S. (1994) *Women, the Environment and Sustainable Development: towards a theoretical synthesis* (London: Zed Press).

Braybrooke, D. (1987) *Meeting Needs* (Princeton: Princeton University Press).

Breslau, N., Davis, G., Andreski, P. and Peterson, E. (1991) 'Traumatic events and post traumatic stress disorder in an urban population of young adults', *Archives of General Psychiatry*, vol. 48, no. 3, pp. 216–22.

Brettle, R. and Leen, C. (1991) 'The natural history of HIV and AIDS in women', *AIDS*, vol. 5, no. 11, pp. 1283–92.

Bridgewood, A. and Savage, D. (1993) *General Household Survey 1991* (UK Office of Population Censuses and Surveys).

Briggs, A. and Oliver, J. (1985) *Caring: experiences of looking after disabled relatives* (London: Routledge and Kegan Paul).

Bronstein, A. (1982) *The Triple Struggle: Latin American peasant women* (War on Want).

Broom, D. (1986) 'Occupational health of houseworkers', *Australian Feminist Studies*, vol. 2, pp. 15–33.

Broom, D. (1993) *Damned if We Do: contradictions in women's health care* (Sydney: Allen and Unwin).

Broverman, I., Broverman, D., Clarkson, H., Rosenkrantz, P. and Vogel, S. (1970) 'Sex role stereotypes and clinical judgements of mental health', *Journal of Consulting and Clinical Psychology*, vol. 34, no. 1, pp. 1–7.

Brown, G. and Harris, T. (1978) *Social Origins of Depression* (London: Tavistock).

Brown, J. (1992) 'Introduction: definitions, assumptions, themes and issues', in D. Counts, J. Brown and J. Campbell (eds) *Sanctions and Sanctuary: cultural perspectives on the beating of wives* (Boulder, Co: Westview Press).

Browne, A. and Finkelhor, D. (1986) 'The impact of child sexual abuse: a review of the research', *Psychological Bulletin*, vol. 99, no. 1, pp. 66–77.

Browne, S. Connors, D. and Stern, D. (1985) *With the Power of Each Breath* (San Francisco, Cleis Press).

Bruce, J. (1987) 'Users' perspectives on contraceptive technology and delivery systems: highlighting some feminist issues', *Technology in Society*, vol. 9, pp. 359–83.

Bruce, J. and Dwyer, D. (1988) 'Purpose and overview', in D. Dwyer and J. Bruce (eds) *A Home Divided: women and income in the third world* (Stanford, Ca: Stanford University Press).

Buckley, M. (1989) *Women and Ideology in the Soviet Union* (Brighton: Harvester).

Buckley, T., Harris, R., Doll, R., Vessey, M. and Williams, P. (1981) 'Case control study of the husbands of women with dysplasia or carcinoma of the cervix uteri', *Lancet* vol. (ii), pp. 1010–15.

Bularzik, M. (1978) 'Sexual harassment in the workplace – historical notes', *Radical America* (July/August), pp. 24–43.

Bullock, S. (1994) *Women and Work* (London: Zed Press).

Bunch, C. and Carillo, R. (1990) *Gender Violence: a development and human rights issue* (Dublin: Attic Press).

Burgess, A. and Holmstrom, L. (1979) *Rape, Crisis and Recovery* (Bowie: Robert, J. Brady).

Busfield, J. (1986) *Managing Madness: changing ideas and practice* (London: Hutchinson).

Buvinic, M., Lycette, M. and McGreevy, W. (eds) (1983) *Women and Poverty in the Third World* (Baltimore, MD: Johns Hopkins Press).

Cairo Women's Health Book Collective (1991) *Women's Lives and Health in Egypt* (Cairo Women's Health Book Collective, c/o Dr Hind Khattab, Delta Consultants, 12 Mohamed El-Hefni Street, 3rd Floor, Apt. 7, Garden City, Cairo).

Camino, L. (1989) 'Nerves, worriation and black women: a community study in the American south', *Health Care for Women International*, vol. 10, nos 2 and 3, pp. 295–314.

Campbell, J. (1992) 'Wife battering: cultural contexts versus western social sciences', in D. Counts, J. Brown and J. Campbell (eds) *Sanctions and Sanctuary: cultural perspectives on the beating of wives* (Boulder, Co: Westview Press).

Campbell, R. and Macfarlane, A. (1990) 'Recent debate on the place of birth', in J. Garcia, R. Kilpatrick and M. Richards (eds) *The Politics of Maternity Care: services for childbearing women in twentieth century Britain* (Oxford: Clarendon Press).

Carovano, K. (1991) 'More than mothers and whores: redefining the AIDS prevention needs of women. *International Journal of Health Services* vol. 21, no. 1, pp. 131–42.

Cartwright, A. (1988) 'Unintended pregnancies that lead to babies', *Social Science and Medicine*, vol. 27, no. 3, pp. 249–54.

Cates, W., Smith, J., Rochat, R. and Grimes, D. (1982) 'Mortality from abortion and childbirth: are the statistics biased?', *Journal of the American Medical Association*, vol. 248, no. 2, pp. 192–6.

Centro de Investigación Para la Acción Femenina (1987) 'Notes on a study of women workers in the Dominican Republic', in M. Davis (ed.) *Third World Second Sex 2* (London: Zed Press).

Cerullo, M. (1990) 'Hidden history: an illegal abortion in 1968', in M. Gerber Fried (ed.) *From Abortion to Reproductive Freedom: transforming a movement* (Boston: South End Press).

Chalmers, I. (1989) 'Evaluating the effects of care during pregnancy and childbirth', in I. Chalmers, M. Enkin and M. Keirse (eds) *Effective Care in Pregnancy and Childbirth*, vol. 2 (Oxford: Clarendon Press).

Chalmers, I., Garcia, J. and Post, S. (1989) 'Hospital policies for labour and delivery', in I. Chalmers, M. Enkin and M. Keirse (eds) *Effective Care in Pregnancy and Childbirth*, vol. 2 (Oxford: Clarendon Press).

Chapkis, W. and Enloe, C. (1983) *Of Common Cloth: women in the global textile industry* (Amsterdam: Transnational Institute).

Chard, T. and Richards, M. (1977) *Benefits and Hazards of the New Obstetrics* (London: Heinemann).

Charlton, A. (1989) 'Smoking and weight control in teenagers', *Public Health*, vol. 98, no. 5, pp. 277–81.

Chavkin, W. (1984) *Double Exposure: women's health hazards on the job and at home* (New York: Monthly Review Press).

Chen, B., Hong, C., Pandey, M. and Smith, K. (1990) 'Indoor air pollution in developing countries', *World Health Statistics Quarterly*, vol. 43, pp. 127–38.

Chen, L., Gesche, M., Ahmed, S., Chowdhury, A. and Mosley, W. (1974) 'Maternal mortality in rural Bangladesh', *Studies in Family Planning*, vol. 5, no. 11, pp. 334–41.

Chen, L., Huq, E. and d'Souza, S. (1981) 'Sex bias in the allocation of food and health care in rural Bangladesh', *Population and Development Review*, vol. 7, no. 1, pp. 55–70.

Chernin, K. (1983) *Womansize: the tyranny of slenderness* (London: Women's Press).

Chollat-Traquet, C. (1992) *Women and Tobacco* (Geneva: World Health Organisation).

Christensen, E. (1989) 'Alcohol as a component of wife battering', in Nordic Council for Alcohol and Drug Research, *Women, Alcohol and Drugs in the Nordic Countries* (Helsinki: NAD).

Christensen, J. (1991) 'In Brazil, sterilising women is the method of choice', *Women's Global Network for Reproductive Rights Newsletter* no. 35, (April–June), pp. 11–13.

Clare, A. (1991) 'The benzodiazepine controversy: a psychiatrist's reaction', in J. Gabe (ed.) *Understanding Tranquilliser Use: the role of the social sciences* (London: Tavistock).

Clarke, A. and Montini, T. (1993) 'The many faces of RU 486: tales of situated knowledges and technological constraints', *Science, Technology and Human Values*, vol. 18, no. 1, pp. 42–78.

Coeytaux, F. (1988) 'Induced abortion in sub-Saharan Africa: what we do know and what we do not know', *Studies in Family Planning*, vol. 19, no. 3, pp. 186–9.

Cohen, B. (1984) *Human Aspects in Office Automation* (Oxford: Elsevier).

Coleman, L. and Dickinson, C. (1984) 'The risks of healing: the hazards of the nursing profession', in W. Chavkin (ed.) *Double Exposure: women's health hazards on the job and at home* (New York: Monthly Review Press).

Colligan, M., Smith, M. and Hurrell, J. (1977) 'Occupational incidence rates of mental health disorders', *Journal of Human Stress*, vol. 3, pp. 34–9.

Commonwealth Department of Community Services and Health (1989) *National Women's Health Policy: advancing women's health in Australia* (Canberra: Australian Government Publishing Service).

Cook, R. (1989) 'Abortion laws and policies: challenges and opportunities', *Int. Journal of Gynaecology and Obstetrics*, Suppl. 3, pp. 61–87.

Cook, R. and Maine, D. (1987) 'Spousal veto over family planning services', *American Journal of Public Health*, vol. 77, no. 3, pp. 339–44.

Cooperstock, R. and Lennard, H. (1986) 'Some social meanings of tranquilliser use', in J. Gabe and P. Williams (eds) *Tranquillisers: social, psychological and clinical perspectives* (London: Tavistock).

Cornelisen, A. (1977) *Women of the Shadows: a study of the wives and mothers of Southern Italy* (New York: Vintage Books).

Correa, S. and Petchesky, R. (1994) 'Reproductive and sexual rights: a feminist perspective', in G. Sen, A. Germain and L. Chen (eds) *Population Policies Reconsidered: health, empowerment and rights* (Boston Mass: Harvard University Press).

Corrigan, E. and Butler, S. (1991) 'Irish alcoholic women in treatment: early findings', *International Journal of the Addictions*, vol. 26, no. 3, pp. 281–92.

Corrin, C. (1992) *Superwomen and the Double Burden: women's experience of change in central and eastern Europe and the former Soviet Union* (London: Scarlet Press).

Cottingham, J. and Royston, E. (1991) *Obstetric Fistulae: a review of available information* (Geneva: WHO).

Cotton, P. (1990) 'Is there still too much extrapolation from data on middle aged white men?', *Journal of the American Medical Association*, vol. 263, no. 8, pp. 1049–50.

Counts, D. Brown, J. and Campbell, J. (eds) (1992) *Sanctions and Sanctuary: cultural perspectives on the beating of wives* (Boulder, Co: Westview Press).

Counts, D. (1987) 'Female suicide and wife abuse: a cross cultural perspective', *Suicide and Life-Threatening Behaviour* vol. 17, no. 3, pp. 194–204.

Covell, D. and Refshauge, C. (1986) 'Jobs for women challenges BHP: unmasking discriminatory safety practices', in *Proceedings of Conference: Women's Health in a*

Changing Society, vol. 2, Adelaide, Australia, September 1985, available office of Women's Advisor 52 Pirie St, Adelaide, SA 5000.

Coward, R. (1989) *The Whole Truth: the myth of alternative health* (London: Faber and Faber).

Cox, E. (1994) 'Gender violence and women's health in Central America', in M. Davis (ed.) *Women and Violence: realities and responses worldwide* (London: Zed Press).

Craig, M. (1981) *The Office Workers' Survival Handbook* (London: British Society for Social Responsibility in Science).

Crofton, J. (1990) 'Tobacco and the third world', *Thorax*, vol. 45, pp. 164–9.

Crull, P. (1984) 'Sexual harassment and women's health', in W. Chavkin (ed.) *Double Exposure: women's health hazards on the job and at home* (New York: Monthly Review Press).

Dalley, G. (1988) *Ideologies of Caring: rethinking community and collectivism* (London: Macmillan).

Daly, M. (1979) *Gyn/Ecology: the meta-ethics of radical feminism* (London: Women's Press).

Daniels, J. (1990) 'Court-ordered Caesareans: a growing concern for indigent women', in M. Gerber Fried (ed.) *From Abortion to Reproductive Freedom: transforming a movement* (Boston, South End Press).

Dankelman, J. and Davidson, I. (1988) *Women and Environment in the Third World: alliance for the future* (London: Earthscan).

Das, L. (1988) 'Violence against women: an Indian view', in Welsh Womens Aid, *Report of the International Women's Aid Conference, Cardiff, 1988* (Available from WWA, 341–342 Crwys Road, Cardiff, Wales).

Das Gupta, M. (1987) 'Selective discrimination against female children in rural Punjab, India. *Population and Development Review*, vol. 13, no. 1, pp. 77–100.

Daswani, M. (1987) 'Women against injectables', in K. Bhate, L. Menon, M. Gupte, M. Savara, M. Daswani, P. Prakash, R. Kashyap and V. Patel (eds) *In Search of our Bodies: a feminist look at women, health and reproduction in India* (Bombay: Shakti).

Datar, C. (1988) 'Reflections on the anti-rape campaign in Bombay', in S. Wieringa (ed.) *Women's Struggles and Strategies* (Aldershot: Gower Press).

Davey, B. (1986) 'Cervical cancer: connections and causes', *Nursing Times* 11 June.

Davin, D. (1987) 'Gender and population in the People's Republic of China', in H. Afshar (ed.) *Women, State and Ideology* (London: Macmillan).

Davin, D. (1992) 'Population policy and reform: the Soviet Union, Eastern Europe and China', in S. Rai, H. Pilkington and A. Phizacklea (eds) *Women in the Face of Change* (London: Routledge).

Davis, A. (1981) *Women, Race and Class* (New York: Random House).

Davis, A. (1990) 'Racism, birth control and reproductive rights', in M. Gerber Fried (ed.) *From Abortion to Reproductive Freedom: transforming a movement* (Boston: South End Press).

Davis, D. and Guarnaccia, D. (1989) 'Wealth, culture and the nature of nerves: an introduction', *Medical Anthropology*, vol. 11, pp. 1–13.

Davis, M. (1994) *Women and Violence: realities and responses worldwide* (London: Zed Press).

Davis, R. (1987) 'Current trends in cigarette advertising and marketing', *New England Journal of Medicine*, vol. 316, no. 12, pp. 725–32.

de Beauvoir, S. (1972) *The Second Sex* (ed.) H. M. Parshlay (Harmondsworth: Penguin) (first published 1949).

de Bruyn, M. (1992) 'Women and AIDS in developing countries', *Social Science and Medicine*, vol. 34, no. 3, pp. 249–62.

De Matteo, B. (1985) *Terminal Shock: the health hazards of video display terminals* (Toronto: NC Press).

DeMaeyer, E. and Adiels-Tegman, M. (1985) 'The prevalence of anaemia in the world', *World Health Statistics Quarterly*, vol. 38, pp. 302–16.

Denenberg, R. (1990a) 'Treatment and trials', in The ACT UP/NY Women and AIDS Book Group, *Women, AIDS and Activism* (Boston, Mass: South End Press).

Denenberg, R. (1990b) 'Unique aspects of HIV infection in women' in: The ACT UP/NY Women and AIDS Book Group, *Women, AIDS and Activism* (Boston, Mass: South End Press).

Devesa, S. and Diamond, E. (1980) 'Association of breast cancer and cervical cancer incidences with income and education among whites and blacks', J. *National Cancer Inst.*, vol. 65, pp. 515–28.

Dietrich, G. (1986) 'Our bodies, ourselves: organising women on health issues', *Socialist Health Review* (March), pp. 179–84.

DiGiacomo, S. (1992) 'Metaphor as illness: postmodern dilemmas in the representation of body, mind and disorder', *Medical Anthropology*, vol. 14, pp. 109–37.

Dixon-Mueller, R. (1993) *Population Policy and Women's Rights: transforming reproductive choice* (Westport Conn: Praeger).

Dixon-Mueller, R. and Wasserheit, J. (1991) *The Culture of Silence: Reproductive Tract Infections among Women in the Third World* (New York: International Women's Health Coalition).

Dobash, R. and Dobash, R. (1980) *Violence against Wives: a case against the patriarchy* (London: Open Books).

Dobash, P. and Dobash, R. (1992) *Women, Violence and Social Change* (London: Routledge).

Dorkenoo, E. and Elworthy, S. (1994) 'Female genital mutilation', in M. Davis (ed.) *Women and Violence: responses and realities worldwide* (London: Zed Press).

Doty, P. (1987) 'Health status and health services among older women: an international perspective', *World Health Statistics Quarterly*, vol. 40, pp. 279–90.

Douglas, M. (1966) *Purity and Danger* (London: Routledge and Kegan Paul).

Dowie, M., Foster, D., Marshall, C., Weir, D. and King, J. (1982) 'The illusion of safety', *Mother Jones*, June, pp. 38–48.

Doyal, L. (1985a) 'Women, health and the sexual division of labour: a case study of the women's health movement in Britain', *Critical Social Policy* vol. 7, pp. 21–32.

Doyal, L. (1985b) 'Women and the National Health Service: the carers and the careless', in E. Lewin and V. Olesen (eds) *Women, Health and Healing: toward a new perspective* (London: Tavistock).

Doyal, L. (1987) 'Infertility – a life sentence? Women and the National Health Service', in M. Stanworth (ed.) *Reproductive Technologies: gender, motherhood and medicine* (Oxford: Polity Press).

Doyal, L. (1994a) 'Changing medicine: the politics of women's health', in J. Gabe, D. Kellehar and G. Williams (eds) *Challenging Medicine* (London: Tavistock).

Doyal, L. (1994b) 'Managing conception: self insemination and the limits of reproductive freedom', *Policy and Politics*, vol. 22, no. 2, pp. 89–93.

Doyal, L. Epstein, S. Green, K. Irwin, A. Russell, D. Steward, F. Williams, R. and Gee, D. (1983) *Cancer in Britain: the politics of prevention* (London: Pluto Press).

Doyal, L. and Doyal, L. (1984) 'Western Scientific Medicine: a philosophical and political prognosis', in L. Birke and J. Silvertown (eds) *More than the Parts: biology and politics* (London: Pluto Press).

Doyal, L. and Gough, I. (1991), A. *Theory of Human Need* (London: Macmillan).

Dreifus, C. (1978) 'Sterilizing the poor', in C. Dreifus (ed.) *Seizing our Bodies: the politics of women's health* (New York: Vintage Books).

Duckert, F. (1989) 'The treatment of female problem drinkers', in Nordic Council for Alcohol and Drug Research, *Women, Alcohol and Drugs in the Nordic Countries* (Helsinki: NAD).

Duggan, L. (1986) 'From birth control to population control: Depo Provera in South East Asia', in K. McDonnell (ed.) *Adverse Effects: women and the pharmaceutical industry* (Penang, Malaysia: International Organisation of Consumer Unions).

Dunne, F. (1988) 'Are women more easily damaged by alcohol than men?', *British Journal of Addiction*, vol. 83, pp. 1135–6.

Durward, L. (1988) *Poverty in Pregnancy: the cost of an adequate diet for expectant mothers (with 1988 update)* (London: Maternity Alliance).

Dworkin, A. (1981) *Pornography: men possessing women* (London: Women's Press).

Dwyer, D. and Bruce, J. (eds) (1988), A. *Home Divided: women and income in the third world* (Stanford, Ca: Stanford University Press).

Editorial (1989) 'Meeting the need for female sterilisation', *The Lancet*, vol. (ii), pp. 1189–90.

Edling, C. (1980) 'Anaesthetic gases as an occupational hazard – a review', *Scandinavian Journal of Work, Environment and Health*, vol. 6, pp. 85–93.

Edwards, A. (1988) *Regulation and Repression* (Sydney, NSW: Allen and Unwin).

Ehrenreich, B., Dowie, M. and Minkin, S. (1979) 'The charge: gynocide. The accused: the US Government', *Mother Jones* (November).

Ehrenreich, B. and English, D. (1979) *For Her Own Good: one hundred and fifty years of the experts' advice to women* (London: Pluto Press).

Eichenbaum, L. and Orbach, S. (1985) *Understanding Women* (Harmondsworth: Penguin).

Eisenberg, L. (1977) 'Disease and illness: distinctions between professional and popular ideas of sickness, *Culture Medicine and Psychiatry*, vol. 1, pp. 9–23.

el Dareer, A. (1982) *Women, Why do you Weep?* (London: Zed Press).

El-Mouelhy, M. (1993) 'Women's lives and health in Egypt', *Reproductive Health Matters*, 1, pp. 113–16.

Elbourne, D., Oakley, A. and Chalmers, I. (1989) 'Social and psychological support during pregnancy', in I. Chalmers, M. Enkin and M. Keirse (eds) *Effective Care in Pregnancy and Childbirth*, vol. 2 (Oxford: Clarendon Press).

Elson, D. and Pearson, R. (1981) 'Nimble fingers make cheap workers: an analysis of women's employment in third world export manufacturing', *Feminist Review*, vol. 7, pp. 87–107.

Epstein, B. (1987) 'Women's anger and compulsive eating', in M. Lawrence (ed.) *Fed Up and Hungry: women, oppression and food* (London: Women's Press).

Ericson, A. and Källen, B. (1986a) 'An epidemiology study of work with video screens and pregnancy outcome: I. registry study', *American Journal of Industrial Medicine*, vol. 9, no. 5, pp. 447–57.

Ericson, A. and Källen, B. (1986b) 'An epidemiology study of work with video screens and pregnancy outcome: II. a case control study', *American Journal of Industrial Medicine*, vol. 9, no. 5, pp. 459–75.

Ernster, V. (1985) 'Mixed messages for women: a social history of cigarette smoking and advertising', *New York State Journal of Medicine*, 312, 384–8.

Estrada-Claudio, S. (1988) 'Maternal deaths in the Philippines', *Health Alert* vol. 73, pp. 237–43.

Ettore, E. (1992) *Women and Substance Use* (London: Macmillan).

Evason, E. (1991) 'Women and poverty', in C. Davies and E. McLaughlin (eds) *Women, Employment and Social Policy in Northern Ireland: a problem postponed* (Belfast: Policy Research Institute).

Evers-Kiebooms, G., Swerts, A. and Van den Berghe, H. (1988) 'Psychological aspects of amniocentesis: anxiety feelings in three different risk groups', *Clinical Genetics*, vol. 33, pp. 196–206.

Ewan, C., Lowy, E. and Reid, J. (1991) 'Falling out of culture: the effects of repetition strain injury on sufferers' roles and identity', *Sociology of Health and Illness*, vol. 13, no. 2, pp. 168–92.

Faden, R. (1991) 'Autonomy, choice and the new reproductive technologies: the role of informed consent in prenatal genetic diagnosis', in J. Rodin and A. Collins (eds) *Women and New Reproductive Technologies: medical, psychosocial, legal and ethical dilemmas* (Hillsdale, NJ: Lawrence Erlbaum Associates).

Faden, R. Geller, G. Powers, M. (eds) (1991) *AIDS, Women and the Next Generation: towards a morally acceptable public policy for HIV testing of pregnant women and newborns.* (Oxford: Oxford University Press).

Falk, K., Gordon, P. and Sora, M. (1979) 'Mutogenicity in urine of nurses handling cytostatic drugs', *Lancet* vol. (i) pp. 1250–1.

Farrant, W. (1985) 'Who's for Amniocentesis? The politics of prenatal screening, in H. Homans (ed.) *The Sexual Politics of Reproduction* (Aldershot: Gower Press).

Fauveau, V., Koenig, M., Chakraborty, J. and Chowdhury, A. (1988) 'Causes of maternal mortality in rural Bangladesh 1970–85', *Bulletin of WHO*, vol. 66, no. 5, pp. 643–51.

Fernandez Kelly, M. (1984) 'Maquiladoras: the view from inside', in K. Sacks and D. Remy (eds) *My Troubles are Going to have Troubles with Me: everyday trials and triumphs of women workers* (New Brunswick, NJ: Rutgers University Press).

Fiebach, N., Viscoli, C. and Horwitz, R. (1990) 'Differences between men and women in survival after myocardial infarction: biology or methodology?', *Journal of the American Medical Association*, vol. 263, no. 8, pp. 1092–6.

Finch, J. and Groves, D. (1983), A. *Labour of Love: women, work and caring* (London: Routledge and Kegan Paul).

Finerman, R. (1989) 'The burden of responsibility: duty, depression and 'nervios' in Andean Ecuador', *Health Care for Women International*, vol. 10, nos 2 and 3, pp. 141–57.

Finkelhor, D. (1991) 'Child sexual abuse', in M. Rosenberg and M. Feinley (eds) *Violence in America: a public health approach* (Oxford: Oxford University Press).

Finkler, K. (1989) 'The universality of nerves', *Health Care for Women International*, vol. 10, nos 2 and 3, pp. 171–9.

Fisher, S. (1986) *In the Patient's Best Interest: women and the politics of medical decisions* (New Brunswick, NJ: Rutgers University Press).

Fleishman, J. (1984) 'The health hazards of office work', in W. Chavkin (ed.) *Double Exposure: women's health hazards on the job and at home* (New York: Monthly Review Press).

Folbre, N. (1988) 'The black four of hearts: towards a new paradigm of household economics' in: D. Dwyer and J. Bruce (eds) A. *Home Divided: women and income in the third world* (Stanford, Ca: Stanford University Press).

Folch-Lyon, E. de la, Macorra, L. and Schearer, S. (1981) 'Focus group and survey research on family planning in Mexico', *Studies in Family Planning*, vol. 12, no. 12, pp. 409–32.

Foley, R. (1985) *Women and Health Care: self help health groups in Britain* (Southampton: Southampton Institute of Higher Education).

Fonn, S., Klugman, B. and Dehaeck, K. (1993) *Towards a National Screening Policy for Cancer of the Cervix in South Africa* (Johannesburg: Centre for Health Policy, University of the Witwatersrand).

Ford, N. and Koetsawang, S. (1991) 'The sociocultural context of the transmission of HIV in Thailand', *Social Science and Medicine*, vol. 33, no. 4, pp. 405–14.

Ford-Smith, H. (1994) 'No! to sexual violence in Jamaica', in M. Davis (ed.) *Women and Violence: responses and realities worldwide* (London: Zed Press).

Fortney, J., Susanti, I., Gadalla, S., Saleh, S., Rogers, S. and Potts, M. (1986) 'Reproductive mortality in two developing countries', *American Journal of Public Health*, vol. 76, no. 2, pp. 134–8

Forum Against the Oppression of Women (1994) 'Report of the National Meeting of Women's Organisations against Rape in India', in M. Davis (ed.) *Women and Violence: responses and realities worldwide* (London: Zed Press).

Foucault, M. (1979) *History of Sexuality, vol. 1 An Introduction*, trans. by Robert Harley (Harmondsworth: Allen Lane).

Fox, S. (1991) *Toxic Work: women workers at GTE Lenkurt.* Temple University Press, Philadelphia.

244 *Bibliography*

Frankenhaueser, M., Lundberg, U. and Chesney, M. (eds) (1991) *Women, Work and Health: stress and opportunities* (New York: Plenum Press).
Free Tibet (1994) 'We have no rights, not even our bodies', in M. Davis (ed.) *Women and Violence: responses and realities worldwide* (London: Zed Press).
Freedman, L. and Maine, D. (1993) 'Women's mortality: a legacy of neglect' in: M. Koblinsky, J. Timyan and J. Gay (eds) *The Health of Women: a global perspective* (Boulder, Co: Westview Press).
Fuentes, A. (1987) 'They call it "la operacion"', *New Internationalist*, October, 14–15.
Funk, N. (1993) 'Abortion and German unification', in N. Funk and M. Mueller (eds) *Gender Politics and Post Communism: reflections from Eastern Europe and the former Soviet Union* (London: Routledge).
Funk, N. and Mueller, M. (eds) (1993) *Gender, Politics and Post Communism: reflections from Eastern Europe and the former Soviet Union* (London: Routledge).
Fuszara, M. (1993) 'Abortion and the formation of the public sphere in Poland', in N. Funk and M. Mueller (eds) *Gender Politics and Post Communism: reflections from Eastern Europe and the former Soviet Union* (London: Routledge).
Gabe, J. and Lipshitz-Phillips, S. (1986) 'Tranquillisers as social control?', in J. Gabe and P. Williams (eds) *Tranquillisers: social, psychological and clinical perspectives* (London: Tavistock).
Gabe, J. and Thorogood, N. (1986) 'Tranquillisers as a resource', in J. Gabe and P. Williams (eds) *Tranquillisers: social, psychological and clinical perspectives* (London: Tavistock).
Gabe, J. and Williams, P. (1986) 'Tranquilliser use: a historical perspective', in J. Gabe and P. Williams (eds) *Tranquillisers: social, psychological and clinical perspectives* (London: Tavistock).
Gahlot, D. (1993) 'A spark of hope for slum dwellers', in Women's Feature Service (ed.) *The Power to Change: women in the third world redefine their environment* (London: Zed Press).
Gallagher, J. (1987) 'Prenatal invasions and interventions: what's wrong with fetal rights', *Harvard Women's Law Journal*, vol. 10, pp. 9–58.
Gamarnikow, E. (1991) 'Nurse or woman: gender and professionalism in reformed nursing, 1860–1923', in P. Holden and J. Littlewood (eds) *Anthropology and Nursing* (London: Routledge).
Game, A. and Pringle, R. (1984) *Gender at Work* (London: Pluto Press).
Gandhi, N. and Shah, S. (1992) *The Issues at Stake: theory and practice in the contemporary women's movement* (New Delhi: Kali for Women).
Garcia, G. and Dacach, S. (1992) 'Norplant – 5 years later', in B. Mintzes (ed.) A. *Question of Control: women's perspectives on the development and use of contraceptive technology* (Amsterdam: Women and Pharmaceuticals Project, Health Action International and WEMOS,).
Garcia, J., Kilpatrick, R. and Richards, M. (1990) *The Politics of Maternity Care: services for childbearing women in twentieth century Britain* (Oxford: Clarendon Press).
Garcia Moreno, C. and Claro, A. (1994) 'Challenges from the women's health move ment: women's rights versus population control', in G. Sen, A. Germain and L. Chen (eds) *Population Policies Reconsidered: health, empowerment and rights* (Cambridge, Mass: Harvard University Press).
Garforth, S. and Garcia, J. (1989) 'Hospital admission practices', in I. Chalmers, M. Enkin and M. Keirse (eds) *Effective Care in Pregnancy and Childbirth*, vol. 2 (Oxford: Clarendon Press).
Gavey, N. (1993) 'Technologies and effects of heterosexual coercion', in S. Wilkinson and C. Kitzinger (eds) *Heterosexuality: a feminism and psychology reader* (London: Sage).
Gerber Fried, M. (ed.) (1990a) *From Abortion to Reproductive Freedom: transforming a movement* (Boston: South End Press).

Gerber Fried, M. (1990b) 'Transforming the reproductive rights movement: the post Webster agenda', in M. Gerber Fried, (ed.) *From Abortion to Reproductive Freedom: transforming a movement* (Boston: South End Press).

Germain, A. and Ordway, J. (1989) *Population Control and Women's Health: balancing the scales* (New York: International Women's Health Coalition).

Germain, A., Holmes, K. Piot, P. and Wasserheit, J. (1992) *Reproductive Tract Infections: global impact and priorities for women's reproductive health* (New York: Plenum Press).

Gillet, J. (1990) *The Health of Women in Papua New Guinea* (Papua New Guinea Institute of Medical Research Monograph no. 9, Kristen Press Inc., PO Box 712, Madang Papua New Guinea)..

Gilliam, A. (1991) 'Women's equality and national liberation', in C. Mohanty, A. Russo and L. Torres (eds) *Third World Women and the Politics of Feminism* (Bloomington, Indiana: Indiana University Press).

Ginsberg, S. and Brown, G. (1982) 'No time for depression: a study of help seeking among mothers of pre-school children', in D. Mechanic (ed.) *Symptoms, Illness Behaviour and Help Seeking* (New York: Prodist).

Glantz, H. and Backenheimer, M. (1988) 'Substance abuse among elderly women', *Clinical Gerontologist*, vol. 8, no. 1, pp. 3–26.

Glazer, N. (1988) 'Overlooked, overworked: women's unpaid and paid work in the health services "cost crisis"', *International Journal of Health Services*, vol. 18, no. 1, pp. 119–37.

Glendinning, C. and Millar, J. (eds) (1987) *Women and Poverty in Britain* (Brighton: Harvester).

Glendinning, C. and Millar, J. (1992) *Women and Poverty in Britain in the 1990s* (Brighton: Harvester Wheatsheaf).

Goddard, V. (1987) 'Women's sexuality and group identity in Naples', in P. Caplan (ed.) *The Cultural Construction of Sexuality* (London: Tavistock).

Goldhaber, M., Polen, M. and Hiatt, R. (1988) 'The risk of miscarriage and birth defects among women who use visual display terminals during pregnancy', *American Journal of Industrial Medicine*, vol. 13, pp. 695–706.

Gordon, L. (1976) *Woman's Body; Woman's Right: a social history of birth control in America* (New York: Grossman Publications).

Graham, H. (1987) 'Women's smoking and family health', *Social Science and Medicine*, vol. 25, no. 1, pp. 47–56.

Graham, H. (1993) *Hardship and Health in Women's Lives* (Brighton: Harvester Wheatsheaf).

Graham, H. and McKee, L. (1980) 'The first months of motherhood', *Health Education Council Research Monograph*, no. 3.

Graham, H. and Oakley, A. (1981) 'Competing ideologies of reproduction: medical and maternal perspectives on pregnancy', in H. Roberts (ed.) *Women, Health and Reproduction* (London: Routledge and Kegan Paul).

Graham, W. and Airey, P. (1987) 'Measuring maternal mortality: sense and sensitivity', *Health Policy and Planning*, vol. 2, no. 4, pp. 323–33.

Grant, A. (1989) 'Monitoring the fetus during labour', in I. Chalmers, M. Enkin and M. Keirse (eds) *Effective Care in Pregnancy and Childbirth*, vol. 2 (Oxford: Clarendon Press).

Greaves, L. (1987) *Background Paper on Women and Tobacco* (Ottawa: Health and Welfare Canada).

Greaves, L. (1990) 'The meaning of smoking to women', in B. Durston and K. Jamrozik (eds) *The global war*, Proceedings of the Seventh World Conference on Tobacco and Health, 1990, Perth, Goverment of Western Australia.

Greaves, L. (1990) 'A historical interpretation of women's smoking', in B. Durston and K. Jamrozik (eds) *The global war*. Proceedings of the Seventh World Conference on Tobacco and Health, 1990, Perth, Goverment of Western Australia.

Green, H. (1988) *Informal Carers: a study carried out as part of the 1985 general household survey* (London: OPCS, HMSO).

Greil, A. L., Leitko, T. and Porter, K. (1988) 'Infertility: his and hers', *Gender and Society*, vol. 2, no. 2, pp. 172–99.

Grossman, R. (1979) 'Women's place in the integrated circuit', in *Changing Role of South East Asian Women, South-East Asian Chronicle*, vol. 66, and *Pacific Research*, vol. 9, no. 5, special joint issue, pp. 2–17.

Gruber, J. and Bjorn, L. (1982) 'Blue collar blues: the sexual harassment of women autoworkers', *Work and Occupations*, vol. 9, no. 3, pp. 271–98.

Grundfest Schoepf, B., Engundu, W., wa Nkera, R., Ntsomo, P. and Schoepf, C. (1991) 'Gender, power and risk of AIDS in Zaire', in M. Turshen (ed.) *Women and Health in Africa* (Trenton, NJ: Africa World Press).

Gulati, L. (1982) *Profiles in Female Poverty: a study of five poor women workers in Kerala* (Oxford: Pergamon).

Haan, M. (1985) 'Job strain and cardiovascular disease: a ten year prospective study. *American Journal of Epidemiology*, vol. 122, no. 3, pp. 532–3.

Hall, R. (1985) *Ask Any Woman: a London inquiry into rape and sexual assault* (Bristol: Falling Wall Press).

Hamblin, A. (1983) 'Is a feminist heterosexuality possible?', in S. Cartledge and J. Ryan (eds) *Sex and Love: new thoughts on old contradictions* (London: Women's Press).

Hamilton, J. (1985) 'Avoiding methodological and policy making biases in gender-related research' in: US Department of Health and Human Services, *Women's Health: report of the Public Health Service Task Force on women's health issues*, vol. II, pp. 54–64 (Washington DC: US Government Printing Office).

Hamilton, S., Popkin, B. and Spicer, D. (1984) *Women and Nutrition in Third World Countries* (New York: Bergin and Garvey).

Hammer, T. and Vaglum, P. (1989) 'The increase in alcohol consumption among women: a phenomenon related to accessibility or stress?, A general population study. *British Journal of Addiction*, vol. 84, pp. 767–75.

Hancock, L. (1991) 'Informed consent: women, surgery and lack of consent', in *Women and Surgery 1990 Conference Proceedings* (Melbourne: Healthsharing Women).

Handy, J. (1991) 'The social context of occupational stress in a caring profession', *Social Science and Medicine*, vol. 32, no. 7, pp. 819–30.

Hansen, E. and Launso, L. (1989) 'Is the controlled clinical trial sufficient as drug technology assessment?', *Journal of Social and Administrative Pharmacy*, vol. 6, pp. 117–26.

Hansson, D. (1991) 'Working against violence against women: recommendations from Rape Crisis (Capetown)', in S. Bazilli (ed.) *Putting Women on the Agenda* (Johannesburg: Ravan Press).

Haraway, D. (1991) 'A manifesto for Cyborgs: science, technology and socialist feminism', in L. Nicholson (ed.) *Feminism/Post-Modernism* (London: Routledge).

Hardee-Cleaveland, K. and Banister, J. (1988) 'Fertility policy and implementation in China, 1986–8', *Population and Development Review*, vol. 14, no. 2, pp. 245–85.

Harding, J. (1986) 'Mood-modifiers and elderly women in Canada: the medicalization of poverty', in K. McDonnell (ed.) *Adverse Effects: women and the pharmaceutical industry* (Penang, Malaysia: International Organisation of Consumer Unions).

Harding, S. (1986) *The Science Question in Feminism* (Ithaca, NY: Cornell University Press).

Harding, S. (1987) 'Introduction: is there a feminist method?', in S. Harding (ed.) *Feminism and Methodology: social science issues* (Milton Keynes: Open University Press).

Hardon, A. (1992) 'Contraceptive research: women's perspectives', in B. Mintzes (ed.) A. *Question of Control: women's perspectives on the development and use of contraceptive technology* (Amsterdam: Women and Pharmaceuticals Project, Health Action International and WEMOS).

Hardon, A. and Achthoven, L. (1991) 'Norplant: a critical review', *Women's Global Network for Reproductive Rights Newsletter 34* (Jan–March), pp. 17–24.

Harlow, S. (1986) 'Function and dysfunction: a historical critique of the literature on menstruation and work', *Health Care for Women International*, vol. 7, no. 39.

Hart, N. (1988) 'Sex, gender and survival: inequalities of life chances between European men and women' in: A. J. Fox (ed.) *Inequality in Health within Europe* (Aldershot: Gower).

Hartmann, B. (1987) *Reproductive Rights and Wrongs: the global politics of population control and contraceptive choice* (New York: Harper and Row).

Hassold, T., Quillen, S. and Yamane, J. (1983) 'Sex ratio in spontaneous abortions', *Annals of Human Genetics*, vol. 47, no. 1, pp. 39–47.

Hatch, M. (1984) 'Mother, father, worker: men and women and the reproduction risks of work', in W. Chavkin (ed.) *Double Exposure: women's health hazards on the job and at home* (New York: Monthly Review Press).

Hatch, S. and Kickbusch, I. (eds) (1983) *Self Help and Health in Europe* (Copenhagen: WHO).

Haw, M. A. (1982) 'Women, work and stress', *Journal of Health and Social Behaviour*, vol. 23, no. 2, pp. 132–44.

Haynes, S. (1991) 'The effect of job demands, job control and new technologies on the health of employed women: a review', in M. Frankenhaueser, U. Lundberg and M. Chesney (eds) *Women, Work and Health: stress and opportunities* (New York: Plenum Press).

Haynes, S. and Feinleib, M. (1980) 'Women, work and coronary heart disease: prospective findings from the Framingham Heart Study', *American Journal of Public Health*, vol. 70, no. 2, pp. 113–41.

Haynes, S., LaCroix, A. and Lippin, T. (1987) 'The effect of high job demands and low control on the health of employed women', in J. Quick, R. Bhagat, J. Dalton and J. Quick (eds) *Work, Stress and Health Care* (New York: Praeger).

Health Department Victoria (1990) *Having a Baby in Victoria: final report of the ministerial review of birthing services in Victoria* (Melbourne: Health Department).

Healthsharing Women (1990) *The Healthsharing Reader: women speak about health* (Syney: Pandora).

Heath, D. B. (1991) 'Women and alcohol: cross cultural perspectives', *Journal of Substance Abuse*, vol. 3, pp. 175–85.

Heikkinen, E., Waters, W. and Brzezinski, Z. (eds) (1983) *The Elderly in Eleven Countries – a socio medical survey* (Public Health in Europe no. 21) (Copenhagen: WHO Regional Office for Europe).

Heise, L. (1993) 'Violence against women: the missing agenda', in M. Koblinsky, J. Timyan and J. Gay (eds) *The Health of Women: a global perspective* (Boulder, Co: Westview Press).

Held, P., Pauly, M., Bovberg, R. *et al* (1988) 'Access to kidney transplantation: has the United States eliminated income and racial differences?', *Archives of Internal Medicine*, vol. 148, pp. 2594–600.

Helman, C. (1986) '"Tonic", "fuel", and "food": social and symbolic aspects of the long-term use of psychotropic drugs', in J. Gabe and P. Williams (eds) *Tranquillisers: social, psychological and clinical perspectives* (London: Tavistock).

Hemminki, K., Niemi M-L, Koskinen, K. and Vainio, H. (1980) 'Spontaneous abortions among women employed in the metal industry in Finland', *International Archives of Occupational and Environmental Health*, vol. 47, pp. 53–60.

Hemminki, K., Mutanen, P., Saloniemi, I. and Luoma, K. (1981) 'Congenital malformations and maternal occupation in Finland: multivariate analysis', *Journal of Epidemiology and Community Health*, vol. 35, pp. 5–10.

Hemminki, K., Mutanen, P., Saloniemi, I., Niemi M-L and Vainio, H. (1982) 'Spontaneous abortions in hospital staff engaged in sterilising instruments with chemical agents', *British Medical Journal*, vol. 285, pp. 1461–3.

Henifin, M. S. (1984) 'The particular problems of video display terminals', in W. Chavkin (ed.) *Double Exposure: women's health hazards on the job and at home* (New York: Monthly Review Press).

Henshaw, S. (1990) 'Induced abortion: a world review, 1990', *Family Planning Perspectives*, vol. 22, no. 2, pp. 76–89.

Hepburn, C. and Gutierrez, B. (1988) *Alive and Well: a lesbian health guide* (Freedom, California: Crossing Press).

Hibbard, B. (1987) 'An obstetric view of population screening programmes', Kings Fund Forum, London, 30 November to 2 December (Kings Fund Centre, 126 Albert Street, London NW1).

Hicks, C. (1988) *Who Cares? Looking after people at home* (London: Virago).

Hicks, E. (1993) *Infibulation: female mutilation in Islamic North Eastern Africa* (New York: Transaction Publishers).

Hillier, S. (1988) 'Women and population control in China: issues of sexuality, power and control', *Feminist Review*, no. 29, pp. 101–13.

Hochschild, A. (1983) *The Managed Heart: commercialisation of human feeling* (San Francisco: University of California Press).

Holck, S. (1987) 'Hormonal contraceptives and the risk of cancer', *World Health Statistics Quarterly*, vol. 40, pp. 225–31.

Holden, P. and Littlewood, J. (1991) *Anthropology and Nursing* (London: Routledge).

Holland J., Ramazanoglou, C., Scott, S., Sharpe, S., Thomson, R. (1990) 'Sex, gender and power: young women's sexuality in the shadow of AIDS', *Sociology of Health and Illness*, vol. 12, no. 3, pp. 336–50.

Hollway, W. (1983) 'Heterosexual sex: power and desire for the other', in S. Cartledge and J. Ryan (eds) *Sex and Love: new thoughts on old contradictions* (London: Women's Press).

Holmberg, P. C. (1978) 'Central nervous system defects in children born to mothers exposed to organic solvents during pregnancy', *Lancet* vol. (i), pp. 177–9.

Holmes, H. and Purdy, L. (1992) *Feminist Perspectives in Medical Ethics* (Bloomington and Indianapolis: Indiana University Press).

hooks, b. (1982) *Ain't, I. a Woman: black women and feminism* (London: Pluto Press).

Horowitz, S. and Kishwar, M. (1984) 'Family life: the unequal deal', in M. Kishwar and R. Vanita (eds) *In Search of Answers: Indian women's voices from Manushi* (London: Zed Press).

Howard, D. (1987) 'Aspects of maternal morbidity: the experience of less developed countries', in D. Jelliffe and E. Jelliffe (eds) *Advances in International Maternal and Child Health*, vol. 7, pp. 1–35 (Oxford, Clarendon Press).

Human Fertilisation and Embryology Authority (1993) *Annual Report 1992* (London).

Humm, M. (ed.) (1992) *Feminisms: a reader* (Brighton: Harvester Wheatsheaf).

Hunt, L. (1991) *Professional Experience Programme Report: women's health promotion, an international perspective* (Perth, Western Australia: School of Community and Language Studies, Edith Cowan University).

Hyndman, S. (1990) 'Housing damp and health among British Bengalis in East London', *Social Science and Medicine*, vol. 30, pt 1. pp. 131–41.

Ibrahim, B. (1985) 'Cairo's factory women', in E. Fernea (ed.) *Women and the Family in the Middle East* (Austin: University of Texas Press).

Illich, I. (1977) *Limits to Medicine: medical nemesis* (Harmondsworth: Penguin).

Infante, P., Wagoner, J., McMichael, A. *et al* (1976) 'Genetic risks of vinyl chloride', *Lancet* vol. (i), pp. 734–5.

International Agency for Research on Cancer (1985) *Tobacco Habits other than Smoking: betel-quid and areca-nut chewing and some related nitrosamines* (Lyon: WHO and IARC).

International Women's Health Coalition (1991) *Reproductive tract infections in women in the Third World: national and international policy implications* (New York: IWHC).

ISIS International (1985) 'Women and health: the Brazilian experience', *Women's Journal*, no. 3.

Jacob, T. and Bremer, D. (1986) 'Assortative mating among men and women alcoholics', *Journal of Studies on Alcohol*, vol. 47, pp. 219–22.

Jacobson, B. (1981) *The Ladykillers: why cigarette smoking is a feminist issue* (London: Pluto Press).

Jacobson, B. (1986) *Beating the Ladykillers: women and smoking* (London: Pluto Press).

Jacobson, J. (1990) *The Global Politics of Abortion* Worldwatch Paper 97 (Washington DC: Worldwatch Institute).

Jacobson, J. (1991) *Women's Reproductive Health: the silent emergency* Worldwatch Paper 102 (Washington DC: Worldwatch Institute).

Jacobson, J. (1992) 'Women's health, the price of poverty', in M. Koblinsky, J. Timyan and J. Gay (eds) *The Health of Women: a global perspective* (Boulder, Co: Westview Press).

Jacobus, H., Keller, E. and Shuttleworth, S. (1990) *Body/Politics: women and the discourses of science* (London: Routledge).

Jain, S. (1991) 'Standing up for trees: women's role in the Chipko movement', in S. Sontheimer (ed.) *Women and the Environment, a Reader: crisis and development in the third world* (London: Earthscan).

'Jane' (1990) 'Just call "Jane"', in M. Gerber Fried (ed.) *From Abortion to Reproductive Freedom: transforming a movement* (Boston: South End Press).

Jankowska, H. (1993) 'The reproductive rights campaign in Poland', *Women's Studies International Forum*, vol. 16: no. 3, pp. 291–6.

Janowitz, B., Nakamura, M., Lins, F., Brown, M. and Clopton, D. (1982) 'Caesarean section in Brazil', *Social Science and Medicine*, vol. 16, no. 1, pp. 19–25.

Jasso, S. and Mazorra, M. (1984) 'Following the harvest: the health hazards of migrant and seasonal farmworking women', in W. Chavkin (ed.) *Double Exposure: women's health hazards on the job and at home* (New York: Monthly Review Press).

Jeffery, P., Jeffery, R. and Lyon, A. (1989) *Labour Pains and Labour Power: women and childbearing in India* (London: Zed Press).

Jelin, E. (ed.) (1990) *Women and Social Change in Latin America* (London: Zed Press).

Jeyeratnam, J. (1990) 'Acute pesticide poisoning: a major global health problem', *World Health Statistics Quarterly*, vol. 43, pp. 139–44.

Jhabvala, R. (1994) 'Self Employed Women's Association: organising women by struggle and development', in S. Rowbotham and S. Mitter (eds) *Dignity and Daily Bread: new forms of economic organising among poor women in the third world and the first* (London: Routledge).

Jochelson, K., Mothibeli, M. and Leger J-P (1991) 'Human Immunodeficiency Virus and migrant labour in South Africa', *International Journal of Health Services*, vol. 21, no. 1, pp. 157–73.

Jordan, B. (1983) *Birth in Four Cultures: a cross-cultural investigation of childbirth in Yucatan, Holland Sweden and the United States*, 3rd edition (Montreal: Eden Press).

Jordan, B. (1986) *Technology Transfer in Obstetrics: theory and practice in developing countries*, Department of Anthropology, Michigan State University, Working Paper 126.

Joseph, G. and Lewis, J. (1981) *Common Differences: conflicts in black and white feminist perspectives* (Boston: South End Press).

Kabeer, N. (1985) 'Do women gain from high fertility?', in H. Afshar (ed.) *Women, Work and Ideology in the Third World* (London: Macmillan).

Kabeer, N. (1991) *Gender, Production and Wellbeing: rethinking the household economy* Discussion Paper 288, (Brighton: Institute of Development Studies, University of Sussex).

Kabir, S. (1992) 'The Bangladesh Women's Health Coalition: an integrated approach to reproductive health services', in B. Mintzes (ed.) A. *Question of Control: women's perspectives on the development and use of contraceptive technologies* (Amsterdam: Women and Pharmaceuticals Project Health Action International and WEMOS).

Kabir, S. and Germain, A. (1992) 'Is RU 486/PG in its current form likely to be appropriate for women in Bangladesh', *Women's Global Network for Reproductive Rights Newsletter*, no. 38, pp. 39–44.

Kandiyoti, D. (1988) 'Bargaining with patriarchy', *Gender and Society*, vol. 2, no. 3, pp. 274–90.

Kaplan, M. and Knutson, S. (1980) 'Women in manufacturing industries – ergonomic factors and deficiencies', in C. Zenz (ed.) *Developments in Occupational Medicine* (Chicago: Year Book Medical Publishers).

Karasek, R. (1979) 'Job demands, job decision latitude and mental strain: implications for job redesign', *Administrative Science Quarterly*, vol. 24, pp. 285–307.

Karasek, R., Baker, D., Marxer, F., Ahlblom, A. and Theorell, T. (1981) 'Job decision latitude, job demands and cardiovascular disease: a prospective study of Swedish men', *American Journal of Public Health*, vol. 71, no. 7, pp. 694–705.

Karasek, R., Russell, R. and Theorell, T. (1982) 'Psychology of stress and regeneration in job-related cardiovascular illness', *Journal of Human Stress*, vol. 8 (March), pp. 29–42.

Karkal, M. (1985) 'How the other half dies in Bombay', *Economic and Political Weekly*, 24 August, p. 1424.

Kass, N. (1991) 'Reproductive decision making in the context of HIV: the case for nondirective counselling', in R. Faden, G. Geller, M. Powers (eds) *AIDS, Women and the Next Generation: towards a morally acceptable public policy for HIV testing of pregnant women and newborns* (Oxford: Oxford University Press).

Keirse, M., Enkin, M. and Lumley, J. (1989) 'Social and professional support during childbirth', in I. Chalmers, M. Enkin and M. Keirse (eds) *Effective Care in Pregnancy and Childbirth*, vol. 2 (Oxford: Clarendon Press).

Kelly, L. (1988) *Surviving Sexual Violence* (Oxford: Polity Press).

Kenyon, S. (1991) *Five Women of Sennar: culture and change in Central Sudan* (Oxford: Clarendon Press).

Keysers, L. and Smyth, I. (1991) 'Reflections on global solidarity for women's health and reproductive rights', *Vena Journal*, vol. 1, no. 3, pp. 26–31.

Khalifa, M. (1988) 'Attitudes of urban Sudanese men toward family planning', *Studies in Family Planning*, vol. 19, no. 4, pp. 236–43.

Khan, T. (1989) 'Recent developments in contraceptive technology: risks and benefits', in E. Kessel and A. Awan (eds) *Maternal and Child Care in Developing Countries* (Thun, Switzerland: Ott Publishers).

Khattab, H. (1992) *The Silent Endurance: social conditions of women's reproductive health in rural Egypt* (Amman, Jordan: UNICEF).

Kirchstein, R. (1991) 'Research on women's health', *American Journal of Public Health* vol. 81, no. 3, pp. 291–93.

Kisekka, M. (1990) 'AIDS in Uganda as a gender issue', in E. Rothblum and E. Cole (eds) *Women's Mental Health in Africa* (New York: Haworth Park Press).

Kisekka, M. (1992) 'Women's organised health struggles: the challenge to women's associations', in M. Kisekka (ed.) *Women's Health Issues in Nigeria* (Zaria, Nigeria: Tamaza Publishing Co).

Kishwar, M. (1984) 'Introduction', in M. Kishwar and R. Vanita (eds) *In Search of Answers: Indian women's voices from Manushi* (London: Zed Press).

Kitzinger, J. (1990) 'Strategies of the early childbirth movement: a case study of the National Childbirth Trust', in J. Garcia, R. Kilpatrick and M. Richards (eds) *The Politics of Maternity Care Services for Childbearing Women in Twentieth Century Britain* (Oxford: Clarendon Press).

Kitzinger, S. (1978) *Women as Mothers* (London: Fontana).

Kitzinger, S. (1989) 'Childbirth and society', in I. Chalmers, M. Enkin and M. Keirse (eds) *Effective Care in Pregnancy and Childbirth*, vol. 1 (Oxford: Clarendon Press).

Kleinman, A. (1988) *The Illness Narratives: suffering, healing and the human condition* (New York: Basic Books).

Kline, A. Kline, E. and Oken, E. (1992) 'Minority women and sexual choice in the age of AIDS', *Social Science and Medicine*, vol. 34, no. 4, pp. 447–57.

Klugman, B. (1993) 'Balancing means and ends – population policy in South Africa', *Reproductive Health Matters* no. 1, pp. 44–57.

Koblinsky, M., Campbell, O. and Harlow, S. (1993) 'Mother and more: a broader perspective on women's health' in: M. Koblinsky, J. Timyan and J. Gay (eds) *The Health of Women: a global perspective* (Boulder, Co: Westview Press).

Koenig, M. and d'Souza, S. (1986) 'Sex differences in mortality in rural Bangladesh', *Social Science and Medicine*, vol. 22, no. 2, pp. 15–22.

Kolder, V., Gallagher, J. and Parsons, M. (1987) 'Court-ordered obstetrical interventions', *New England Journal of Medicine*, vol. 316, no. 19, pp. 1192–6.

Korvick, J. (1993) 'Trends in federally sponsored clinical trials', in A. Kurth (ed.) *Until the Cure: caring for women with HIV* (London and New Haven: Yale University Press).

Koso-Thomas, O. (1987) *The Circumcision of Women: a strategy for eradication* (London: Zed Press).

Koss, M. (1988) 'Hidden rape: sexual aggression and victimisation in a national sample of students in higher education', in A. Burgess (ed.) *Rape and Sexual Assault* (New York: Garland Publishing).

Koss, M. (1990) 'The women's mental health research agenda: violence against women', *American Psychologist*, vol. 45, no. 3, pp. 374–80.

Krahn, D. (1991) 'The relationship of eating disorders to substance abuse', *Journal of Substance Abuse*, vol. 3, pp. 239–53.

Kurth, A. (1993) 'Introduction: an overview of women and HIV disease', in A. Kurth (ed.) *Until the Cure: caring for women with HIV* (London and New Haven: Yale University Press).

Kwast, B. (1987) *Roads to Maternal Death: case histories including comments on preventive strategy*, background paper prepared for Safe Motherhood Conference, Nairobi, Kenya, 10–13 February.

Kynch, J. (1985) 'How many women are enough? Sex ratios and the right to life', *Third World Affairs* (London: Third World Foundation) pp. 156–72.

Kynch, J. and Sen, A. (1983) 'Indian women: well-being and survival', *Cambridge Journal of Economics*, vol. 7, pp. 363–80.

LaCheen, C. (1986) 'Population control and the pharmaceutical industry', in K. McDonnell (ed.) *Adverse Effects: women and the pharmaceutical industry* (Penang, Malaysia: International Organisation of Consumer Unions).

LaCroix, A. and Haynes, S. (1987) 'Gender differences in the health effects of work-place roles', in R. Barnett, L. Biener and G. Baruch (eds) *Gender and Stress* (New York: Free Press).

Ladipo, O. (1989) 'Preventing and managing complications of induced abortion in third world countries', *International Journal of Gynaecology and Obstetrics*, suppl. 3, pp. 21–8.

LaDou, J. (1986) 'Health issues in the microelectronics industry', *State of the Art Reviews: Occupational Medicine*, vol. 1, no. 1 (Jan–March), pp. 1–11.

Laga, M. (1992) 'Human immunodeficiency virus infection prevention: the need for complementary STD control', in A. Germain, K. Holmes, P. Piot and J. Wasserheit (eds) *Reproductive Tract Infections: global impact and priorities for women's reproductive health* (New York: Plenum Press).

La Rosa, J. (1990) 'Executive women and health: perceptions and practices', *American Journal of Public Health*, vol. 80, no. 12, pp. 1450–4.

Latif; A. (1989) 'Genital ulcers and transmission of HIV among couples in Zimbabwe', *AIDS*, 3, pp. 519–23.

Lawrence, M. (ed.) (1987) *Fed Up and Hungry: women, oppression and food* (London: Women's Press).

Léon, R. (1990) 'Bartolina Sisa: the Peasant Women's Organisation in Bolivia', in E. Jelin (ed.) *Women and Social Change in Latin America* (London: Zed Press).

Levinson, D. (1989) *Family Violence in Cross Cultural Perspective* (Newbury Park, Ca: Sage).

Lightfoot-Klein, H. (1989) *Prisoners of Ritual: an odyssey into female genital circumcision in Africa* (New York: Haworth Press).

Lim, L. (1978) *Women Workers in Multinational Corporations: the case of the electronics industry in Malaysia and Singapore*, Michigan University Occasional Papers in Women's Studies, (Ann Arbor, University of Michigan).

Lin, V. (1986) *Health, Women's Work and Industrialisation: women workers in the semiconductor industry in Singapore and Malaysia*, working paper no. 130, Michigan State University, Women in International Development.

Lincoln, R. and Kaeser, L. (1988) 'Whatever happened to the contraceptive revolution?', *Family Planning Perspectives*, vol. 20, no. 1, pp. 20–4.

Lindbohm, M-L, Taskinen, H. and Hemminki, K. (1985) 'Reproductive health of working women: spontaneous abortions and congenital malformations', *Public Health Review*, vol. 13, pp. 55–87.

Lindbohm M-L, Taskinen, H. and Sorsa, M. (1993) 'Reproductive health', in K. Kauppinen (ed.) *OECD Panel Group on Women's Work and Health* National Report: Finland (Helsinki: Ministry of Social Affairs and Health).

Ling, C. (1991) 'Women and the environment: the Malaysian experience', in T. Wallace and C. March (eds) *Changing Perceptions: writings on gender and development* (Oxford: Oxfam).

Lisansky Gomberg, E. (1982) 'Historical and political perspective: women and drug use', *Journal of Social Issues*, vol. 38, no. 2, pp. 9–23.

Little, R. and Wendt, J. (1991) 'The effects of maternal drinking in the reproductive period: an epidemiological review', *Journal of Substance Abuse*, vol. 3, pp. 187–204.

Llewellyn Davies, M. (1978) *Maternity: letters from working women* (London: Virago).

Lock, M. and Gordon, D. (eds) (1988) *Biomedicine Examined* (Dordrecht: Kluwer).

Lodl, K., McGettigan, A. and Bucy, J. (1985) 'Women's responses to abortion: implications for post abortion support groups', *Journal of Social Work and Sexuality*, vol. 3, nos 2–3, pp. 119–32.

Loewenson, R. (1991) 'Harvests of disease: women at work on Zimbabwean plantations', in M. Turshen (ed.) *Women and Health in Africa* (Trenton NJ: Africa World Press).

London Hazards Centre (1988) *Repetition Strain Injury: hidden harm from overuse* (London: London Hazards Centre Trust).

Lorber, J. (1984) *Women Physicians: careers, status and power* (London: Tavistock).

Louis M.-V. (1994) 'Sexual harassment in France: what stakes for feminists?', in M. Davis (ed.) *Women and Violence: responses and realities worldwide* (London: Zed Press).

Lovell, T. (1990) *British Feminist Thought: a reader* (Oxford: Basil Blackwell).

Low, S. (1989a) 'Health, culture and the nature of nerves: a critique', *Medical Anthropology*, vol. 11, pp. 91–5.

Low, S. (1989b) 'Gender, emotion and "nervios" in urban Guatemala', *Health Care for Women International*, vol. 10, nos 2 and 3, 115–40.

Lown, J. and Chenut, H. (1983) 'The patriarchal thread – a history of exploitation', in W. Chapkis and C. Enloe (eds) *Of Common Cloth: women in the global textile industry* (Amsterdam: Transnational Institute).

Luker, K. (1984) *Abortion and the Politics of Motherhood* (Berkeley: University of California Press).

Lupton, D. (1994) *Medicine as Culture: illness, disease and the body in western societies* (Newbury Park, Ca: Sage).

Macfarlane, A. and Mugford, M. (1984) *Birth Counts: statistics of pregnancy and childbirth* (London: HMSO).

Marschall, D. and Gregory, J. (1983) *Office Automation: Jekyll or Hyde?* (Cleveland Ohio: Working Women Education Fund).

Mann, J., Tarantola, D. and Netter, T. (1992) *AIDS in the World: a global report* (Cambridge, Mass: Harvard University Press).

Marcelis, C. and Shiva, M. (1986) 'EP drugs: unsafe by any name', in K. McDonnell (ed.) *Adverse Effects: women and the pharmaceutical industry* (Penang, Malaysia: International Organisation of Consumer Unions).

Marshall, J. (1980) 'Stress amongst nurses', in C. Cooper and J. Marshall (eds) *White Collar and Professional Stress* (Chichester: John Wiley).

Marte, C. (1992) 'Cervical cancer', in J. Mann, D. Tarantola and T. Netter (eds) *AIDS in the World: a global report* (Cambridge, Mass: Harvard University Press).

Martin, E. (1987) *The Woman in the Body: a cultural analysis of reproduction* (Milton Keynes: Open University Press).

Matsui, Y. (1989) *Women's Asia* (London: Zed Press).

Mauldin, W. and Segal, S. (1988) 'Prevalence of contraceptive use: trends and issues', *Studies in Family Planning*, vol. 19, no. 6, pp. 335–53.

Maynard, M. (1994) 'Methods, practice and epistemology: the debate about feminism and research', in M. Maynard and J. Purvis (eds) *Redefining Women's Lives from a Feminist Perspective* (London: Taylor and Francis).

Maynard, M. and Purvis, J. (eds) (1994) *Redefining Women's Lives from a Feminist Perspective* (London: Taylor and Francis).

Maynard-Tucker, G. (1989) 'Women's status as a factor in male and female decision making about the use of contraception: a case study from rural Peru', Working Paper 191, Michigan State University, Women in International Development.

Mbivso, H. and Adamchak, D. (1989) 'Condom use and acceptance: a survey of male Zimbabweans', *Central African Journal of Medicine*, vol. 35, pp. 519–58.

McCarthy, P. *et al.* (1985) 'Respiratory conditions: effects of housing and other factors', *Journal of Epidemiology and Community Health*, vol. 39, pt 1, pp. 15–19.

McCurdy, S. A., Schenker, M. and Lassiter, D. (1989) 'Occupational injury and illness in the semiconductor manufacturing industry', *American Journal of Industrial Medicines*, vol. 15, no. 5, pp. 499–510.

McDonald, A. D., Cherry, N. Delorme, C. and McDonald, J. (1986) 'Visual display units and pregnancy: evidence from the Montreal Survey', *Journal of Occupational Medicine*, vol. 28, no. 12, pp. 1226–31.

McDonnell, K. (1987) 'At cross purposes on abortion', *New Internationalist*, vol. 176, pp. 18–20.

McDowell, L. and Pringle, R. (1992) *Defining Women* (Oxford: Polity Press).

McFarlane, J., Parker, B., Soeken, K. and Bullock, L. (1992) 'Assessing for abuse during pregnancy: severity and frequency of injuries and associated entry into prenatal care', *Journal of the American Medical Association*, vol. 267, no. 23, pp. 92–4.

McLaney, H. and Hurrell, J. (1988) 'Control, stress and job satisfaction in Canadian nurses', *Work and Stress*, vol. 3, pp. 217–24.

Mebrahtu, S. (1991) 'Women, work and nutrition in Nigeria', in M. Turshen (ed.) *Women and Health in Africa* (Trenton NJ: Africa World Press).

Medicine in Society (1983) special issue on nurses and nursing, vol. 8, no. 4, pp. 14–35.

Meehan, E. (1985) *Women's Rights at Work: campaigns and policy in Britain and the United States* (London: Macmillan).

Meirik, O., Källen, B., Gauffin, U. and Ericson, A. (1979) 'Major malformations in infants born of women who worked in laboratories while pregnant', *Lancet* vol. (ii), p. 91.

Merchant, K. and Kurz, K. (1993) 'Women's nutrition through the life cycle: social and biological vulnerabilities', in M. Koblinsky, J. Timyan and J. Gay (eds) *The Health of Women: a global perspective* (Boulder, Co: Westview Press).

Mergler, D. and Vézina, N. (1985) 'Dysmenorrhoea and cold exposure', *Journal of Reproductive Medicine*, vol. 30, no. 2, pp. 106–111.

Mernissi, F. (1975) 'Obstacles to family planning practice in urban Morocco', *Studies in Family Planning*, vol. 6, no. 12, pp. 418–25.

Messing, K., Dumais, L. and Romito, P. (1993) 'Prostitutes and chimney sweeps both have problems: towards full integration of both sexes in the study of occupational health', *Social Science and Medicine*, vol. 36, no. 1, pp. 47–55.

Mies, M. (1986) *Patriarchy and Accumulation on a World Scale: women in the international division of labour* (London: Zed Press).

Miles, A. (1988) *Women and Mental Illness: the social context of female neurosis* (Brighton: Wheatsheaf Books).

Miles, A. (1991) *Women, Health and Medicine* (Milton Keynes: Open University Press).

Miller, B. (1981) *The Endangered Sex: neglect of female children in rural North India* (Ithaca, NY: Cornell University Press).

Minority Rights Group (1980) 'Female circumcision, excision and infibulation', *MRG*, edited by Scilla Mclean, report no. 47.

Mintzes, B. (ed.) (1992), *A Question of Control: women's perspectives on the development and use of contraceptive technology* (Amsterdam: Women and Pharmaceuticals Project, Health Action International and WEMOS).

Mintzes, B,. Hardon, A. and Hanhart, J. (1993) *Norplant: under the skin* (Amsterdam: Women's Health Action Foundation, Women and Pharmaceuticals Project and WEMOS).

Mitchell, J., Hatsukami, P. Eckert, E. and Pyle, R. (1985) 'Characteristics of 275 patients with bulimia', *American Journal of Psychiatry*, vol. 142, no. 4, pp. 482–85.

Mitter, S. (1986) *Common Fate, Common Bond: women in the global economy* (London: Pluto Press).

Mohanty, C. (1991) 'Introduction: Cartographies of struggle: third world women and the politics of feminism', in C. Mohanty, A. Russo and L. Torres (eds) *Third World Women and the Politics of Feminism* (Bloomington and Indianapolis: Indiana University Press).

Mohanty, C., Russo, A., and Torres, L. (1991) *Third World Women and the Politics of Feminism* (Bloomington and Indianapolis: Indiana University Press).

Momsen, J. and Townsend, J. (1987) *Geography of Gender in the Third World* (London: Hutchinson).

Montini, T. and Ruzek, S. (1989) 'Overturning orthodoxy: the emergence of breast cancer treatment policy', *Research in the sociology of health care*, vol. 8, pp. 3–32. (Greenwich CT: JAI Press).

Moore, H. (1988) *Feminism and Anthropology* (Oxford: Polity Press).

Morgall, J. (1993) 'Medical technology assessment: a useful occupation or useless diversion?', *Women's Studies International Forum* vol. 16, no. 6, pp. 591–604.

Morgan, D. and Scott, S. (1993) 'Bodies in a social landscape', in S. Scott and D. Morgan (eds) *Body Matters, essays on the sociology of the body* (Brighton: Falmer Press).

Morgan, L. (1987) 'Dependency theory in the political economy of health: an anthropological critique', *Medical Anthropology*, vol. 1, no. 2, pp. 131–54.

Morgan, P. (1987) 'Women and alcohol: the disinhibition rhetoric in an analysis of domination', *Journal of Psychoactive Drugs*, vol. 19, no. 2, pp. 129–33.

Morris, L. (1990) *The Workings of the Household* (Oxford: Polity Press).

Morton, W. and Ungs, T. (1979) 'Cancer mortality in the major cottage industry', *Women and Health*, vol. 4, pp. 345–54.

Moser, C. (1987) 'Mobilisation is women's work: struggles for infrastructure in Guayaquil, Ecuador', in C. Moser and L. Peake (eds) *Women, Human Settlements and Housing* (London: Tavistock).

Moser, C. (1989) 'Gender planning in the third world', *World Development*, vol. 17, no. 11.

Moser, C. and Peake, L. (eds) (1987) *Women, Human Settlements and Housing* (London: Tavistock).

Mosher, W. and Pratt, W. (1985) *Fecundity and Infertility in the United States 1965–1982* (Washington, DC: National Center for Health Statistics, Public Health Services).

Motsei, M. (1993) *Detection of Woman Battering in Health Care Settings, the case of Alexandra Health Clinic*. Centre for Health Policy, Paper 30 (Johannesburg: University of Witwatersrand).

Mpangile, G. Leshabari, M. and Kihwele, D. (1993) 'Factors associated with induced abortion in public hospitals in Dar es Salaam, Tanzania', *Reproductive Health Matters*, no. 2, pp. 21–31.

Mtimavalye, L. and Belsey, M. (1987) *Infertility and Sexually Transmitted Disease: major problems in maternal and child health and family planning* (New York: Population Council).

Murphy, M. (1981) 'Social consequences of vesico-vaginal fistula in Northern Nigeria', *Journal of Biosocial Science*, vol. 13, pp. 139–50.

Murphy-Lawless, J. (1993) 'Fertility, bodies and politics: the Irish case', *Reproductive Health Matters*, no. 2, pp. 53–64.

Muvman Liberasyon Fam of Mauritius (1989) 'Mauritius: ongoing campaign for legal abortion', *Women's Global Network for Reproductive Rights Newsletter* (Jan–March), pp. 19–20.

Nairne, K. and Smith, G. (1984) *Dealing with Depression* (London: Women's Press).

National Occupational Health and Safety Commission (1986) *Repetitive Strain Injury: a report and model code of practice* (Canberra: Australian Government Publishing Service).

Nicholson, L. (1991) 'Introduction', in L. Nicholson (ed.) *Feminism/Post Modernism* (London: Routledge).

Norboo, T., Yahya, M., Bruce, N., Heady, J. and Ball, K. (1991) 'Domestic pollution and respiratory illness: a Himalayan village', *International Journal of Epidemiology*, vol. 20, no. 3, pp. 749–57.

Nordstrom, S., Beckman, L. and Nordenson, I. (1979a) 'Occupational and environmental risks in and around a smelter in Northern Sweden, V. Spontaneous abortion among female employees and decreased birth weight in their offspring', *Hereditas*, vol. 90, pp. 291–6.

Nordstrom, S., Beckman, L. and Nordenson, I. (1979b) 'Occupational and environmental risks in and around a smelter in Northern Sweden. VI. Congenital malformations', *Hereditas*, vol. 90, pp. 297–302.

Nowrojee, S. (1993) 'Speaking out for sexual and reproductive health', *Women's Global Network for Reproductive Rights Newsletter*, no. 44, pp. 16–17.

Oakley, A. (1974) *The Sociology of Housework* (London: Martin Robertson).

Oakley, A. (1976) *Housewife* (Harmondsworth: Penguin).

Oakley, A. (1979) *Becoming a Mother* (Oxford: Martin Robertson).

Oakley, A. (1981) *From Here to Maternity: becoming a mother* (Harmondsworth: Penguin).

Oakley, A. (1984) *The Captured Womb: a history of the medical care of pregnant women* (Oxford: Basil Blackwell).

Oakley, A. (1987) 'From walking wombs to test tube babies', in M. Stanworth (ed.) *Reproductive Technologies: gender, motherhood and medicine* (Oxford: Polity Press).

Oakley, A. and Richards, M. (1990) 'Women's experiences of Caesarean delivery', in J. Garcia, R. Kilpatrick and M. Richards (eds) *The Politics of Maternity Care: services for childbearing women in twentieth century Britain* (Oxford: Clarendon Press).

Office of Health Economics (1987) *Women's Health Today* (London: OHE).

Office of Population Censuses and Surveys (OPCS) (1986) *Occupational Mortality: Decennial Supplement, England and Wales 1979–80* (London: HMSO).

Orbach, S. (1978) *Fat is a Feminist Issue* (London: Hamlyn).

Orbach, S. (1986) *Hunger Strike: the anorectic's struggle as a metaphor for our age* (London: Faber and Faber).

Oren, L. (1974) 'The welfare of women in labouring families in England 1860–1950', in M. Hartman and L. Banner (eds) *Clio's Consciousness Raised: new perspectives on the history of women* (London: Harper and Row).

O'Sullivan, S. (1987) *Women's Health: a Spare Rib reader* (London: Pandora).

Otto, R. (1986) *Teachers under Stress* (Melbourne: Hill of Content).

Pahl, J. (1989) *Money and Marriage* (London: Macmillan).

Palmer, R., Chaloner, D. and Oppenheimer, R. (1992) 'Childhood sexual experience with adults reported by female patients', *British Journal of Psychiatry*, vol. 160, pp. 261–5.

Paltiel, F. (1987) 'Women and mental health: a post Nairobi perspective', *World Health Statistics Quarterly*, vol. 40, pp. 233–66.

Panos Institute (1990) *Triple Jeopardy: woman and AIDS* (London: Panos Publications).

Panos Institute (1992) *The Hidden Cost of AIDS: the challenge of HIV to development* (London: Panos Publications).

Papanek, H. (1990) 'To each less than she needs, from each more than she can do: allocations, entitlements and value', in I. Tinker (ed.) *Persistent Inequalities: women and world development* (Oxford: Oxford University Press).

Paykel, E. (1991) 'Depression in women', *British Journal of Psychiatry*, vol. 158 (suppl. 10), pp. 22–9.

Payne, S. (1991) *Women, Health and Poverty: an introduction* (Brighton: Harvester Wheatsheaf).

Peay, M. and Peay, E. (1988) 'The role of commercial sources in the adoption of a new drug', *Social Science and Medicine*, vol. 26, no. 12, pp. 1183–9.

Pember Reeves, M. (1980) *Round About a Pound a Week* (London: Virago).

Petchesky, R. (1979) 'Workers, reproductive hazards and the politics of protection: an introduction', *Feminist Studies*, 5 (Summer), pp. 233–45.

Petchesky, R. (1986) *Abortion and Women's Choice: the state, sexuality and reproductive freedom* (London: Verso).

Petticrew, M., McKee, M. and Jones, J. (1993) 'Coronary artery surgery: are women discriminated against?', *British Medical Journal*, vol. 306, pp. 1164–6.

Pfeffer, N. (1992) 'From private patients to privatization', in M. Stacey (ed.) *Changing Human Reproduction: social science perspectives* (London: Sage).

Pfeffer, N. and Woollett, A. (1983) *The Experience of Infertility* (London: Virago).

Phillips, A. and Rakusen, J. (1989) *The New Our Bodies Ourselves: a health book by and for women* (Harmondsworth: Penguin).

Piepe, T., Cattermole, B., Charlton, P., Motley, F., Morey, J. and Yerrell, P. (1988) 'Girls smoking and self-esteem – the adolescent context', *Health Education Journal*, vol. 47, pp. 83–5.

Pies, C. (1985) *Considering Parenthood: a workbook for lesbians* (San Francisco: Spinsters Ink).

Placek, P., Taffel, S. and Moien, M. (1988) '1986: C-sections rise; VBAC's inch upward', *American Journal of Public Health*, vol. 78, pp. 562–3.

Plichta, S. (1992) 'The effects of woman abuse on health care utilisation and health status', *Women's Health* (Jacobs Institute), vol. 2, no. 3, pp. 154–62.

Pollack, S. (1985) 'Sex and the contraceptive act', in H. Homans (ed.) *The Sexual Politics of Reproduction* (Aldershot: Gower Press).

Popay, J. (1992) 'My health is all right, but I'm just tired all the time: women's experiences of ill health', in H. Roberts (ed.) *Women Health Matters* (London: Routledge).

Popay, J. and Jones, G. (1990) 'Patterns of wealth and illness among lone parents', *Journal of Social Policy*, vol. 19, pp. 499–534.

Pope, H., Hudson, J., Jonas, J. and Yurgelun-Todd, D. (1983) 'Bulimia treated with imipramine: a placebo-controlled double-blind study', *American Journal of Psychiatry*, vol. 140, pt 5, pp. 554–8.

Population Information Programme (1980) 'Complications of abortion in developing countries', *Population Reports Series* F, no. 7, (Baltimore, Md: Johns Hopkins University).

Prather, L. (1991) 'Decoding advertising: the role of communication studies in explaining the popularity of minor tranquillisers', in J. Gabe (ed.) *Understanding Tranquilliser Use: the role of the social sciences* (London: Tavistock).

Prather, L. and Fidell, S. (1986) 'Sex differences in the content and style of medical advertisements', in J. Gabe and P. Williams (eds) *Tranquillisers: social, psychological and clinical perspectives* (London: Tavistock).

Pringle, R. (1992) 'Absolute sex? Unpacking the sexuality/gender relationship', in R. Connell and G. Dowsett (eds) *Rethinking Sex: social theory and sexuality research* (Melbourne: Melbourne University Press).

Protein-Calorie Advisory Group (PAG) (1977) *Women in Food Production, Food Handling and Nutrition: with special emphasis on Africa – final report* (New York: Protein-Calorie Advisory Group of the United Nations System, UN).

Pugh, H., Power, C., Goldblatt, P. and Arber, S. (1991) 'Women's lung cancer mortality, socio-economic status and changing smoking patterns', *Social Science and Medicine*, vol. 32, no. 10, pp. 1105–10.

Raikes, A. (1989) 'Women's health in East Africa', *Social Science and Medicine*, vol. 28, no. 5, pp. 447–59.

Ramazanoglou, C. (1993) *Up Against Foucault: explorations of some tensions between Foucault and feminism* (London: Routledge).

Rapp, R. (1987) 'Moral pioneers: women, men and fetuses on a frontier of reproductive technology', *Women and Health*, vol. 13, nos 1–2, pp. 101–16.

Ray, L. (1991) 'The political economy of long-term minor tranquilliser use', in J. Gabe (ed.) *Understanding Tranquilliser Use: the role of the social sciences* (London: Tavistock).

Raymond, J., Klein, R. and Dumble, L. (1991) *RU 486: Misconceptions, Myths and Morals* (Cambridge, Mass: Institute of Women and Technology).

Reed, B. (1985) 'Drug misuse and dependency in women: the meaning and implications of being considered a special population or minority group', *International Journal of the Addictions*, vol. 20, no. 1, pp. 13–62.

Reid, E. (1992) 'Gender, knowledge and responsibility', in J. Mann, D. Tarantola and T. Netter (eds) *AIDS in the World: a global report* (Cambridge, Mass: Harvard University Press).

Reid, J., Ewan, C. and Lowy, E. (1991) 'Pilgrimage of pain: the illness experiences of women with repetition strain injury and the search for credibility', *Social Science and Medicine*, vol. 32, no. 5, pp. 601–12.

Reid, M. and Garcia, J. (1989) 'Women's views of care during pregnancy and child birth', in I. Chalmers, M. Enkin and M. Keirse (eds) *Effective Care in Pregnancy and Childbirth* (Oxford: Clarendon Press).

Remennick, L. (1991) 'Epidemiology and determinants of induced abortion in the USSR', *Social Science and Medicine*, vol. 33, no. 7, pp. 841–8.

Rennie, S. (1993) 'Breast cancer prevention: diet versus drugs', *MS Magazine*, (May/June), pp. 38–46.

Repetti, R., Matthews, K. and Waldron, I. (1989) 'Employment and women's health: effects of paid employment on women's mental and physical health', *American Psychologist*, vol. 44, no. 11, (November), pp. 1394–401.

Rich, A. (1980) 'Compulsory heterosexuality and lesbian existence', *Signs*, vol. 5, no. 4, pp. 631–60.

Richgels, P. (1992) 'Hypoactive sexual desire in heterosexual women: a feminist analysis', *Women and Therapy*, vol. 12, nos 1/2, pp. 123–35.

Richie, B. (1990) 'AIDS: in living color', in E. White (ed.) *The Black Women's Health Handbook* (Seattle: Seal Press).

Roberts, H. (1985) *The Patient Patients: women and their doctors* (London: Pandora).

Robertson, M. (1992) 'Lesbians as an invisible minority in the health services arena', *Health Care for Women International*, vol. 13, no. 2, pp. 155–64.

Robinson, J. (1982) 'Cancer of the cervix: occupational risks of husbands and wives and possible preventive strategies', in J. Jordan, F. Sharp and A. Singer *Preclinical Neoplasia of the Cervix*. Royal College of Obstetricians and Gynaecologists.

Robinson, J., Hibbard, B. and Laurence, K. (1984) 'Anxiety during a crisis: emotional effects of screening for neural tube defects', *Journal of Psychosomatic Research*, vol. 28, no. 2, pp. 163–9.

Rochat, R., Koonin, L., Atrash, H., Jewett, J. and the Maternal Mortality Collaborative (1988) 'Maternal mortality in the United States: report from the maternal mortality collaborative', *Obstetrics and Gynaecology*, vol. 72, no. 1, pp. 91–7.

Rodda, A. (1991) *Women and the Environment* (London: Zed Press).

Rodin, J. and Ickovics, J. (1990) 'Women's health: review and research agenda as we approach the 21st century', *American Psychologist*, vol. 45, no. 9, pp. 1018–34.

Rogers, R. and Salvage, J. (1988) *Nurses at Risk: a guide to health and safety at work* (London: Heinemann).

Rogow, D. (1986) 'Quality of care in international family planning: a feminist contribution', in *Contraceptive Development Process and Quality of Care in Reproductive Health Services* (New York: International Women's Health Coalition and Population Council).

Rohsenow, D., Corbett, R. and Devine, D. (1988) 'Molested as children: a hidden contribution to substance abuse?', *Journal of Substance Abuse Treatment*, vol. 5, no. 1, pp. 13–18.

Roldàn, M. (1985) 'Industrial outworking: struggles for the reproduction of working class families and gender subordination', in N. Redcliff and E. Mingione (eds) *Beyond Employment* (Oxford: Basil Blackwell).

Rom, W. (1976) 'Effects of lead on the female and reproduction: a review', *Mount Sinai Journal of Medicine*, vol. 43, no. 5, pp. 542–52.

Romito, P. (1990) 'Post-partum depression and the experience of motherhood', *Acta Obstetricia and Gynecologica, Scandinavica*, vol. 69, Supplement 154, pp. 1–37.

Romito, P. (1993) 'Work and health in mothers of young children: who cares?', *Proceedings of Conference on Women, Health and Work*, CAPS, Barcelona, 11–12 November.

Romito, P. and Zalateo, C. (1992) 'Social history of a research project: a study on early post-partum discharge', *Social Science and Medicine*, vol. 34, no. 3, pp. 227–35.

Rooney, C. (1992) *Antenatal Care and Maternal Health: how effective is it?, A review of the evidence* (Geneva: WHO).

Rosa, K. (1987) 'Organising women workers in the free trade zone, Sri Lanka', in M. Davis (ed.) *Third World – Second Sex 2* (London: Zed Press).

Rosa, K. (1994) 'The conditions and organisational activities of women in Free Trade Zones: Malaysia, Philippines and Sri Lanka 1970–1990', in S. Rowbotham and S. Mitter (eds) *Dignity and Daily Bread: new forms of economic organising among poor women in the third world and the first* (London: Routledge).

Rose, H. and Hanmer, J. (1976) 'Women's liberation: reproduction and the technological fix', in D. Barker and S. Allen (eds) *Sexual Divisions and Society: process and change* (London: Tavistock).

Rosenberg, H. (1984) 'The home is the workplace: hazards, stress and pollutants in the household', in W. Chavkin (ed.) *Double Exposure: women's health hazards on the job and at home* (New York: Monthly Review Press).

Rosenberg, M., Feldblum, P. and Marshall, E. (1987) 'Occupational influences on reproduction: a review of recent literature', *Journal of Occupational Medicine*, vol. 29, no. 7, pp. 584–91.

Rosenfeld, J. (1992) 'Maternal work outside the home and its effect on women and their families', *Journal of the American Women's Association*, vol. 47, no. 2, pp. 47–53.

Ross, L. (1993) 'African-American women and abortion 1800–1970', in S. James and A. Busia (eds) *Theorizing Black Feminisms: the visionary pragmatism of black women* (London: Routledge).

Rosser, S. (1992) 'Re-visioning clinical research: gender and the ethics of experimental design', in H. Holmes and L. Purdy (eds) *Feminist Perspectives in Medical Ethics* (Bloomington and Indianapolis: Indiana University Press).

Rothenberg, R., Woelfel, M., Stoneburner, R., Milberg, J., Parker, R. and Truman, B. (1987) 'Survival with the acquired immune deficiency syndrome', *New England Journal of Medicine*, vol. 317, no. 21, pp. 1297–302.

Rothman, B. (1988) *The Tentative Pregnancy: prenatal diagnosis and the future of motherhood* (London: Pandora).

Rothman, B. (1989) *Recreating Motherhood: ideology and technology in a patriarchal society* (New York: W.W. Norton).

Rowbotham, S. and Mitter, S. (1994) *Dignity and Daily Bread: new forms of economic organising among poor women in the third world and the first* (London: Routledge).

Royston, E. and Armstrong, S. (1989) *Preventing Maternal Deaths* (Geneva: World Health Organisation).

Rubin, G. (1975) 'The traffic in women: notes on the "political economy" of sex', in R. Reiter (ed.) *Toward an Anthropology of Women* (Boston: Monthly Review Press).

Russell, D. (1982) *Rape in Marriage* (New York: Macmillan).

Russell, D. (1986) *The Secret Trauma: incest in the lives of women and girls* (New York: Basic Books).

Ruzek, S. (1978) *Women's Health Movement: feminist alternatives to medical control* (New York: Praeger).

Ruzek, S. (1980) 'Medical responses to women's health activists: conflict, accommodation and co-optation', *Research in Sociology of Health Care* (Greenwich, CT: JAI Press) vol. 1, pp. 335–4.

Ruzek, S. (1991) 'Women's reproductive rights: the impact of technology, in J. Rodin and A. Collins (eds) *Women and the New Reproductive Technologies: medical, psychosocial, legal and ethical dilemmas* (Hillsdale, NJ: Lawrence Erlbaum Associates).

Sachs, B., Layde, P., Rubin, G. and Rochat, R. (1982) 'Reproductive mortality in the United States', *Journal of the American Medical Association*, vol. 247, no. 20, pp. 2789–792.

Saffron, L. (1983) 'Cervical cancer: the politics of prevention', *Spare Rib*, 29 April.

Salvage, J. (1985) *The Politics of Nursing* (London: Heinemann).

Salzberger, L., Magidor, S., Avgar, A. and Baumgold-Land J. (1991) *Patterns of Contraceptive Behaviour among Jerusalem Women Seeking Pregnancy Counselling* (Hebrew University, Jerusalem: Paul Baerwald School of Social Work).

Sanday, P. R. (1981) 'The socio-cultural context of rape: a cross cultural study', *Journal of Social Issues*, vol. 37, no. 4, pp. 5–27.

Sandmaier, M. (1992) *The Invisible Alcoholics: women and alcohol*, 2nd ed. (Blue Ridge Summit, Pennsylvania: TAB Books).

Schei, B. and Bakketeig, L. (1989) 'Gynaecological impact of sexual and physical abuse by a spouse: a study of a random sample of Norwegian women', *British Journal of Obstetrics and Gynaecology*, vol. 96, no. 12, pp. 1379–83.

Scheper-Hughes, N. and Lock, M. (1987) 'The mindful body: a prolegomenon to future work in medical anthropology', *Medical Anthropology Quarterly*, vol. 1, no. 1, pp. 6–41.

Schrijvers, J. (1988) 'Blueprint for undernourishment: the Mahaweli River Development Scheme in Sri Lanka', in B. Agarwal (ed.) *Structures of Patriarchy: the state, the community and the household* (London: Zed Press).

Schwartz, E. (1990) 'The engineering of childbirth: a new obstetric programme as reflected in British obstetric textbooks 1960–1980', in J. Garcia, R. Kilpatrick and M. Richards (eds) *The Politics of Maternity Care: services for childbearing women in twentieth century Britain* (Oxford: Clarendon Press).

Scott, H. (1984) *Working your Way to the Bottom: the feminisation of poverty* (London: Pandora).

Scott, J. (1984) 'Keeping women in their place: exclusionary policies and reproduction', in W. Chavkin (ed.) *Double Exposure: women's health hazards on the job and at home* (New York: Monthly Review Press).

Scott, J. (1993) 'The impact of Norplant on poor women and women of colour in the US', *Women's Global Network for Reproductive Rights Newsletter*, no. 42, pp. 16–18.

Scritchfield, S. (1989) 'The infertility enterprise: IVF and the technological construction of reproductive impairments', in D. Wertz (ed.) *Research in the Sociology of Health Care* (Greenwich, CT: JAI Press).

Seager, J. and Olson, A. (1986) *Women in the World: an international atlas* (London: Pan).

Segal, L. (1987) *Is the Future Female: troubled thoughts on contemporary feminism* (London: Virago).

Segal, L. (1990) *Slow Motion: changing masculinities, changing men* (London: Virago).

Seidel, G. (1993) 'The competing discourses of HIV/AIDS in sub-Saharan Africa: discourses of rights and empowerment vs discourses of control and exclusion', *Social Science and Medicine*, vol. 36, no. 3, pp. 175–94.

Sen, A. (1988) 'Family and food: sex bias in poverty' in: T. Srinivasan and P. Bardham (eds) *Rural Poverty in South Asia* (New York: Columbia University Press).

Sen, A. (1985) *Commodities and Capabilities* (Amsterdam: Elsevier).

Sen, A. (1990a) 'Gender and co-operative conflicts', in I. Tinker (ed.) *Persistent Inequalities: women and world development* (Oxford: Oxford University Press).

Sen, A. (1990b) 'More than 100 million women are missing', *The New York Review of Books*, 20 December, pp. 61–6.

Sen, G. and Grown, C. (1988) *Development, Crises and Alternative Visions* (London: Earthscan).

Shah K. (1989) *Enquiry on the Epidemiology and Surgical Reapir of Obstetric Related Fistulae in South-East Asia*, background paper prepared for WHO Technical Working Group on Vesico-Vaginal Fistulae.

Shaaban, B. (1988) *Both Right and Left Handed: Arab women talk about their lives* (London: Women's Press).

Shapiro, T. (1985) *Population Control Politics: women, sterilisation and reproductive choice* (Philadelphia: Temple University Press).

Shearer, H. (1989) 'Maternity patients' movements in the United States 1826–1985', in I. Chalmers, M. Enkin and M. Keirse (eds) *Effective Care in Pregnancy and Childbirth* (Oxford: Clarendon Press).

Shiva, V. (1989) *Staying Alive: women, ecology and development* (London: Zed Press).

Shiva, M. (1992) 'Women equal tubes, wombs and targets?', *Women's Global Network for Reproductive Rights Newsletter*, (Jan-March), pp. 9–12.

Shorter, E. (1984), *A History of Women's Bodies* (Harmondsworth: Penguin).

Siklova, J. and Hradlikova, J. (1994) 'Women and violence in post-communist Czechoslovakia', in M. Davis (ed.) *Women and Violence: responses and realities worldwide* (London: Zed Press).

Silverman, M. and Lee, P. (1974) *Pills, Profits and Politics* (Berkeley: University of California Press,).

Simkin, P. (1986) 'Is anyone listening? Lack of clinical impact of randomised controlled trials of electronic fetal monitoring', *Birth*, vol. 13, pp. 219–22.

Simmons, J. (1990) 'Abortion: a matter of choice', in E. White (ed.) *The Black Women's Health Book: speaking for ourselves* (Seattle: Seal Press).

Sinclair, D. (1985) *Understanding Wife Assault: a training manual for counsellors and advocates* (Ontario: Ministry of Community and Social Services).

Smith, B. (1992) 'Choosing ourselves: black women and abortion', in M. Gerber Fried (ed.) *Abortion to Reproductive Freedom: transforming a movement* (Boston: South End Press).

Smith, G., Taylor, G. and Smith, K. (1985) 'Comparative risks and costs of female sterilisation', *American Journal of Public Health*, vol. 75, no. 4, pp. 370–4.

Smith, P. (1992) *The Emotional Labour of Nursing: how nurses care* (London: Macmillan).

Smyke, P. (1991) *Women and Health* (London: Zed Press).

Snell, W., Belk, S. and Hawkins, R. (1987) 'Alcohol and drug use in stressful times: the influence of the masculine role and sex-related personality attributes', *Sex Roles*, vol. 16, nos 7/8, pp. 359–73.

Snitow, A., Stansell, C. and Thompson, S. (1984) *Powers of Desire: the politics of sexuality* (London: Virago).

Sontheimer, S. (1991) *Women and the Environment, a Reader: crisis and development in the third world* (London: Earthscan).

Sorensen, G. and Verbrugge, L. (1987) 'Women, work and health', *American Review of Public Health*, vol. 8, pp. 235–51.

Stacey, M. (1992) 'Social dimensions of assisted reproduction', in M. Stacey (ed.) *Changing Human Reproduction: social science perspectives* (London: Sage).

Stafford, R. (1990) 'Alternative strategies for controlling rising Caesarian rates', *Journal of the American Medical Association*, vol. 263, no. 5, pp. 683–7.

Stanko, E. (1985) *Intimate Intrusions: women's experience of male violence* (London: Routledge and Kegan Paul).

Stanley, K., Stjernsward, J. and Koroltchouk, V. (1987) 'Women and cancer', *World Health Statistics Quarterly*, vol. 40, pp. 267–78.

Stanworth, M. (1987) *Reproductive Technologies: gender, motherhood and medicine* (Oxford: Polity Press).

Stark, E. and Flitcraft, A. (1991) 'Spouse abuse', in M. Rosenberg and M. Fenley (eds) *Violence in America: a public health approach* (Oxford: Oxford University Press).

Starrs, A. (1987) *Preventing the Tragedy of Maternal Deaths: a report on the International Safe Motherhood Conference, Nairobi* (Washington DC: World Bank, World Health Organisation and United Nations Fund for Population Activities).

Stebbins, K. (1991) 'Tobacco, politics and economics: implications for global health', *Social Science and Medicine*, vol. 33, no. 12, pp. 1317–26.

Stein, A., Cooper, P., Campbell, E., Day, A. and Altham, P. (1989) 'Social adversity and perinatal complications: their relation to postnatal depression', *British Medical Journal*, vol. 298, pp. 1073–4.

Stein, Z. (1990) 'HIV prevention: the need for methods women can use', *American Journal of Public Health*, vol. 80, no. 4, pp. 460–2.

Stein, Z. and Hatch, M. (1986) *Reproductive problems in the Workplace* (Philadelphia: Hanley and Belfus).

Stellman, J. (1977) *Women's Work, women's health: myths and realities* (New York: Pantheon).

Stellman, J. and Henifin, M. (1989) *Office Work Can be Dangerous to Your Health* (New York: Pantheon).

Stevens, P. (1992) 'Lesbian health care research: a review of the literature from 1970 – 1990', *Health Care for Women International*, vol. 13, no. 2, pp. 91–120.

Stevens, P. and Meleis, A. (1991) 'Maternal role of clerical workers: a feminist analysis', *Social Science and Medicine*, vol. 32, no. 12, pp. 1425–33.

Stewart, S. and Glazer, G. (1986) 'Expectations and coping of women undergoing in vitro fertilisation', *Maternal-Child Nursing Journal*, vol. 15, no. 2, pp. 103–13.

Strandberg, M., Sandbäck, K., Axelson, O. and Sundell, L. (1978) 'Spontaneous abortions among women in hospital laboratories', *Lancet*, vol. (i), pp. 384–5.

Sundari Ravindran, T. (1986) *Health Implications of Sex Discrimination in Childhood: a review paper and annotated bibliography prepared for WHO/UNICEF* (Geneva: WHO, UNICEF/FHE 86.2).

Sundari Ravindran, T. (1993) 'Women and the politics of population development', *Reproductive Health Matters*, no. 1, pp. 26–38.

Swett, C., Cohen, C., Surrey, J., Compaine, A. and Chavez, R. (1991) 'High rates of alcohol use and history of physical and sexual abuse among women out-patients', *American Journal of Drug and Alcohol Abuse*, vol. 17, no. 1, pp. 49–60.

Taattola, K. and Susitaival, P. (1993) 'Occupational health and safety problems among women in Finnish agriculture', in K. Kauppinen (ed.) *OECD Panel Group on Women's Work and Health* National Report: Finland (Helsinki: Ministry of Social Affairs and Health) .

Taylor, D. (1987) 'Current usage of benzodiazepines in Britain', in H. Freeman and Y. Rue (eds) *Benzodiazepines in Current Clinical Practice* (London: Royal Society of Medicine).

Thaddeus, S. and Maine, D. (1991) *Too Far to Walk: maternal mortality in context* (New York: Centre for Population and Family Health, Faculty of Medicine, Columbia University).

Thiam, A. (1986) *Black Sisters Speak Out: feminism and oppression in black Africa* (London: Pluto Press).

Tirado, S. (1994) 'Weaving dreams, constructing realities: the Nineteenth of September National Union of Garment Workers in Mexico', in S. Rowbotham and S. Mitter (eds) *Dignity and Daily Bread: new forms of economic organising among poor women in the third world and the first* (London: Routledge).

Tobin, J. Wassertheil-Smoller, S., Wexler, J. *et al* (1987) 'Sex bias in considering coronary bypass surgery', *Annals of Internal Medicine*, vol. 107, pp. 19–25.

Toubia, N. (1985) 'The social and political implications of female circumcision: the case of Sudan', in E. Warnock Fernea (ed.) *Women and the Family in the Middle East: new voices of change* (Austin: University of Texas Press).

Toubia, N. (1993) Female Genital Mutilation: A call for global action (New York: Women Ink).

Tudiver, S. (1986) 'The strength of links: international women's health networks in the eighties', in K. McDonnell (ed.) *Adverse Effects: women and the pharmaceutical industry* (Penang, Malaysia: International Organisation of Consumer Unions).

Turner, B. (1992) *Regulating Bodies: essays in medical sociology* (London: Routledge).

UK Royal College of General Practitioners (1974) *Oral Contraceptives and Health* (Pitman Medical).

UK Royal College of General Practitioners (1986) *Morbidity Statistics from General Practice 1981–2 Third National Survey* (London: HMSO).

Ulin, P. (1992) 'African women and AIDS: negotiating behavioural change', *Social Science and Medicine*, vol. 34, no. 1, pp. 63–73.

Ulrich, H. (1987) 'A study of change and depression among Havik Brahmin women in a South Indian village', *Culture Medicine and Psychiatry*, vol. 11, pp. 261–87.

Ungerson, C. (1987) *Policy is Personal: sex, gender and informal care* (London: Tavistock).

UNICEF (1990) *The State of the World's Children 1989* (Oxford: Oxford University Press).

United Nations (1991) 'The world's women 1970–1990: trends and statistics', *Social Statistics and Indicators*, Series, K, no. 8. (New York: UN).

United Nations (1989a) 'Levels and trends of contraceptive use as assessed in 1988', *Population Studies* no. 110. (New York: United Nations).

United Nations (1989b) *Violence against Women in the Family* (Vienna: Centre for Social Development and Humanitarian Affairs).

United Nations Institute for the Advancement of Women (INSTRAW) (1991) 'Women, water and sanitation', in S. Sontheimer (ed.) *Women and the Environment, a Reader: crisis and development in the third world* (London: Earthscan).

United States National Institutes of Health (1992) *Opportunities for Research on Women's Health* (NIH Publication no. 92–3457) (Washington, DC: US Department of Health and Human Services).

United States Public Health Service (1985) *Women's Health: report of the Public Health Service task force on women's health issues* (Washington DC: US Department of Health and Human Services).

US Congress Office of Technology Assessment (1988) *Infertility: medical and social choices* (Washington DC: US Government Printing Office).

US Department of Health and Human Services) (1989) *Reducing the Health Consequences of Smoking: 25 years of progress* (Washington, DC: DHHS).

US Merit Systems Protection Board (1981) *Sexual Harassment in the Federal Workplace: is it a problem?* (Washington DC: US Government Printing Office).

Ussher, J. (1989) *The Psychology of the Female Body* (London: Routledge).

Valverde, M. (1985) *Sex, Power and Pleasure* (Toronto: Women's Press).

Vance, C. (ed.) (1984) *Pleasure and Danger: exploring female sexuality* (London: Routledge).

Vannicelli, M. and Nash, L. (1984) 'Effects of sex bias on women's studies on alcoholism', *Clinical and Experimental Research*, vol. 8, no. 3, pp. 334–6.

Venkatramani, S. (1986) 'Female infanticide: born to die', *India Today*, June 15 10–17. Reprinted in J. Radford and D. Russell (eds) (1992) *Femicide: the politics of women killing* (Buckingham: Open University Press).

Verbrugge, L. (1984) 'How physicians treat mentally distressed men and women', *Social Science and Medicine*, vol. 18, no. 1, pp. 1–9.

Verbrugge, L. (1985) 'An epidemiological profile of older women' in: M. Haug, A. Ford and M. Sheafor (eds) *The Physical and Mental Health of Older Women* (New York: Springer).

Verbrugge, L. (1986) 'From sneezes to adieux: stages of health for American men and women', *Social Science and Medicine* vol. 22, no. 11, pp. 1195–212.

Verbrugge, L. and Steiner, R. (1981) 'Physician treatment of men and women patients: sex bias or appropriate care? *Medical Care*, vol. 19, no. 6, pp. 609–32.

Vessey, M. and Nunn, J. (1980) 'Occupational hazards of anaesthesia', *British Medical Journal*, vol. 281, pp. 696–8.

Vickers, J. (1991) *Women and the World Economic Crisis* (London: Zed Press).

Waldron, I. (1986a) 'What do we know about the causes of sex differences in mortality?', *Population Bulletin of the United Nations*, vol. 18, pp. 59–76.

Waldron, I. (1986b) 'The contributions of smoking to sex differences in mortality', *Public Health Reports*, vol. 101, no. 2, pp. 163–73.

Waldron, I. (1987) 'Patterns and causes of excess female mortality among children in developing countries', *World Health Statistics Quarterly*, vol. 40, pp. 194–210.

Waldron, I. (1991) 'Effects of labour force participation on sex differences in mortality and morbidity', in M. Frankenhaeuser, U. Lundberg and M. Chesney (eds) *Women, Work and Health: stress and opportunities* (New York: Plenum Press).

Waldron, I. and Jacobs, J. (1989) 'Effects of labor force participation on women's health: new evidence from a longitudinal study', *Journal of Occupational Medicine*, vol. 30, no. 12, pp. 977–83.

Walker, J. (1990) 'Mothers and children', in ACT UP/NY Women and AIDS Book Group. *Women, AIDS and Activism* (Boston, Mass: South End Press).

Walker, L. (1979) *The Battered Woman* (New York: Harper and Row).

Warnock, M. (1985), A. *Question of Life: the Warnock Report on human fertilisation and embryology* (Oxford: Basil Blackwell).

War on Want (1988) *Women Working Worldwide: the international division of labour in the electronics, clothing and textiles industries* (Available from War on Want, 37–39 Great Guildford Street, London SE1).

Warr, P. and Parry, G. (1982) 'Paid employment and women's psychological wellbeing', *Psychological Bulletin*, vol. 91, no. 3, pp. 498–516.

Warren, M. (1987) 'Better safe than sorry', *New Internationalist*, October, p. 22.

Wasserheit, J. (1989) 'The significance and scope of reproductive tract infections among third world women', *International Journal of Gynaecology and Obstetrics* Suppl. 3, pp. 145–68.

Wasserheit, T. and Holmes, K. (1992) 'Reproductive tract infections: challenges for international health policy, programs and research', in A. Germain, K. Holmes, P. Piot and J. Wasserheit (eds) *Reproductive Tract Infections: global impact and priorities for women's reproductive health* (New York: Plenum Press).

Watson, S. (ed.) (1990) *Playing the State* (London: Verso).

Weeks, J. (1986) *Sexuality* (London: Tavistock).

Weissman, M. and Klerman, G. (1977) 'Sex differences and the epidemiology of depression', *Archives of General Psychiatry*, vol. 24, pp. 98–111.

Wells, J. and Batten, L. (1990) 'Women smoking and coping: an analysis of women's experience of stress', *Health Education Journal*, vol. 49, no. 2, pp. 57–60.

Wenger, N. (1990) 'Gender, coronary heart disease and coronary bypass surgery', *Annals of Internal Medicine*, vol. 112, no. 8, pp. 557–8.

Westlander, G. and Magnusson, B. (1988) 'Swedish women and new technology', in G. Westlander and J. Stellman (eds) *Women and Health*, vol. 13, (New York: Haworth Press).

Whatley, M. (1988) 'Beyond compliance: towards a feminist health education', in S. Rosser (ed.) *Feminism Within the Science and Health Care Professions: overcoming resistance* (Oxford: Pergamon).

Whelehan, M. (1988) *Women and Health: cross cultural perspectives* (Granby, Mass: Bergin and Garvey).

Whitbeck, C. (1991) 'Ethical issues raised by the new medical technologies', in J. Rodin and A. Collins (eds) *Women and New Reproductive Technologies: medical, psychosocial, legal and ethical dilemmas* (Hillsdale, NJ: Lawrence Erlbaum).

White, C. (1993) '"Close to home in Johannesburg": gender oppression in township households', *Women's Studies International Forum*, vol. 16, no. 2, pp. 149–63.

Whitehead, M. (1988) *The Health Divide: inequalities in health in the 1980s* (Harmondsworth: Penguin).

Williams, P. and Bellantuono, C. (1991) 'Long-term tranquilliser use: the contribution of epidemiology', in J. Gabe (ed.) *Understanding Tranquilliser Use: the role of the social sciences* (London: Tavistock).

Wilsnack, R. and Cheloha, R. (1987) 'Women's roles and problem drinking across the lifespan', *Social Problems*, vol. 34, no. 3, pp. 231–48.

Wilsnack, S. and Wilsnack, R. (1991) 'Epidemiology of women's drinking', *Journal of Substance Abuse*, vol. 3, pp. 133–57.

Wilsnack, R. Wilsnack, S. and Klassen, A. (1984) 'Women's drinking and drinking problems: patterns from a 1981 national survey', *American Journal of Public Health*, vol. 74, no. 11, pp. 1231–8.

Witz, A. (1992) *Professions and Patriarchy* (London: Routledge).

Wolfson, D. and Murray, J. (1986) *Women and Dependency: women's personal accounts of drug and alcohol problems* (London: DAWN).

Womankind Worldwide (n.d.) *Our Health is Our Only Wealth*. Women's Lives no. 3 (available from 122 Whitechapel High Street, London E1 7PT).

Womankind Newsletter (1994) no. 1, 'Changes in Chingleput', p. 5,

Women's Global Network for Reproductive Rights (WGNRR) (1992) *Report of the Maternal Morbidity and Mortality Campaign 1992* (Amsterdam: WGNRR).

Women's Health Matters (1993) Research Round-Up, no. 1, p. 101.

Worcester, N. and Whatley, M. (1988) 'The response of the health care system to the women's health movement: the selling of women's health centers', in S. Rosser (ed.) *Feminism within the Science and Health Care Professions: overcoming resistance* (Oxford: Pergamon).

Working Woman (1984) *9 to 5 Stress Survey* (Cleveland Ohio: Working Women's Education Fund).

World Bank (1993) *World Development Report 1993: investing in health* (Oxford: Oxford University Press).

World Health Organisation, Special Programme of Research, Development and Research Training in Human Reproduction (1981) 'A cross cultural study of menstruation: implications for contraceptive development and use', *Studies in Family Planning*, vol. 12, no. 1, pp. 3–16.

World Health Organisation, Regional Office for Europe (1983) *Women and Occupational Health Risks*. EURO Reports and Studies, 76, Copenhagen.

World Health Organisation (1984) *Biomass Fuel Combustion and Health* (Geneva: WHO).

World Health Organisation (1985) 'Appropriate technology for birth', *Lancet*, vol. (ii), pp. 436–7.

World Health Organisation (1986a) *Having a Baby in Europe* (Copenhagen: WHO Regional Office for Europe).

World Health Organisation (1986b) *Maternal Mortality Rates: a tabulation of available information* (Geneva: WHO).

World Health Organisation (1986c) 'Control of cancer of the cervix uteri', *Bulletin of the World Health Organisation*, vol. 64, no. 4, pp. 607–18.

World Health Organisation (1989) *The Risks to Women of Pregnancy and Childbearing in Adolescence* (Geneva: WHO/MCH/89.5, Division of Family Health, WHO).

World Health Organisation (1990) *Global Programme on AIDS: report of the meeting on research priorities relating to women and HIV/AIDS*, Geneva, 19–20 November (Geneva: WHO).

World Health Organisation (1991) *Infertility: a tabulation of available data on prevalence of primary and secondary fertility*, Programme on Maternal and Child Health and Family Planning (Geneva: WHO).

World Health Organisation and International Women's Health Coalition (1991) *Creating Common Ground: report of a meeting between women's health advocates and scientists* (WHO/HRP/ITT/91 (Geneva: WHO).

World Health Organisation (1992) *Women's Health: across age and frontier* (Geneva: WHO).

World Health Organisation (1993) *Fertility Regulating Vaccines: report of a meeting between women's health advocates and scientists to review the current status of the development of fertility regulating vaccines* (Geneva: WHO).

World Health Organisation (1994) *Women's health counts*, Proceedings of a conference on the health of women in Eastern and Central Europe, Vienna, February 1994, Comparative analysis and country reports (Copenhagen: WHO).

Worth, D. (1989) 'Sexual decision making and AIDS: why condom promotion among vulnerable women is likely to fail', *Studies in Family Planning*, vol. 20, no. 6, pp. 297–307.

Wright, P. and Treacher, A. (eds) (1982) *The Problem of Medical Knowledge: examining the social construction of medicine* (Edinburgh: Edinburgh University Press).

Young, K. (1993) *Planning Development with Women: making a world of difference* (London: Macmillan).

Young, K., Wolkowitz, C. and McCullagh, R. (1981) *Of Marriage and the Market* (London: CSE Books).

Yuval Davis, N. (1989) 'National reproduction and the "demographic race" in Israel', in H. Afshar (ed.) *Woman, Nation, State* (London: Macmillan).

Zimmerman, M. (1987) 'The women's health movement: a critique of medical enterprise and the position of women', in B. Hess and M. Marx Ferree (eds) *Analyzing Gender: a handbook of social science research* (Newbury Park, Ca: Sage).

Zola, I. (1975) 'Medicine as an institution of social control', in C. Cox and A. Mead (eds) *A Sociology of Medical Practice*. Collier Macmillan.

Zopf, P. (1989) *American Women in Poverty* (New York: Greenwood Press).

Zwi, A. and Cabral, A. (1991) 'Identifying high risk situations for preventing AIDS', *British Medical Journal*, vol. 303, pp. 1527–9.

Index

266